STO

ACPL ITEM
DISCARDED

3·14·77

Advertising, Competition, and Public Policy: A Simulation Study

Advertising, Competition, and Public Policy: A Simulation Study

Paul N. Bloom

College of Business and Management
University of Maryland

Ballinger Publishing Company • Cambridge, Mass.
A Subsidiary of J.B. Lippincott Company

Copyright ©1976 by Ballinger Publishing Company. All rights reserved. No part of this publication may be reproduced, stored in a retrieval system, or transmitted in any form or by any means, electronic mechanical photo-copy, recording or otherwise, without the prior written consent of the publisher.

International Standard Book Number: 0-88410-280-7

Library of Congress Catalog Card Number: 75-37590

Printed in the United States of America

Library of Congress Cataloging in Publication Data

Bloom, Paul N.
    Advertising, competition, and public policy.

    Includes bibliographical references.
    1. Advertising. 2. Competition. 3. Advertising—Costs. 4. Computer sim-
ulation. I. Title.
HF5827.B575   659.1   75-37590
ISBN 0-88410-280-7

To Diane

Contents

List of Figures

List of Tables

Acknowledgments

There are a large number of individuals and organizations who helped me in writing this book. Philip Kotler of Northwestern University deserves mention first, since it was he who offered me the most advice and assistance. I am also deeply grateful to Louis W. Stern, Robert T. Masson, Morton I. Kamien, Philip C. Burger, and Fred C. Allvine (all presently or formerly at Northwestern) for their helpful suggestions.

The American Marketing Association provided the bulk of the financial support for this research in the form of a research grant. In addition, the Vogelback Computer Center of Northwestern University provided a portion of the necessary computer time and the College of Business and Management of the University of Maryland supplied the necessary secretarial support.

I must also thank the six executives from the breakfast cereal industry who allowed me to interview them.

Lastly, I would like to express my gratitude to my wife, Diane, for the support, encouragement, and affection she has given me while I have been working on this research. It is with great pleasure that I dedicate this book to her.

Chapter One

Introduction

In recent years, advertising has been under an almost constant barrage of criticism. Advertising has been accused of being misleading, expensive, wasteful, anticompetitive, inflationary, offensive, intrusive, and even immoral. As criticism of advertising has become more vocal and persistent, the volume of laws and regulations governing advertising has grown in size.[1] Moreover, the critics of advertising are continually proposing new ways for governments to gain tighter control over advertising.

In the following pages, a description is presented of a study that systematically evaluated a few of the more controversial proposals for controlling advertising that have appeared during the past few years. The proposals that were examined have been made by a number of economists, consumer advocates, and other individuals who feel that advertising can be anticompetitive and who believe that certain industries would become more competitive if their firms were required or encouraged to spend less on advertising. Experiments were performed with a computer simulation model of an oligopolistic grocery manufacturing industry in order to explore the competitive effects of seven proposed controls on advertising expenditures—two advertising taxes, three limits on advertising outlays, and two depreciation requirements for advertising. In general, the simulation results failed to provide support for advertising's critics. Instead, the results indicated that there is a possibility that the introduction of certain controls on advertising expenditures would lead to *less* competition in some industries.

Before examining the objectives, methodology, and results of this study in greater detail, however, it is necessary to review briefly the arguments, proposals, and research that have emerged from the controversy over advertising's effect on competition. This review should demonstrate that there is a definite need for the type of research performed in this study.

THE ADVERTISING AND COMPETITION
CONTROVERSY

The question of how advertising affects competition has received a vast amount of attention from industrial organization economists and marketing scholars. Hundreds of articles and at least six books[2]—volumes by Comanor and Wilson, Ferguson, and Lambin are the most recent—have appeared in which this question has received primary consideration. The future promises to bring even more writing on the subject, as many issues remain unresolved.

The interest that has developed in the relationship between advertising and competition is a natural outgrowth of the long-standing interest that has existed within the United States and other countries in preserving competition (or rivalry characterized by independent behavior) in the marketplace. Competitive markets are considered desirable because they are supposed to provide lower prices, better service, better quality, more frequent innovations, and more efficient use of scarce resources. Competitive markets are also considered desirable because they are supposed to be essentially self-regulating—that is, they are considered less likely to require the development of bureaucratic government regulatory mechanisms to keep them serving the public in a responsible fashion.[3] Thus, anything that presents a potential threat to the maintenance of competitive markets has, traditionally, received considerable attention from public policy makers and scholarly researchers. Advertising—or "mass paid communication, the ultimate purpose of which is to impart information, develop attitudes, and induce action beneficial to the advertiser (generally the sale of a product or service)"[4]—has been perceived as presenting just such a threat.

A complex, entangled set of reasons have been put forth to explain why, in theory, advertising should lead to less competition in certain industries. These theoretical arguments are summarized below.

1. Advertising can suppress competition by helping firms erect *product differentiation barriers to entry*. These barriers can develop when the firms in an industry are successful at using advertising to create loyalty among consumers for their brands. Potential entrants to such an industry typically find that to achieve any given level of output (sales), they must spend more on advertising than established rivals would have to spend. This absolute-cost disadvantage is often large enough to keep potential rivals from entering.[5]

2. Economies of scale in advertising[a] put small advertisers at a disadvantage. Also, small advertisers are often at a disadvantage because they are unable to stimulate enough demand to allow them to benefit from economies of scale in manufacturing and physical distribution. These disadvantages make it difficult for small firms to survive in markets with large advertisers. Without small firms, these markets tend to become less competitive.[6]

---

[a]Economies of scale in advertising exist where (1) there is a need to reach some threshold level of advertising expenditures in order to reach peak effectiveness or (2) there are quantity discounts offered by the media.

3. Imperfections in the capital markets make it difficult for new firms to enter industries where existing firms spend large amounts on advertising. Lenders and investors feel advertising campaigns are too risky to "invest" in, especially since no tangible assets are purchased in these campaigns that can be resold in the event of failure. Thus, potential entrants to certain industries cannot accumulate the funds needed to climb over the barriers to entry mentioned above.[7]

4. In some industries, the occurrence of escalations in advertising expenditures seems to lead to less competition in the long run. Firms in moderately concentrated industries are reluctant to cut prices on one another because they fear retaliations, but they are not at all hesitant to increase advertising expenditures. Thus, an escalation occurs that eventually results in the failure, or absorption (by larger firms), of some of an industry's smaller firms who cannot survive these "advertising wars." The existence of these wars also frightens away potential competitors.[8]

Of course, not all people accept the above arguments. Many individuals feel that advertising is generally pro-competitive. These people have offered the following arguments and rebuttals to support their position.

1. Information is a valuable resource. Advertising provides consumers with information at a very low cost and thereby saves them from incurring considerable expenses in searching for information upon which to base purchasing decisions. The more informed consumers are about the product alternatives available in a market, the more difficult it is for sellers to extract noncompetitive prices or to pass off shoddy merchandise or services. Therefore, in markets where advertising is prevalent, sellers are forced to compete vigorously for the dollars of *informed* consumers. In short, "advertising is a productive and pro-competitive activity, substituting cheaply provided information for expensive search costs, rather than being a wasteful activity producing monopolistic results."[9]

2. Advertising is a *means* of entry for new brands, not a barrier to entry. All new entrants have the opportunity to use this powerful tool for prying away consumers from their favorite brands. Advertising is used to make industries more competitive, not less competitive.[10]

3. It is unlikely that economies of scale in advertising exist in more than a few industries. Moreover, in those cases where they do, they "need not lead to increased concentration within markets, but rather can lead to many efficient multi-market conglomerate firms."[11]

4. Advertising is only one element of the "marketing mix" of most firms. To single out advertising as being anticompetitive ignores the fact that the effects of advertising are confounded considerably by such other factors in the mix as consumer and dealer promotion, sales calls, and product quality. One must determine exactly what advertising's role is in the marketing mixes of an industry's firms before condemning it for damaging competition in that industry.[12]

To be sure, there is no way to make a fair evaluation of the arguments on both sides without looking at empirical findings. However, it is not possible to reach a conclusion that advertising is or is not anticompetitive based on the empirical work that has been done thus far. Such work contains a group of contradictory and questionable findings.[13] If these empirical studies have revealed anything, it is the unsurprising finding that advertising can be *both* anticompetitive and pro-competitive. The effect that advertising has on competition seems to depend on the industry being observed. For example, Greer has accumulated evidence that competition in the brewing industry has been affected adversely by advertising.[14] On the other hand, Benham has shown that advertising has had a pro-competitive effect in the retail eyeglass industry.[15]

PUBLIC POLICY PROPOSALS IN THE LITERATURE

A number of the works that explore the relationship between advertising and competition conclude by endorsing controls on advertising expenditures or other public policy measures. The proposals that have been made call for advertising to be taxed, limited, or depreciated, or for other policy actions designed to increase competition. The various proposals that have appeared and the logic behind them are reviewed below.

Advertising Taxes

Taxes on advertising are typically proposed as means of raising revenue for governmental bodies. Several states, municipalities, and foreign countries have imposed taxes on advertisers, advertising agencies, or media suppliers in order to accumulate additional funds.[16] None of the taxes that have appeared to date were introduced to encourage competition, although it is possible that some legislators may have had this in mind when they voted in favor of these measures.

A few economists, however, have endorsed a *progressive* tax on advertising expenditures as a means of encouraging competition in certain industries. Walter Adams, for example, has stated:

> The advisability of a progressive tax on advertising—with a generous exemption of say $3,000,000—should be examined, in an effort to prevent excessive advertising expenditures from acting as an obstacle to free entry in some concentrated industries.[17]

Advertising Limitations

Rather than providing a disincentive to large advertising outlays, some individuals would prefer simply to cut off spending on advertising in certain industries at "reasonable" levels. Limitations could be placed on the percentage of sales that could be spent on advertising, the absolute dollar amount spent on advertising, or the growth rate of spending on advertising. A Ralph Nader study group has, in essence, endorsed the first of these three approaches:

> The Study Group recommends that a 100 percent tax be levied on all advertising expenditures of firms possessing "incipient market power" in excess of a percent of sales revenues, to be determined by the FTC after a major study of the link between advertising and concentration.[18]

Presumably, "reasonable" cut-off levels would be determined after assessing how much advertising was needed to adequately inform consumers of a product's existence, its qualities, and its price. The limitations would supposedly make it easier for small competitors to enter an industry and, also, provide an incentive for firms to compete on a price basis.

Advertising Depreciation Requirements

Joel Dean has recommended that for planning purposes, firms should treat advertising as an *investment* that provides returns over a long period of time.[19] Some people have gone one step further than Dean's recommendation and have endorsed the treatment of advertising as a capital investment *for tax purposes.* In other words, some individuals feel that the tax laws should require firms to capitalize their advertising expenditures and to amortize [or depreciate] the resulting intangible asset over an extended period of time. Some favor this approach because they feel it would lead to more accurate financial reporting, while others, such as economist Leonard Weiss, see it as a way to encourage firms to spend less on advertising. As Weiss has put it:

> . . . our corporate income tax as it now stands, gives special favor to those who invest heavily in advertising and expand such investment rapidly. The relative subsidy to advertising is unimportant in most industries, but in a handful of cases where the effects of heavy advertising are most severe it often exceeds the investment credit available to investors in tangibles. The subsidy is greater the heavier the advertising expenditures, the more rapidly they grow, and the most lasting their effect. As a result, the tax law probably biases advertising decisions upward and in favor of promotion designed to create long lasting brand loyalties. A revision of the tax law to require the "capitalization" and depreciation of advertising which is of lasting value seems justified on both equity and economic efficiency grounds, and may be more attainable than straightforward limitations on promotional expenditures.[20]

Thus, Weiss and others believe that firms would make smaller investments in advertising if they could not write off their investments quite as rapidly.[b] By discouraging firms from escalating their advertising expenditures, a depreciation requirement would supposedly encourage firms to compete in other ways and make entry less difficult.[c]

Other Proposals

A number of other public policy alternatives have been proposed by those who feel that advertising can be anticompetitive. For example, F.M. Scherer, who recently directed the Bureau of Economics of the Federal Trade Commission, has suggested that consumers could be provided with more objective information about the relative qualities of rival sellers' products. This information could be provided through the use of uniform quality grading systems, the subsidization of organizations like Consumers Union, or the publication of the results of government tests on consumer products. A more informed consumer would presumably be less influenced by the persuasive aspects of advertising and, thus, sellers would not be able to maintain product differentiation barriers to entry where product differences were minor or nonexistent. Scherer has also suggested that more vigorous policing of misleading advertising would help to avoid the creation of these barriers.[21]

Paul Scanlon, associate editor of the *Antitrust Law and Economics Review*, has made a detailed proposal that is quite consistent with Scherer's thinking. Scanlon has advocated that firms that meet certain criteria (belonging to highly-concentrated, advertising-intensive industries) should be required to submit all their advertisements to the Federal Trade Commission before the ads are shown. The FTC would evaluate the truthfulness and informational content of the ads and would allow them to be used only if they were honest and informative.[22]

Other ideas that have appeared for remedying the *alleged* anticompetitive effects of advertising include: (1) the use of media bans similar to the one recently imposed on the cigarette industry; (2) the encouragement of industry self-regulation in the area of advertising expenditures; (3) the prevention of mergers where advertising barriers to entry could be raised; and (4) the breaking-up of industries where advertising has contributed to a lack of competition.[23]

In this study, only the consequences of taxing, limiting, or requiring

---

[b]The exact reaction to a depreciation requirement would actually depend upon the goals or objectives of the firms on which it would be imposed. For further discussion, see Chapter Four of this work.

[c]An extreme form of a depreciation requirement—an income tax disallowance—has been suggested by Preston. With a disallowance, firms could *never* deduct a portion of a year's advertising expenditures for tax purposes. See Lee E. Preston, "Advertising Effects and Public Policy," in Robert L. King, ed., *Marketing and the New Science of Planning* (Chicago: American Marketing Association, 1968), pp. 558-66.

depreciation of expenditures on advertising were explored. These types of controls can be tested in a reasonable fashion by using the relatively simple simulation model that was built for this study. To test consumer information programs, media bans, self-regulation attempts, or structural reforms, one would have to build a substantially more complex model.

THE RESPONSE OF PUBLIC POLICY MAKERS

Although public policy makers in the United States have yet to adopt and enforce any of the proposals that have just been discussed, they have shown signs of having accepted the viewpoint that advertising can be anticompetitive and that remedial action may be necessary. They have exhibited agreement with this viewpoint on a number of occasions, including the six discussed in the following paragraphs.

In 1966 Donald F. Turner, while serving as Assistant Attorney General for Antitrust, delivered a widely quoted speech in which he stated his belief that advertising could help to create entry barriers. Turner went as far as to say that "it would be quite appropriate to impose, for a period of time, an absolute or percentage limitation on promotional expenditures by a firm or firms that have obtained undue market power through violations of the Sherman Act. A classic purpose of a remedial decree in such cases is to dissipate the consequences of unlawful acts, and if limitations on promotional expenditures would help, they are appropriate even though the promotional expenditures as such were and are lawful."[24]

In 1967, the Supreme Court stopped a merger between Procter and Gamble and Clorox Chemical Company. One of the arguments that was put forth to justify this decision was that if the merger were allowed, Procter could use its enormous advertising expenditures to frighten away potential competition in the liquid bleach market.[25]

Later, in 1972, the Federal Trade Commission issued a complaint against the four major manufacturers of ready-to-eat breakfast cereals that charged them with maintaining a "shared monopoly." The complaint states that "practices of proliferating brands, differentiating similar products and promoting trademarks through intensive advertising result in high barriers to entry into the RTE cereal market."[26]

Also in 1972, and again in 1975, Senator Philip Hart, chairman of the Senate Antitrust and Monopoly Subcommittee, submitted a bill to Congress titled the Industrial Reorganization Act. This bill calls for the establishment of an Industrial Reorganization Commission that would be empowered to investigate highly concentrated industries. According to Senator Hart, the Commission would have recourse to the following remedies: "A company could [be required to] spin off subsidiaries—or replace long-term supply contracts with frequently negotiated contracts—or alter its financial backing commitments—or eliminate exclusive dealerships—*or alter its advertising expenditures*—or license patents and trademarks—or actually divest" [emphasis added] .[27]

In 1974, Representative Edward Mezvinsky, a member of the House Antitrust and Monopoly Subcommittee, stated that he thought the FTC should develop guidelines limiting advertising in highly concentrated food industries. He felt that if the FTC could determine that mergers will have an adverse effect on competition, it could also determine whether competition is being adversely affected by advertising expenditures. His remarks were made before a Senate subcommittee hearing on rising food prices.[28]

Finally, in 1975, the FTC announced an investigation into the structure, conduct, and performance of the heavy-duty detergent industry. One of the major areas it planned to explore was "barriers to significant entry into the industry, including advertising and promotional expenditures."[29]

Thus, it is conceivable that, in the near future, certain firms could be subjected to controls on advertising expenditures. These controls could be imposed as part of a settlement or court ruling in an antitrust case like the cereal case (or future detergent case), or as part of a ruling by an Industrial Reorganization Commission or other governmental body.

PREVIOUS EVALUATIONS OF CONTROLS ON ADVERTISING EXPENDITURES

In spite of the interest that public policy makers have shown in using controls on advertising expenditures to stimulate more vigorous competition in certain industries, very few researchers have conducted *systematic* evaluations of controls of this type. Except for a few cases, most researchers have based their forecasts of the effects of controls on advertising expenditures upon *a priori* reasoning. Some of the forecasts that have been made are discussed in this section. However, the forecasts that were made by Pogue and Uhl,[30] Bass and Wildt,[31] and Comanor and Wilson[32] in their more rigorous evaluations of controls on advertising expenditures are not discussed here. These studies are given special attention in the appendix to this chapter.

Almost all of the people who have evaluated controls on advertising expenditures warn of numerous potential dangers and difficulties. For example, there appears to be some consensus that there would be enormous definitional problems associated with determining exactly what constituted *controllable* advertising expenditures and what did not. Should allowances for cooperative advertising be considered advertising expenditures? What about the costs of erecting in-store displays, developing fancy packages, or painting signs on company buildings and delivery trucks? Unless care were taken in defining what was controllable, a mass rush to noncontrollable forms of advertising could result.

In a similar vein, several authors have expressed concern over the unfair advantage that advertising controls might give to firms that had managed to differentiate their brands *without* the aid of large advertising outlays. Why should firms that utilize huge, inefficient sales forces or costly, superficial, annual-style changes to develop loyalty for their brands be given an edge over their competitors?[33]

Concern has also been expressed that controls on advertising expenditures could actually make industries *less* competitive. It is feared that the controls themselves could frighten potential entrants away, even if an exemption were given to new rivals. Firms might feel that entry could not, in the long run, be profitable without unrestricted use of advertising.[34] Furthermore, it has been suggested that controls on advertising might only benefit the most deeply entrenched firms with their strong sales forces and well-developed distribution systems. Without being able to use advertising to maintain their market position, weaker brands might not survive.[35]

In addition to the more general qualms mentioned above, the following reservations about specific types of controls have appeared:

1. Progressive taxes on advertising would discriminate against multi-brand firms. They also could encourage the creation of joint ventures and holding companies.[36] In addition, if demand for a product were price inelastic, sellers might simply pass along the tax burden to consumers.[37]
2. Limitations on advertising expenditures could be set too small to allow firms to adequately inform consumers or to achieve economies of scale in either marketing or production.[38] Moreover, if a limit were placed on the size of the advertising-sales ratio, larger firms would be able to spend more and thereby maintain their advantage over smaller firms.[39]
3. If a depreciation requirement were tried, there would be difficulties in determining appropriate depreciation schedules.[40]

There are, of course, many individuals who have concluded that the disadvantages of introducing controls on advertising expenditures are outweighed by the advantages. Several people have decided that certain controls could do much to enhance competition in selected industries, but they have stopped short of endorsing advertising controls on an across-the-board basis for all industries.[41] It has also been conjectured that the introduction of controls could produce a productive and permanent "cease fire" in some industries. The resulting truce could lead to much lower advertising expenditures, higher profits for the participating firms, and possibly lower prices for consumers.[42]

OBJECTIVES OF THE STUDY

In order to go at least a step further than what has been accomplished in past evaluations of controls on advertising expenditures, a computer simulation approach was used in this study. A model of a hypothetical grocery manufacturing industry was built and then used to pretest seven different proposed controls. This model was designed to possess many of the characteristics of an industry that must be considered a potential target of these controls—the ready-to-eat breakfast cereal industry. A group of structure and performance variables (see Chapter Four for their description) were monitored in each computer run to give an indication of how competition in the simulated industry was affected by a control. The validity of the model and of its predictions were tested by comparing its assumptions and output to information about the breakfast cereal industry obtained from a series of personal interviews and from an examination of published materials.

Thus, the major objective behind building, experimenting with, and attempting to validate the simulation model was to be able to make some tentative statements about the competitive consequences of placing taxes, limits, or depreciation requirements on the advertising expenditures of firms in certain types of oligopolistic industries. In other words, this study was a piece of *exploratory* research that was designed to generate some interesting and counterintuitive hypotheses about the competitive effects of controlling advertising expenditures—hypotheses that could be refined and tested in future research. Given the shortage of past systematic research on the effects of controlling advertising expenditures [from which one could draw hypotheses to test], an exploratory research effort was all that was called for at the start of this study.

WHY SIMULATION?

Three research approaches other than computer simulation were considered for use in this study: (1) case studies of real-world controls on advertising expenditures, (2) a behavioral laboratory simulation, and (3) mathematical analysis. Although all three were felt to be adequate for hypothesis-generating purposes, computer simulation was judged to have better potential in this area. As Forrester has pointed out, computer simulation can be particularly useful for discovering the *counterintuitive* nature of systems.[43] Since it was hoped that this study could suggest some hypotheses about the consequences of controlling advertising expenditures that had not appeared elsewhere, the possibility of discovering some counterintuitive results through the use of computer simulation seemed attractive.

Each of the three alternative approaches was also rejected for other reasons. Case studies were rejected because it was felt that it would be difficult to make any statements about what might happen in certain U.S. industries based upon studies of the reactions to measures such as Sweden's or Iowa's advertising taxes[44] or Mexico's depreciation requirements;[45] especially since these measures were introduced to raise revenue and not to encourage competition. Similarly, a behavioral laboratory simulation in which subjects would be required to play games that would test out different controls was rejected because (1) it would be difficult to control for the development of different learning patterns in different games, (2) the games would have to be quite complex to get a true feel for the effect on competition of various controls, and (3) it would be difficult to find suitable subjects to use in these games. Finally, mathematical analysis, the type of approach a theoretical economist might employ, was rejected because of a desire by the author to build a complex model that had decision makers within business firms (1) manipulating a large number of decision variables and (2) acting like "satisficers" rather than "maximizers." Mathematical analysis becomes extremely difficult with highly complex models.

Computer simulation was selected as the research methodology of this study for one other reason. It was felt that by utilizing a computer simulation approach, this study would produce—as a byproduct—a model of industry behavior that other researchers could build upon in an effort to formulate a richer theory of the firm or theory of oligopoly. As several organization theorists and economists have recognized, computer simulation models of firms and industries can be considerably more useful for certain purposes than many of the abstract analytical models traditionally found in the microeconomics literature.[46] However, most of the simulation models of firms and industries that have been built to date have not been very *marketing* oriented.[47] Therefore, the model that has been built in this study attempts to fill this gap. It includes several marketing variables that have not been included in other industry models.

OUTLINE OF CHAPTERS TWO TO SIX

The chapter that follows contains a discussion of the job of the product manager. This material is presented to help give the reader an understanding of the type of decision makers represented in the industry model built for this study.

In Chapter Three, this industry model is described. First, the procedures followed in designing and refining the model are discussed. Next, a detailed description of the model is provided along with a discussion of the theory and empirical findings that provide support for the model's numerous assumptions.

The results of the various computer runs that were performed are reported in Chapter Four. These results are analyzed to see whether there are logical reasons for the controls to have the different effects on competition that were discovered in the runs.

A review of the steps that were taken to test the validity of the industry model is found in Chapter Five. The results of a series of personal interviews that were used to test the face validity of the model are examined at some length. In addition, a comparison is made between the benchmark (no controls) run of the simulation and available real-world data on the ready-to-eat breakfast cereal industry. Some possible improvements and extensions of the model are also discussed.

Lastly, the conclusions of this study are presented in Chapter Six. A few of the implications of these conclusions are also discussed. In addition, some suggestions for future research that could build upon what was done in this study are found at the end of this chapter.

APPENDIX TO CHAPTER ONE
A REVIEW OF THREE PRIOR STUDIES

A review is presented here of three important studies by Pogue and Uhl, Bass and Wildt, and Comanor and Wilson. Although these studies were not designed primarily to test how controls on advertising expenditures would affect *competition*, each did reach conclusions that are extremely relevant to this study.

Pogue and Uhl Study

Pogue and Uhl[48] analyzed the economic implications of direct state taxes on the suppliers of advertising services (e.g., advertising agencies, and so forth). While they basically relied on economic theory and analysis to make predictions and statements about the effects of such taxes, they also conducted a field study in Iowa to assess the effects of a sales tax on advertising, which was imposed there in 1967 and repealed in 1969. The following conclusions were reached about the income-distribution effects and resource-allocation effects of state advertising taxes:

> A tax on advertising seems likely to act in the long-run as a tax paid by individuals as a part of the price of final products. The rate of such implicit taxation would be greater for heavily advertised products than for slightly advertised and unadvertised products. These conclusions rest on the plausible assumption that the factors employed in production of advertising services are mobile and adaptable.
>
> There are potentially many ways in which an advertising tax might affect the allocation of resources. Such allocative effects stem from the tax-induced increase in the prices of advertising services and advertised products (relative to the prices of other products and services). These changes in relative prices tend to discourage advertising, thus diverting resources from advertising to other uses. The diverted resources may be used to produce substitutes for advertising, in which case their use tends to counter the effects of decreased advertising; the effects of decreased advertising tend to be offset or attenuated by increased use of advertising substitutes. The tax may also change the mix of communication activities and the total value of resource absorbed in the promotion and distribution of goods and services. To the extent that the diverted resources are not used to produce advertising substitutes, they will be used to produce other goods and services that have more or less value than the foregone advertising services.[49]

These conclusions were supported by the results of the Iowa field study. It was found that the demand for advertising services and for advertised products in Iowa tended to be inelastic. Consequently, the tax burden was passed forward from agencies to advertisers to ultimate consumers in the form of higher prices. In addition, no evidence was discovered that suppliers of advertising services tended to relocate to avoid the tax or that buyers of these services went outside the state to get lower prices.

Pogue and Uhl also commented on the effects that advertising taxes might have on freedom of entry in certain industries. They concluded that available evidence did not allow them to judge whether an advertising tax would discourage potential entrants who would not want to pay the tax or would encourage them by making it more costly for existing competitors in an industry to build up barriers to entry. This last conclusion underscores the fact that there is a need for more careful study of the consequences of taxing advertising for purposes of encouraging competition.

Bass and Wildt Study

Bass and Wildt[50] conducted a three-stage study. First, they estimated an industry demand equation for a three-firm grocery manufacturing industry by using proprietary data made available to them from industry sources. Second, they built a model with nine simultaneous equations (three market share equations, three advertising budget decision rules, and three promotion budget decision rules) to simulate the competitive activity of the industry. Third, they used the data base to study the relationship between the structure and performance of the industry *over time*. This three-stage approach helped them to gain insights into the competitive behavior that existed in the industry and to make predictions about how the industry would react to various public policy changes.

In the first part of their study, they found industry demand to be relatively insensitive to industry advertising expenditures. In spite of this, they found the industry to be characterized by vigorous non-price competition. Apparently, the market shares of each of the three firms *were* quite sensitive to changes in the marketing activities of the other two, and thus the firms tended to react sharply to changes in one another's strategy in setting advertising and promotion budgets. The time-series study of the structure and performance variables yielded the following conclusions:

> There is not any significant association between product differentiation activity, as measured by new variety introductions or advertising intensity, and seller concentration, but a significant positive relation does exist between change in advertising intensity and change in concentration.
>
> The level of new variety introduction is positively related to industry profit.
>
> Advertising intensity bears a very significant negative relationship to industry profit and it appears that a reduction in industry advertising expenditures would enhance the profits of each firm

providing firms maintained relative advertising ratios at existing levels. Reductions in the level of industry advertising in a way such that each firm maintains its market share would certainly increase the profit of each firm.

No significant relationship was found between industry profits and degree of seller concentration.[51]

These results were interpreted as providing support for the notion that in some industries a competitive escalation of advertising expenditures occurs and can actually be unprofitable for participating firms.[52] Bass and Wildt therefore reached a conclusion that a policy of limiting advertising to some fixed percentage of sales in the industry would only tend to substantially increase the profits of existing firms. But in arguing that this result would occur, Bass and Wildt basically turned to *a priori* reasoning for support and not to any predictions made by their nine-equation model. They implicitly assumed that existing firms would all recognize the mutual benefits that would result from discontinuing their competitive behavior and would cut back on advertising *without* increasing promotion or starting to change prices. They also assumed that only a few new entrants would be attracted, even if given an exemption from controls, for reasons that are not really explained.

Hopefully, Bass and Wildt will someday use their rich data base to develop a more complex model of industry behavior that would portray the *decision processes behind the decision rules* appearing in their simultaneous-equation model. An understanding of the decision processes used in determining a firm's marketing mix is needed before one can accurately predict that it will recognize its interdependence with its rivals or do anything else following a major policy change.

Comanor and Wilson Study

In a recent study, Comanor and Wilson[53] tried to demonstrate that advertising is an important determinant of the level of sales in many industries. In other words, they attempted to show that besides influencing the market shares of brands within an industry, advertising can also be responsible for keeeping up the total demand in that industry. Using an extended Houthakker-Taylor consumer demand model[54] that included advertising as a determinant of consumer expenditures, they estimated demand equations for forty-one consumer goods industries. The coefficients of the demand equation were then used to compute price and advertising elasticities for each of the industries. These elasticities represent the total response of consumer demand to change in price or advertising when equilibrium levels of demand are attained. As was anticipated, price elasticities were found to be generally negative while advertising elasticities were found to be uniformly positive. More significantly, a 1 percent increase in the advertising-sales ratio of most industries was found to lead to substantially greater increases in sales than a 1 percent decline in price would produce.

To reinforce their finding that advertising is a very important determinant of sales in many consumer goods industries, Comanor and Wilson then estimated what would happen to sales in fourteen industries that spent more than 3 percent of sales on advertising if they were restricted to a 3 percent maximum spending level. Their estimates revealed that in a few industries, such as drugs, wines, soft drinks, clocks and watches, and cereals, a restriction of this type could lead to rather large declines in industry sales.

Although Comanor and Wilson made no statements about how a 3 percent limit on the advertising-sales ratio might affect competition in the fourteen industries, it seems reasonable to assume that declining industry sales could lead firms to try drastically different marketing strategies. In addition, declining sales could also make entry look less attractive. Thus, Comanor and Wilson's results make it clear that the relationship between an industry's sales and its advertising expenditures must be understood before the competitive effects of advertising controls can be completely assessed. If the industry is one in which sales are not sensitive to advertising, such as the industry studied by Bass and Wildt, controls could have a much different impact than they would where the opposite relation existed.

Conclusions about Prior Studies

The results of these three studies indicate that there are several important things that must be done in a study of the competitive effects of controls on advertising expenditures. The Pogue and Uhl study pointed out a need to examine how controls on advertising expenditures would affect entry barriers; the Bass and Wildt study suggested that there is a need to build models of the decision processes *behind* the decision rules that decision makers appear to use; and the Comanor and Wilson study highlighted the need to pay close attention to how industry sales are influenced by industry advertising expenditures. The study described in the following pages attempted to heed this advice.

NOTES TO CHAPTER ONE

1. For descriptions of public policy toward advertising in the United States, see S. Watson Dunn, *Advertising: Its Role in Modern Marketing* (New York: Holt, Rinehart and Winston, 1969), Ch. 7; and Robert E. Wilkes and James B. Wilcox, "Recent FTC Actions: Implications for the Advertising Strategist," *Journal of Marketing* (January 1974), pp. 55-61.

2. Jules Backman, *Advertising and Competition* (New York: New York University Press, 1967); Julian L. Simon, *Issues in the Economics of Advertising* (Urbana, Ill.: University of Illinois Press, 1970); Richard Schmalen-

see, *The Economics of Advertising* (Amsterdam: North-Holland Publishing, 1972); William S. Comanor and Thomas A. Wilson, *Advertising and Market Power* (Cambridge, Mass.: Harvard University Press, 1974); James M. Ferguson, *Advertising and Competition: Theory, Measurement, Fact* (Cambridge, Mass.: Ballinger Publishing, 1974); and Jean-Jacques Lambin, *Advertising, Competition and Market Conduct* (Amsterdam: North-Holland Publishing, 1975).

3. See Harlan M. Blake and William K. Jones, "In Defense of Antitrust," *Columbia Law Review* (March 1965), pp. 376-400.

4. Russell H. Colley, *Defining Advertising Goals for Measured Advertising Results* (New York: Association of National Advertisers, 1961), p. 1.

5. See Joe S. Bain, *Barriers to New Competition* (Cambridge, Mass.: Harvard University Press, 1956); and William S. Comanor and Thomas A. Wilson, "Advertising, Market Structure and Performance," *Review of Economics and Statistics* (November 1967), pp. 423-40.

6. See Nicholas Kaldor, "The Economic Aspects of Advertising," *Review of Economic Studies* (1949-51), pp. 1-27; Bain, *Barriers*; and Comanor and Wilson, "Advertising, Market Structure."

7. See Comanor and Wilson, "Advertising, Market Structure."

8. See Douglas F. Greer, "Product Differentiation and Concentration in the Brewing Industry," *Journal of Industrial Economics* (July 1971), pp. 201-19.

9. See Yale Brozen, "New FTC Policy From Obsolete Economic Doctrine," *Antitrust Law Journal*, no. 3 (1973), pp. 477-87. Brozen's argument is based essentially on what is found in George J. Stigler, "The Economics of Information," *Journal of Political Economy* (June 1961), pp. 213-25. For a similar line of reasoning, see Lester G. Telser, "Advertising and Competition," *Journal of Political Economy* (December 1964), pp. 537-62; and Ferguson, *Advertising and Competition*, Chapters 1 and 2.

10. See Backman, *Advertising and Competition*; Brozen, "FTC Policy"; and Telser, "Advertising and Competition."

11. Ferguson, *Advertising and Competition*, pp. 16-17.

12. See Robert D. Buzzell, "The Role of Advertising in the Marketing Mix," Remarks delivered at the Federal Trade Commission's Hearings on Modern Advertising Practices, October 1971; and Backman, *Advertising and Competition*.

13. Reviews of this work can be found in Backman, *Advertising and Competition*; Peter Doyle, "Economic Aspects of Advertising: A Survey," *Economic Journal* (September 1968), pp. 570-602; Lee E. Preston, "Advertising Effects and Public Policy," in Robert L. King, ed., *Marketing and the New Science of Planning* (Chicago: American Marketing Association, 1968), pp. 558-66; Simon, *Issues*; Schmalensee, *The Economics of Advertising*; John M. Vernon, *Market Structure and Industrial Performance: A Review of Statistical Findings* (Boston: Allyn and Bacon, 1972); and Ferguson, *Advertising and Competition*.

14. Greer, "Product Differentiation."

15. Lee Benham, "The Effect of Advertising on the Price of Eyeglasses," *Journal of Law and Economics* (October 1972), pp. 337-52.

16. For a review of existing taxes, see Thomas F. Pogue and Kenneth P. Uhl, *Direct State Taxes on Advertising Services: Economic Implications* (Washington, D.C.: Consumer Research Institute, 1972).

17. Walter Adams, *The Structure of American Industry* (New York: Macmillan, 1971), p. 490. See also W.H. Nicholls, *Price Policies in the Cigarette Industry* (Nashville: The Vanderbilt University Press, 1951), pp. 412-15; and Max Corden, *A Tax on Advertising?* (London: Fabian Society Research Series 222, 1961).

18. Mark J. Green et al., *The Closed Enterprise System* (New York: Grossman Publishers, 1972), p. 318. See also Donald F. Turner, "Advertising and Competition," *Federal Bar Journal* (Spring 1966), p. 96.

19. Joel Dean, "Does Advertising Belong in the Capital Budget?" *Journal of Marketing* (October 1966), pp. 15-21.

20. Leonard W. Weiss, "Advertising, Profits, and Corporate Taxes," *Review of Economics and Statistics* (November 1969), pp. 421-30. For additional support for a depreciation requirement, see Simon, *Issues*, p. 281.

21. F.M. Scherer, *Industrial Market Structure and Economic Performance* (Chicago: Rand McNally, 1970), pp. 344-45.

22. Paul D. Scanlon, "Anti-Competitive Advertising and the FTC: A Ban on Oligopoly-Creating Ads?" *Antitrust Law and Economics Review* (Spring 1970), pp. 21-30.

23. For a discussion of these alternatives see Philip Kotler, Fred C. Allvine, and Paul N. Bloom, "Public Policy Alternatives for Regulating Advertising Expenditures: An Evaluation," in Fred C. Allvine, ed., *Public Policy and Marketing Practices* (Chicago: American Marketing Association, 1973).

24. Turner, "Advertising and Competition."

25. See John M. Kuhlman, "The Procter and Gamble Decision," *Quarterly Review of Economics and Business* (Spring 1966), pp. 29-36.

26. "The Cereal Case: Opening Shot in FTC War on 'Structural' Shared-Monopoly or Attack on 'Marketing' Irregularities?" *Antitrust Law and Economics Review* (Fall 1971). For additional discussion of the cereal case, see Louis W. Stern and Thomas Dunfee, "Public Policy Implications of Non-Price Marketing Strategies and De-Oligopolization in the Cereal Industry," in Allvine, ed., *Public Policy*; and William E. Huth, "The Advertising Industry–An Unlikely Monopolizer," *Antitrust Bulletin* (Winter 1974), pp. 653-79.

27. Senate bill introduced by Senator Philip Hart. See the *Congressional Record* (July 24, 1973) and "Anti-Monopoly Bill Offered," *The Washington Post*, June 13, 1975, p. D1.

28. See "Food Industry Structure to Be Focus of FTC Probe," *Advertising Age* (March 11, 1974), p. 2.

29. "Investigation of Heavy-Duty Detergent Industry Announced," *Federal Trade Commission News Summary*, June 20, 1975, p. 4.

30. Pogue and Uhl, *Direct State Taxes.*

31. Frank M. Bass and Albert R. Wildt, *Analysis of the Dynamics of Competition in a Heavily Advertised Food Product Category* (Washington, D.C.: Consumer Research Institute, 1972).

32. William S. Comanor and Thomas A. Wilson, "Advertising and the

Distribution of Consumer Demand," Research paper No. 169, Stanford University Graduate School of Business, May 1973.

33. See, for example, Robert Pitofsky, "Changing Focus in the Regulation of Advertising," Speech given before the Advertising and Society Lecture Series of the University of Chicago, April 1972; Kotler et al., "Alternatives"; and Preston, "Advertising Effects."

34. Reed Moyer, *Macro Marketing: A Social Perspective* (New York: Wiley, 1972), p. 52.

35. Raymond A. Bauer and Stephen A. Greyser, *Advertising in America: The Consumer View* (Boston: Harvard Business School, 1968), p. 375.

36. Simon *Issues*, p. 279; and Scherer, *Industrial*, p. 344.

37. Doyle, "Economic Aspects."

38. Moyer, *Macro*; and Doyle, "Economic Aspects."

39. Preston, "Advertising Effects"; and Doyle, "Economic Aspects."

40. Doyle, "Economic Aspects."

41. Pitofsky, "Changing Focus."

42. Kotler, et al., "Alternatives"; and Bauer and Greyser, *America*.

43. Jay W. Forrester, *Industrial Dynamics* (Cambridge, Mass.: M.I.T. Press, 1961).

44. See Bertil Klinte, *The Swedish Tax on Advertising* (London: Institute of Practitioners in Advertising, 1974); and Pogue and Uhl, *Direct State Taxes*.

45. See Banco National de Mexico, "The Tax on Advertising: Its Effect on the Economy," *Review of the Economic Situation of Mexico* (February 1971), pp. 62-64.

46. See Richard M. Cyert and James G. March, *A Behavioral Theory of the Firm* (Englewood Cliffs, N.J.: Prentice-Hall, 1963); Charles P. Bonini, *Simulation of Information and Decision Systems in the Firm* (Englewood Cliffs, N.J.: Prentice-Hall, 1963); Richard M. Cyert and Charles L. Hendrick, "Theory of the Firm: Past, Present, and Future: An Interpretation," *Journal of Economic Literature* (June 1972), pp. 398-412; Julian L. Simon et al., "A Duopoly Simulation: An End to Cournot," *Review of Economic Studies* (July 1973), pp. 353-66, and F. Gerard Adams, "From Econometric Models of the Nation to Models of Industries and Firms," *Wharton Quarterly* (Supplement, 1973), pp. 6-11.

47. Exceptions include Thomas A. Klein, "The Performance Implications of Brand Advertising: Simulation of a Typical Market for Packaged Whole Milk," Unpublished Ph.D. Dissertation, The Ohio State University, 1964; A.A. Kuehn and D.L. Weiss, "Marketing Analysis Training Exercise," *Behavioral Science* (January 1965), pp. 51-67; Lee E. Preston and Norman R. Collins, *Studies in a Simulated Market* (Berkeley: IBER Special Publications, 1966); and Philip Kotler, "Competitive Strategies for New Product Marketing Over the Life Cycle," *Management Science* (December 1965), p. 104.

48. Pogue and Uhl, *Direct State Taxes*.

49. Ibid., p. 22.

50. Bass and Wildt, *Analysis*.

51. Ibid., p. 146-47.

52. For a similar conclusion, see Greer, "Product Differentiation."

53. Comanor and Wilson, "Advertising and the Distribution of Consumer Demand."

54. H.S. Hothakker and L.D. Taylor, *Consumer Demand in the United States* (Cambridge, Mass.: Harvard University Press, 1970).

Chapter Two

The Product Manager

The product management system has been widely adopted within the advertising-intensive, consumer products manufacturing industries that can be considered potential targets of government controls on advertising expenditures (e.g., the breakfast cereal, detergent, cosmetic, and beer industries). Product managers play a major role within these industries in determining marketing strategies and tactics. Thus, in building the industry model used in this study, it was deemed necessary, among other things, to depict how product managers influence the actions of their respective firms. The manner in which this was done is described fully in Chapter Three. In the present chapter, some background is provided on the product management system and the product manager's job. This background material should give the reader a better understanding of a group of individuals who could play a key role in determining how much controls on advertising expenditures would stimulate or suppress competition.

HISTORY OF THE PRODUCT MANAGEMENT SYSTEM

It is generally agreed that Procter and Gamble, the giant soap and detergent manufacturer, was the first company to assign one of its employees to a position of product (or brand) manager. Accounts differ, however, as to the date, the product, and the manager involved. One author has reported that Procter and Gamble appointed Neil H. McElroy (who later became the company's president) as brand manager of Camay soap in 1927.[1] Other authors have claimed that the company assigned its first brand manager (no name given) to Lava soap in 1928.[2] Regardless of when and how it was first used, the product (brand) management system rapidly became an important and productive part of Procter and Gamble's organizational design. Under the leadership of McElroy, the company had eighteen brand managers as early as 1939.[3]

Despite the success achieved by Procter and Gamble with the product management system, other companies were slow to adopt it. A few innovative firms such as General Electric, General Foods, Monsanto, and Johnson & Johnson were early users of the system, but widespread acceptance of this form of marketing organization did not occur until the 1960s.[4] Although firms apparently recognized the value of having one individual coordinating all activities pertinent to the successful marketing of a particular product, they also saw many potential problems in switching to a product management system. They did not want to encounter the problems associated with using product managers identified by a McKinsey and Co. speaker during an American Management Association seminar in 1960:

1. Confusion with other jobs.
2. Tendency to interfere with line activities.
3. Background too limited for "total marketing" approach.
4. Misunderstood "profit responsibility."
5. "Veto" of creative advertising.
6. Difficulty of measuring performance.
7. Dominance by the field sales manager.
8. Isolation from field conditions.
9. Abdication of related responsibility by line management.
10. Detail involvement.
11. Difficulty of defining decision-making role.[5]

Since 1960, the vast majority of consumer products manufacturing firms in the United States have overcome their fears of changing to a product management system. In a 1973 survey of product managers and other marketing personnel in the food, soap and cleanser (and allied), paper products, and health and beauty aids industries, Clewett and Stasch discovered that over 98 percent of their 160 respondents felt that the product management system is "definitely here to stay" (63.8 percent) or that "its use is likely to continue" (34.4 percent).[6] Product management has received such widespread acceptance because it possesses many benefits, including those identified by Evans in an American Management Association research study:

1. Greater attention is paid by the corporation to the performance of each product or brand. . . .
2. The product manager is, by necessity, an information center to which higher management can turn for quick and specific up-to-date information on any product in the line.
3. With one person specifically charged with planning in relation to specific product groups, there will be a stronger tendency for the detail planning to get done. . . .
4. The job of coordination . . . becomes easier under the product manager system. . . . If nothing else, the product manager's job enables him to bring

continually to the attention of each department the information by which proper coordination can be achieved.

5. Because the product manager knows daily how well the organization is proceeding against plan in his product area, he is instantly aware of problems as they arise, and works with the line organization to resolve any problem or to revise the marketing plan to a new set of circumstances. . . .

6. The product manager position is—or can be—an excellent training ground on which to breed the kinds of generalists needed to fill vacancies or new positions as they occur in higher management echelons.[7]

In addition, the product management system can help to restore an entrepreneurial spirit to managers in large-scale, multi-product organizations.[8]

PRODUCT MANAGEMENT IN THEORY

Thus far, no attempt has been made to define what a product manager is or to describe his duties and responsibilities. In this section, therefore, an effort is made to present what is typically found in textbooks and job descriptions about how a product manager *should* operate; the following section is devoted to describing what empirical research studies have discovered about how product managers *actually* operate.

Clewett and Stasch have provided the following comprehensive description of what a product manager should theoretically be:

> The product manager's job is to serve as the focal point for planning and coordinating all of the activities required for the growth and profitability of his product. This does not mean that he does all the planning for his product, but it does mean that he sees that all the activities affecting his product are properly planned. The product manager is clearly not a line executive in the classic sense, for he has no line authority. Nor is he staff in the sense of support staff, as are, for example, the market research or advertising managers. The difference is that he does have the unqualified responsibility for seeing that everything related to his product gets done well and on time.
>
> To carry out this role effectively, he must be able to work with experts on all matters relating to his product, both inside and outside the company. He must be able to rely on his broad product and market knowledge, management skills, and sheer persuasiveness to get things planned and accomplished. He has to do this by working through executives who do have line authority.[9]

Thus, a product manager should be, to some extent, a "little general manager" for his product and, to some extent, an assistant to his company's line management. He should be given responsibility for the performance of his product and rewarded if it does well, but he should be given only limited authority to make the decisions that affect his product's performance. He should be primarily a recommender and influencer of decisions, not a line decision maker. To give him more decision-making authority could create undesirable conflicts within an organization (e.g., among product managers).

To be more specific, the *good* product manager (or *brand* manager, if he is responsible for only a single brand within a product category) should, in theory, have well-developed skills in five important areas. First, the product manager should be skillful at gathering relevant, timely, useful information about the performance of his product, the activities of competitors, the attitudes and habits of dealers and consumers, the policies of government agencies, and so on—that is, he should be responsible for any data that can help his firm do a more effective job of marketing his product. The product manager should have, virtually at his fingertips, the data that can tell him whether there is a need to revise or abandon his product, change a package or advertising theme, or increase production or inventories. Such data should be acquired from internal marketing research departments, accounting records, syndicated data reporting services, salespersons, and a host of other sources.

Second, the product manager should be adept at planning marketing strategies and programs. He should develop both annual and long-range marketing plans for his product that are workable and effective. The annual plan should contain recommendations on advertising, promotion, and sales call budgets, pricing strategy, packaging changes, product revisions, and distribution policies, as well as the yearly objectives for the product. The long-range plan should focus on how the product should be marketed over a four- or five-year period and, in part, on what the long-run implications would be of continuing to use the strategies recommended in the annual plan.

The product manager should also be good at making forecasts. He should be able to make reasonably accurate predictions of what sales will be if certain marketing strategies and tactics are used. These predictions are frequently needed by personnel in production, inventory control, finance, and distribution.

Fourth, the product manager should be proficient at coordinating the activities of a wide variety of persons and organizations. He needs to make sure that the firm's advertising agency and internal advertising department are working together productively, that the production department has shipments ready to go when the salesmen promised them, and that the results of an important marketing research study are available when requested by top management.

Finally, the product manager should be competent at monitoring the progress of the marketing program for his product. He should be able to identify quickly when the marketing plan is not being adhered to or when deviations from the plan are required to avoid disappointing performance. He should also be able to recommend the remedial steps required to make a product perform as previously planned.

To briefly summarize, then, the product manager should, in theory, be given only limited authority to make decisions about how his product should be marketed. The product manager should be primarily an information gatherer, planner, forecaster, coordinator, and performance monitor, not a line decision maker.

PRODUCT MANAGEMENT IN PRACTICE

Do product managers, in reality, have very little decision making authority? If so, how much influence do they have on the marketing decisions made by higher management? In what areas do product managers tend to have the most influence? Although it is difficult to generalize about how decisions are made in different organizations, three recent studies have produced results that can help to answer these questions. In surveys of the role of product managers in large consumer products manufacturing companies, Lucas,[10] Buell,[11] and Clewett and Stasch[12] have found certain similarities to exist across firms and industries. Their findings are summarized in the following paragraphs.

Lucas conducted a mail questionnaire survey of 60 product managers from consumer products manufacturing companies found in the "Top 125 National Advertisers of 1969" list of *Advertising Age*. The survey was designed to examine the influence of product managers in making decisions on all aspects of marketing (and on production, budget control, and legal questions). Respondents were asked about their degree of control over fifteen specific decision areas.

Lucas' findings led him to conclude that product managers enjoy much greater decision-making authority than most textbooks or job descriptions indicate. More specifically, he found that:

> Altogether, of 15 decision areas studied, the product managers claimed to be dominant in seven: advertising strategy, copy approval, media planning, agency relations, sales promotion, marketing tests, and more general marketing research. They admitted to only limited control of advertising agency selection, budgeting for personal selling, selection of salesmen, scheduling production, logistics of distribution and problems involving legal considerations. Only two areas seemed to involve more shared authority: advertising expenditures . . . [and] pricing.[13]

However, he found that more than one-half claimed full, or almost full, control (and seventeen claimed about one-half control) over advertising expenditures;

and that more than one-half (35) indicated full, or almost full, control (and fifteen claimed about one-half control) over pricing.[14] Lucas summarized his findings in the following statement:

> Only seven of the 60 respondents complained of a serious lack of control over decisions affecting profit. This hardly reflects the image of a product manager as a pseudo-executive whose level of responsibility and authority are neither defined nor assigned.[15]

Buell's survey of upper level managers—*not* product managers—produced findings that tend to contradict those of Lucas. Buell conducted personal interviews with 63 executives from 20 major consumer products companies, and with 23 executives from 10 major advertising agencies. He was primarily concerned with discovering how the advertising decision-making process works in large, multi-product consumer products companies. His findings led him to make the following statements:

> There is no question that, in the sixteen companies in this study that use product managers, major advertising decisions are made at division middle management levels (including group product managers) and above—and primarily at the division chief marketing executive and division manager level . . . the common observation made by executives interviewed is that *advertising is too important to leave decisions regarding it to lower and less experienced levels.* Advertising agency executives confirmed the above findings.[16]

Buell's report contains explanations by both his respondents and himself for the inconsistencies between his findings and those of Lucas. Buell's respondents expressed the opinion that product managers were reinforcing their own self-images when answering the Lucas questionnaire.[17] On the other hand, Buell, himself, believed that the inconsistencies could be caused by (1) his own smaller sample of firms—all of which were industry leaders—or (2) the fact that a product manager might "perceive that he has authority if his recommendations are normally accepted, even though his management, in fact, does not delegate final decision-making authority to him."[18]

In a more recent study, Clewett and Stasch conducted a mail survey of 160 product managers and other marketing personnel (including people in higher management) from firms listed among *Advertising Age's* "100 Leading National Advertisers of 1971." All respondents were from the food, soap and cleanser (and allied), paper products, and health and beauty aids industries. The survey attempted to discover, among other things (1) the management tasks performed by product managers, (2) the set of marketing decisions influenced by product managers, and (3) the influence product managers have in establishing the size of their products' budgets and the freedom they have in using these budgets. It was found that product managers tend to have decision-making authority that falls somewhere in between what they were reported to have by Lucas and by Buell.

To be more specific, Clewett and Stasch found that:

1. Product managers saw themselves as playing more than a major role in seeing that management tasks such as "establishing marketing objectives for your product," "communicating the marketing plan," and "determining expense budgets for each marketing activity" are completed. In fact, many saw themselves as being solely responsible for these tasks.[19]
2. Product managers saw themselves as being slightly less than major participants in making marketing decisions on behalf of their products. They viewed themselves as being very major participants in decisions regarding sales promotions; as somewhat less active (but still influential) in decision making on marketing research, advertising, product quality, packaging, and pricing; and as minor participants, at best, in decisions about their company's sales force.[20]
3. Approximately 65 percent of product managers felt that they had at least a "strong voice" in determining their product's budget.[21]
4. Higher management personnel attributed (1) noticeably more management task responsibility, (2) somewhat more decision authority, and (3) slightly more budget recommendation influence to product managers than product managers did to themselves.[22]

As one examines the results of the three studies reviewed above as well as those of other studies on product management,[23] a relatively clear picture begins to emerge of the role played by product managers in large, multi-product, consumer products companies. In a majority of cases, the product manager is the focal point of all corporate marketing activity related to a particular product. It is the product manager who initially develops his product's annual marketing plan, who acts as the chief watchdog over competing products, and who monitors his product's performance. Moreover, it is the product manager who tends to inject some competitive fervor into his product's marketing program; he is constantly urging other personnel in sales, advertising, and elsewhere to give their best efforts to help his product outperform its competitors. In short, the product manager is the person who, in spite of his lack of final decision-making authority, probably has more influence over the nature of his product's marketing program than any other single individual in his organization.

IMPLICATIONS FOR THIS STUDY

Since product managers seem to have considerable influence over the marketing decisions made in multi-product, consumer products manufacturing companies, it was judged to be reasonable to have the industry model used in this study consist, essentially, of several competing product or brand managers. A model was thus constructed to represent how the brand managers in an oligopolistic grocery manufacturing industry develop the yearly marketing plans followed by their firms. Brand managers are assumed to go through a decision process each year in which they (1) gather information about their respective industries, (2) forecast how rival managers will behave, (3) set objectives for their brands, (4) test the consequences of using various marketing plans, and (5) select a plan to employ. A complete description of this model is presented in the next chapter.

SUMMARY

After taking several decades to become accepted by American business firms, the product management form of organization now enjoys widespread use. In the vast majority of consumer products manufacturing companies, product managers play a major role in the formation of marketing programs, despite the fact that they are rarely given final decision-making authority. It therefore seems reasonable to have the industry model used in this study consist, essentially, of several competing product or brand managers.

NOTES TO CHAPTER TWO

1. Philip Kotler, *Marketing Management: Analysis, Planning, and Control* (Englewood Cliffs, N.J.: Prentice-Hall, 1972), p. 287.

2. Gordon H. Evans, *The Product Manager's Job* (New York: American Management Association, 1964), p. 12; and George S. Dominguez, *Product Management* (New York: American Management Association, 1971), p. 6.

3. Evans, *Product Manager's*, p. 12.

4. Dominguez, *Product Management*, p. 7.

5. Evans, *Product Manager's*, p. 19.

6. Richard M. Clewett and Stanley F. Stasch, *Product Managers in Consumer Packaged Goods Industries* (Evanston, Ill.: Northwestern University Graduate School of Management, 1974), p. 9.

7. Evans, *Product Manager's*, p. 19.

8. Kotler, *Marketing Management*, p. 287.

9. Clewett and Stasch, *Product Managers*, p. 23.

10. Darrell B. Lucas, "Point of View: Product Managers in Advertising," *Journal of Advertising Research* (June 1972), p. 41-44.

11. Victor P. Buell, *Changing Practices in Advertising Decision-Making and Control* (New York: Association of National Advertisers, 1973).

12. Clewett and Stasch, *Product Managers*. See also Richard M. Clewett and Stanley F. Stasch, "Shifting Role of the Product Manager," *Harvard Business Review* (January-February 1975), pp. 65-73.

13. Lucas, "Point of View," pp. 42-43.

14. Ibid., p. 43.

15. Ibid., p. 42.

16. Buell, *Changing*, pp. 51-52.

17. Ibid., p. 51.

18. Ibid., p. 51.

19. Clewett and Stasch, *Product Managers*, p. 10.

20. Ibid., p. 10.

21. Ibid., p. 11.

22. Ibid., p. 2.

23. Evans, *Product Manager's*; Dominguez, *Product Management*; Gordon Medcalf, *Marketing and the Brand Manager* (Oxford: Pergamon Press, 1967); and The Conference Board, *The Product Management System: A Symposium* (New York: National Industrial Conference Board, 1965).

Chapter Three

The Model

The model used in this study and the procedure that was followed in constructing it are described in this chapter. The model was built to represent a *hypothetical*, oligopolistic, grocery manufacturing industry that possesses many of the characteristics of the nutritional submarket ("Special K," "Total," "Life," and so forth) of the ready-to-eat breakfast cereal industry.[a] The emphasis in the model is on how marketing decisions in the areas of advertising, promotion, sales calls, product quality, and price are made for each brand in the industry.

The model was patterned after the nutritional submarket of the cereal industry for two reasons. First, some data were available about this submarket from the Harvard Business School "Life Cereal Case,"[1] and about the entire cereal industry from a study published by the National Commission on Food Marketing.[2] However, there was not enough data available to allow one to build a model of the actual submarket. Second, the cereal industry has frequently been accused of using its advertising expenditures in an anti-competitive manner (see, for example, the discussion of the FTC complaint against the cereal industry in Chapter One). If any industry is to be subjected to controls on its advertising expenditures, it is likely to be the cereal industry or one very similar to it.

CONSTRUCTION PROCEDURE

A procedure consisting of basically five steps was followed in constructing the model. First, an extensive survey of the economics and marketing literature was

---

[a]Simulation models of *hypothetical* systems have been found to be valuable for gaining insights into the nature of *real* systems. See, for example, Charles P. Bonini, *Simulation of Information and Decision Systems in the Firm* (Englewood Cliffs, N.J.: Prentice-Hall, 1963).

conducted. This survey was carried out to insure that the assumptions about the behavior of manufacturers, potential rival manufacturers, retailers, and consumers found in the model could be supported by economic theory, marketing theory, or empirical evidence. The literature that was covered included work on the theory of the firm, oligopoly theory, advertising decision making, pricing behavior, and marketing model building.

The second step consisted of a survey of available materials on the grocery manufacturing industry and, in particular, on the breakfast cereal manufacturers. This was done to gain familiarity with the various marketing tools and strategies used by grocery manufacturers and to acquire a feeling for the character of past and current competition in the cereal market. The materials surveyed included several works that were an outgrowth of the National Commission on Food Marketing studies,[3] trade journals, and a few Harvard cases.[4]

Following these two surveys, a set of *starting* assumptions were determined and then used in designing a first approximation to the model.[5] A computer program was written at this time to test the feasibility, from a cost standpoint, of using such a model to study the consequences of controlling advertising expenditures.

The fourth step of the construction procedure involved an analysis of the limited amount of data available on the nutritional submarket of the cereal industry. Figures from the "Life Cereal Case," the National Commission study, a publication called *National Advertising Investments,*[6] and a few trade journal articles[7] were used to make estimates of the market shares, profits, advertising budgets, consumer-directed promotion budgets, availability, prices, and several other variables for all the brands in the submarket during the decade of the 1960s. These estimates served as an artificial data base to use in estimating, via regression analysis, a set of parameters for the response function in the model that determines a brand's expected and actual market share.[b] The estimated parameters were used as starting points in the search process necessary to finalize the model (see below). In addition, four years of the artificial data base were used to provide starting conditions for all the runs of the model.

The fifth step of the construction procedure put the model into its final form. A search was conducted for a set of assumptions, response functions, and parameter values which would produce output data that seemed "reasonable." An attempt was made to match the output from an eight-year computer run, in which no controls on advertising expenditures were operative, to the available data from the 1960s on the nutritional submarket. Various aspects of

---

[b]The market share response function used in the model is presented later in this chapter. The transformation that was done to put this nonlinear equation into linear form was suggested by Masao Nakanishi, "Measurement of Sales Promotion Effect at the Retail Level—A New Approach," in Boris W. Becker and Helmut Becker, eds., *Marketing Education and the Real World* (Chicago: American Marketing Association, 1973), pp. 338-43.

the model were successively changed to produce output that appeared more realistic. A comparison of the output produced by the final model to available industry data can be found in Chapter Five.

It should be noted that most of the changes made in the model were not made merely to get a closer fit to the available data. The search process led to the discovery of certain properties of the model that were theoretically weak and changes were made to correct these properties. The changes that were made to improve the fit to the data were made simply to parameter values.

A detailed description of the final version of the model is found in the next section. This description contains a small amount of critical commentary about the model. A more complete critical analysis of the model can be found at the end of Chapter Five.

DESCRIPTION OF THE MODEL

The model contains four basic components: (1) a manufacturers' submodel, (2) a potential rival manufacturers' submodel, (3) a retailers' submodel, and (4) a consumers' submodel. These four submodels interact in a yearly cycle. Each year, all existing manufacturers make a set of seven strategic marketing decisions for each of their brands to carry them through that year. While existing manufacturers are reaching their decisions, potential rival manufacturers look into the industry and go through a decision procedure in which they decide whether to enter or not. Once all the old and new manufacturers have decided how to market their brands for a given year, the retailers decide whether they should stock and support the various brands. After this, consumers determine how much of each brand they want to purchase. The results that each brand achieves in the marketplace for a year are finally fed back to the manufacturers, adjustments are made, and the cycle starts over again for another year.

A description of each submodel is found below. These descriptions include some discussion of the theoretical arguments and empirical evidence that support the various assumptions that were made. The computer program of the model and the output from the benchmark (no controls) run of the model can be found in Appendix A and Appendix B of this book.

Manufacturers' Submodel

Since the overall model was designed to have a marketing orientation, it was deemed appropriate to assume that the decision makers for the manufacturers are brand or product managers. In other words, the seven yearly marketing decisions made for each of the manufacturers' brands are assumed to be made by brand managers. As discussed in Chapter Two, in a majority of consumer products firms, brand or product managers probably have more influence over the nature of their products' marketing programs than anyone else.

In those cases where a manufacturer has more than one brand, no cooperation is assumed to take place among the managers of those brands. Brand managers are assumed to compete with managers from both outside and inside their firms.[c]

A representation of the decision procedure that each brand manager goes through during a year is found in Figure 3-1. Each step in this procedure is discussed extensively in a separate section below. The procedure can be viewed as representing what a manager does in planning his marketing *strategy* for a year (or his annual marketing plan). His marketing strategy is defined by the settings he chooses for seven marketing variables: consumer advertising expenditures, consumer-directed promotion expenditures (coupons, premiums, and so forth), dealer-directed promotion expenditures (allowances, discounts, and so forth), sales call expenditures, retail price, wholesale price, and brand quality (e.g., level of nutrients). No decision is made on levels of production because it is assumed that each manager can produce the exact quantity demanded. Moreover, *tactical* decisions in areas such as media selection, copy selection, packaging, and salesmen's compensation are also not made in the model. Only marketing decisions of a more aggregate and strategic nature are included.[8]

Profit Equation Estimation. To keep the model simple, each brand manager is assumed to have perfect knowledge of (1) what future population levels will be, (2) how consumers and retailers will behave given certain marketing strategies are used by the manufacturers, and (3) what his brand's manufacturing and transportation costs will be at various levels of production, retail availability, and product quality. The only thing a brand manager is assumed to be uncertain about is the behavior of his existing and potential rivals. Thus, each brand manager is, in effect, a player in an *n-person nonzero-sum game* in which he knows all the payoffs in the game's payoff matrix, but does not know what strategies the other players are going to use.[d] This simplification creates a situation where all brand managers in the model make a correct estimate of the form of their brand's profit equation during the first step presented in Figure 3-1. This simplification also makes the entire model *deterministic.*

The profit equation that is estimated by the brand managers and that is also used to compute each brand's actual after-tax profits is found in Table 3-1. The equation makes a brand's profits a function of several variables,

---

[c]Brand managers from the same firm have been known to compete vigorously with one another. See Victor P. Buell, *Changing Practices in Advertising Decision-Making and Control* (New York: Association of National Advertisers, 1973), pp. 39-40.

[d]Several individuals have suggested that game theory provides a useful framework for describing oligopolistic behavior. See, for example, R. Duncan Luce and Howard Raiffa, *Games and Decisions* (New York: Wiley, 1957); Martin Shubik, *Strategy and Market Structure* (New York: Wiley, 1959); and Lester G. Telser, *Competition, Collusion, and Game Theory* (Chicago: Aldine-Atherton, 1972).

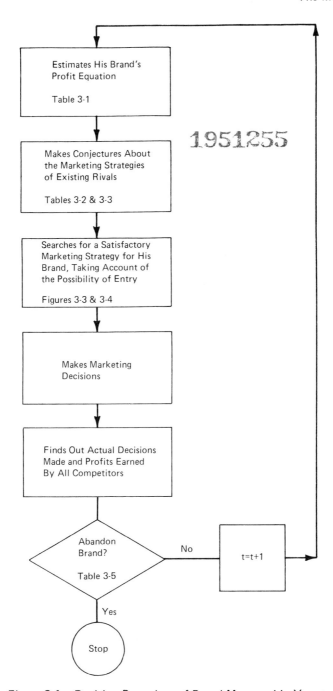

Figure 3-1. Decision Procedure of Brand Manager i in Year t.

Table 3-1. The Model's Profit Equation

$$Z_{it} = [SB_{it} - (VC_{it} \cdot Q_{it}) - FC_{it} - A_{it} - CP_{it} - DP_{it} - SC_{it}] \, .52$$

Where:

$$SB_{it} = PW_{it} \cdot Q_{it}$$

$$Q_{it} = SI_t \cdot SHARE_{it}.$$

CONSUMER BEHAVIOR SUBMODEL

$$SI_t = POP_t \cdot PCAP_{t-1} \cdot \left[\frac{TAG_t}{TAG_{t-1}}\right]^{ETA_t} \left[\frac{TCP_t}{TCP_{t-1}}\right]^{ETC} \left[\frac{APR_t}{APR_{t-1}}\right]^{EAP}$$

$$SHARE_{it} = \frac{PR_{it}^{EPR} \cdot D_{it}^{ED} \cdot AG_{it}^{EA} \cdot CI_{it}^{ECI} \cdot B_{it}^{EB} \cdot CP_{it}^{ECP}}{\Sigma_j PR_{jt}^{EPR} \cdot D_{jt}^{ED} \cdot AG_{jt}^{EA} \cdot CI_{jt}^{ECI} \cdot B_{jt}^{EB} \cdot CP_{jt}^{ECP}}$$

$$ETA_t = b - mTAG_t$$

$$AG_{it} = .4A_{it} + .3A_{it-1} + .2A_{it-2} + .1A_{it-3}$$

RETAILER BEHAVIOR SUBMODEL

$$D_{it} = \left[\frac{CI_{it}}{DIV}\right]\left[\frac{DREV_{it}}{ADREV}\right]^{EREV} \left[\frac{SC_{it}}{ASC_t}\right]^{ESC}$$

$$CI_{it} = CI_{it-1} + 10(FSH_{kt-1} - FSH_{kt-2})$$

$$DREV_{it} = SI_t \cdot S\hat{H}ARE_{it}(PR_{it} - PW_{it} - .10) + DP_{it}$$

$$S\hat{H}ARE_{it} = \frac{PR_{it}^{EPR} \cdot D_{it-1}^{ED} \cdot AG_{it}^{EA} \cdot CI_{it}^{ECI} \cdot B_{it}^{EB} \cdot CP_{it}^{ECP}}{\Sigma_j PR_{jt}^{EPR} \cdot D_{jt-1}^{ED} \cdot AG_{jt}^{EA} \cdot CI_{jt}^{ECI} \cdot B_{jt}^{EB} \cdot CP_{jt}^{ECP}}$$

$$D_{it-1} = \frac{CI_{it}}{DIV} \text{ if } NAGE_{it} \leqslant 1$$

$$VC_{it} = .18 + .0002B_{it} + .10D_{it}$$

$$FC_{it} = 2,000,000$$

Table 3-1 (cont.)

Variables defined as:

Z_{it}	=	After-tax profits of Brand i in year t
SB	=	Sales in dollars
VC	=	Variable manufacturing and transportation cost per pound
Q	=	Sales in pounds
FC	=	Fixed manufacturing and transportation costs
A	=	Consumer advertising expenditures
CP	=	Consumer-directed promotion expenditures
DP	=	Dealer-directed promotion expenditures
SC	=	Sales-calls expenditures
PW	=	Average wholesale price per pound
SI	=	Industry sales in pounds
$SHARE$	=	Market share of brand
POP	=	U.S. population
$PCAP$	=	Per capita consumption of industry's product
TAG	=	Total industry advertising goodwill
TCP	=	Total industry consumer-directed promotion expenditures
APR	=	Average retail price in industry
ETA	=	Sensitivity parameter of advertising goodwill
ETC, EAP	=	Sensitivity parameters
PR	=	Average retail price per pound
D	=	Distribution effectiveness
AG	=	Advertising goodwill
CI	=	Corporate image
B	=	Brand quality
$EPR, ED, EA, ECI, EB, ECP$	=	Sensitivity parameters
b, m	=	Parameters
$DREV$	=	Expected retail gross profits
ASC	=	Average sales-calls expenditures in industry
$DIV, ADREV, EREV, ESC$	=	Parameters
FSH_{kt}	=	Market share of firm k in year t
$\hat{SHARE}$	=	Share brand would receive with previous year's distribution effectiveness
$NAGE$	=	Age of brand in years

including the marketing decisions made by all the brands in the industry. A corporate tax rate of 48 percent is utilized.

As shown in Table 3-1, the sales (in pounds) of a brand (Q) are determined by multiplying industry sales in pounds (SI) by the brand's market share (SHARE). Industry sales are assumed to be a function of population and of the previous year's per capita consumption of the industry's product, adjusted for changes in the industry's total advertising goodwill (TAG), total consumer-directed promotion expenditures (TCP), and average retail price (APR). A brand's share is assumed to be equal to its share of the industry's total "marketing effort." Together, the industry sales response function and market share response function make up the model's consumer behavior submodel. This submodel is described more fully later in this chapter.

A response function that determines a brand's "distribution effectiveness" (D) is also found in Table 3-1. A brand's distribution effectiveness can be viewed as an expression of the availability of the brand and of the reseller support it receives. The distribution effectiveness response function represents the model's retailer behavior submodel. This submodel is described in more detail later in this chapter.

The cost equations found in Table 3-1 were selected to produce a downward sloping average manufacturing and transportation cost curve of the type typically used in economic analysis. Data from the National Commission study and the "Life Cereal Case" were also used to provide some guidance in determining the cost equations.[9] An approximation of the average cost curve that is used is found in Figure 3-2. The sharp downward slope at the start of this curve indicates the presence of significant economies of scale in manufacturing and transportation. The upward turn at high levels of production is caused by an assumed positive relationship between transportation costs and distribution effectiveness. As distribution improves, longer trips are presumably added to transportation schedules and inventories are presumably replenished more frequently. Another important characteristic of the cost curve is that it shifts upward when improvements are made in a brand's quality.

Returning to Figure 3-1, one sees that a brand manager goes through a number of other activities as part of his annual decision procedure besides estimating his brand's profit equation. He must (1) make conjectures about what he thinks his existing rivals' marketing strategies, or *marketing mixes*, will be for the next four years; (2) go through a search procedure in which he locates a satisfactory marketing strategy to use for the coming year; (3) make conjectures about what he thinks potential rivals will do over the next four years; and (4) decide at the end of the year whether to continue marketing his brand. The remainder of this section on the manufacturers' submodel focuses on what the brand manager does in each of these four areas.

Conjectures Made about Existing Rivals. In the model, a brand manager's existing rivals can be of two types—established and new. An estab-

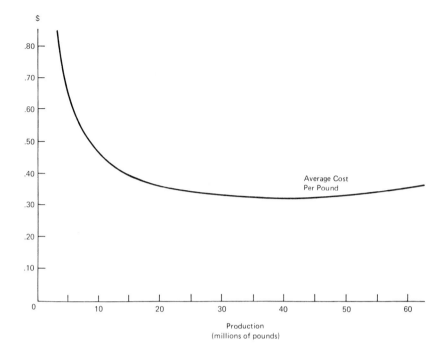

Figure 3-2. The Average Manufacturing and Transportation Cost Curve of the Brand Manager.

lished rival is a brand that has been in existence for at least four years. A new rival is a brand that is one to four years old. Brand managers make different conjectures about the behavior of established rivals and that of new rivals.

Because all established brand managers are assumed to have four-year planning horizons, they must make conjectures about four years of rival behavior. The planning horizon for them was extended to four years to avoid having managers take actions that would be helpful to them in the short run but harmful to their long-run interests. The horizon was limited to four years because it was felt that real-world brand managers do not generally look beyond this point.[e]

It should also be noted that managers of one- or two-year old brands are assumed to have only one-year planning horizons. They were believed to be concerned primarily with having their brands survive past each of the first two years. Nevertheless, the managers of these infant brands must still make conjectures about how their rivals will behave in the coming year before they can determine their marketing strategies for that year.

[e]This belief was tested during the interviews that were conducted as part of this study (see Chapter Five).

Conjectures made about established rivals. The conjectures that a manager of an established or new brand makes about his *established* rivals in almost all years are shown in Table 3-2. Unless an advertising control has just been introduced (the conjectures made in this situation are discussed later), the manager conjectures that his rivals will continue to utilize the decision rules that they appeared to use in the previous year for the next four years (year t to year $t+3$). The manager believes that his rivals always employ rules that (1) set advertising, consumer-directed promotion, dealer-directed promotion, and sales call budgets at certain proportions of their previous year's sales; (2) set retail price and wholesale price at certain proportions of the average retail price

Table 3-2. Conjectures Made by the Brand Manager About the Behavior of Established Rivals

The brand manager conjectures that established rival i will follow the following decision rules during any given year t of the next four years:

$$A_{it} = p1_i \cdot SB_{it-1}$$

$$CP_{it} = p2_i \cdot SB_{it-1}$$

$$DP_{it} = p3_i \cdot SB_{it-1}$$

$$SC_{it} = p4_i \cdot SB_{it-1}$$

$$PR_{it} = p5_i \cdot APR_{t-1}$$

$$PW_{it} = p6_i \cdot APR_{t-1}$$

$$B_{it} = B_{it-1}$$

Where:

$p1_i = A_{it-1}/SB_{it-2}$ (or the decision parameter used in the first decision rule during the previous year)

$p2_i = CP_{it-1}/SB_{it-2}$

$p3_i = DP_{it-1}/SB_{it-2}$

$p4_i = SC_{it-1}/SB_{it-2}$

$p5_i = PR_{it-1}/APR_{t-2}$

$p6_i = PW_{it-1}/APR_{t-2}$

and all other variables are defined in Table 3-1.

charged in the industry during the previous year; and (3) set brand quality at the same level it was during the previous year. The proportions, or *decision parameters*, that appear to have been used in the previous year's rules are assumed by the manager to remain the same throughout the next four years. The brand manager is assumed to collect information from various data reporting services—such as the Nielsen Retail Index or SAMI (Selling Area Marketing Incorporated)—to compute these parameters. Thus, if one rival spent $1 million on advertising in the previous year and had $10 million in sales in the year before that, it will be conjectured by his rivals that he will continue using a decision rule for the next four years that sets advertising expenditures at 10 percent of the past year's sales.[f] In short, brand managers conjecture that rival managers of established brands will basically behave in the future as they have in the past.

This assumption concerning the conjectures brand managers make about their established rivals is one of many that could be made in this type of model. The simplest possible assumption would be to have each brand manager conjecture that his rivals will continue spending the exact same amount, charging the same prices, and producing the same quality merchandise as they did in the previous year, regardless of what he does with his brand. This simple assumption is analogous to the Cournot assumption of classical duopoly theory in which one firm was assumed to conjecture that its rival would continue producing at the same output level.[10]

The major problem with using a Cournot-like assumption is that it amounts to assuming that the brand manager does not give his rivals credit for having enough sense to *react* in some way to his strategy changes. By assuming instead that each brand manager conjectures that his rivals will use only the same *decision rules* in the future, not make the same decisions, it is possible to let the brand manager conjecture that some type of reaction can occur. For example, in this model, the decision rules that a brand manager assumes his rivals will follow have him conjecturing that (1) rivals will spend *less* on advertising, consumer-directed promotion, dealer-directed promotion, and sales calls if he does something that lowers their sales; and (2) rivals will follow his increases (decreases) in retail price with relatively smaller increases (decreases) in their retail *and* wholesale prices. These reactions are conjectured because the rules that rivals are assumed to follow make spending in the four areas a constant fraction of past sales and make prices a constant fraction of past average retail price in the industry.

But although the assumption found in Table 3-2 represents an improvement over a straightforward Cournot assumption, it has serious weaknesses. For example, it is difficult to accept the assumption that brand managers think their rivals will always react to declines in sales by lowering their

---

[f]If a limit on advertising expenditures is being enforced, managers conjecture that their rivals will not exceed this limit.

marketing expenditures. Even though there is empirical evidence to support the notion that firms tend to base their advertising expenditures on past sales,[11] it has not been established that firms actually believe this evidence and therefore think their rivals set advertising budgets in this way. Furthermore, the assumption in Table 3-2 still basically models the brand manager as someone who gives his rivals credit for having very little ingenuity and competitive spirit. A more complex model than the one used in this study might have brand managers go through a learning process over time in which they discovered how competitors tended to react to certain strategy changes.[g]

A more complicated assumption than that found in Table 3-2 was not utilized, however, because it was felt that such an improvement would add substantially to the computer time for each run of the model. Moreover, it was also felt that there is a strong possibility that brand managers may actually make rather simple conjectures of the type found in Table 3-2.[h] Managers may feel that competitive reactions are not worth worrying about unless very major strategy changes are planned.

Conjectures made about new rivals. Brand managers must also make conjectures about the behavior of rivals that are four years old or less. It was reasoned that managers do not conjecture that new rivals will continue using the same decision rules as the past year, but, instead, conjecture that new rivals will employ some type of new product introduction strategy to help them gain a foothold in the market. Managers would presumably expect different introduction strategies to be used by a company already in the industry, a major consumer products marketer that is not in the industry, or a private brander.

The conjectures that all brand managers in the model make about the behavior of new rivals are found in Table 3-3. These rivals are expected to employ decision rules that differ according to the type of firm marketing the brand and the age of the brand. The rules, in general, set spending levels and prices at selected proportions of the industry averages of the previous year.

Established companies are conjectured to always enter with average quality brands (index of 100) that sell for the same retail price as the average brand in the industry did in the previous year and are supported by consumer-directed promotion and sales call budgets that are the same as past-year averages for the industry. These brands are also expected to spend 25 percent more than the past year's industry average on advertising, in order to create awareness for their new item, and 100 percent more than the past year's industry average on dealer-directed promotion, in order to get effective distribution. The conjectured

---

[g]For an example of a model where learning about competitive reactions is represented see Julian L. Simon, Carlos M. Puig, and John Aschoff, "A Duopoly Simulation: An End to Cournot," *Review of Economic Studies* (July 1973), pp. 353-66.

[h]This belief was tested during the interviews that were conducted as part of this study (see Chapter Five).

Table 3-3. Conjectures Made by the Brand Manager About the Behavior of New Rivals

The brand manager conjectures that new rival i will follow the following decision rules at various ages:

If Marketed by an Established Company:

One Year Old:	Two Years Old:	Three or Four Years Old:
$A_{it} = 1.25\overline{A}_{t-1}$*	$A_{it} = 1.25\overline{A}_{t-1}$	$A_{it} = \overline{A}_{t-1}$
$CP_{it} = \overline{CP}_{t-1}$	$CP_{it} = \overline{CP}_{t-1}$	$CP_{it} = \overline{CP}_{t-1}$
$DP_{it} = 2\overline{DP}_{t-1}$	$DP_{it} = 2\overline{DP}_{t-1}$	$DP_{it} = \overline{DP}_{t-1}$
$SC_{it} = \overline{SC}_{t-1}$	$SC_{it} = \overline{SC}_{t-1}$	$SC_{it} = \overline{SC}_{t-1}$
$PR_{it} = \overline{PR}_{t-1}$	$PR_{it} = PR_{it-1}$	$PR_{it} = PR_{it-1}$
$PW_{it} = .82\overline{PR}_{t-1}$	$PW_{it} = PW_{it-1}$	$PW_{it} = PW_{it-1}$
$B_{it} = 100$	$B_{it} = B_{it-1}$	$B_{it} = B_{it-1}$

If Marketed by a Consumer Products Firm:

One Year Old:	Two Years Old:	Three or Four Years Old:
$A_{it} = 1.5\overline{A}_{t-1}$	$A_{it} = 1.5\overline{A}_{t-1}$	$A_{it} = \overline{A}_{t-1}$
$CP_{it} = 1.2\overline{CP}_{t-1}$	$CP_{it} = 1.2\overline{CP}_{t-1}$	$CP_{it} = \overline{CP}_{t-1}$
$DP_{it} = 3\overline{DP}_{t-1}$	$DP_{it} = 3\overline{DP}_{t-1}$	$DP_{it} = \overline{DP}_{t-1}$
$SC_{it} = 1.2\overline{SC}_{t-1}$	$SC_{it} = 1.2\overline{SC}_{t-1}$	$SC_{it} = \overline{SC}_{t-1}$
$PR_{it} = \overline{PR}_{t-1}$	$PR_{it} = PR_{it-1}$	$PR_{it} = PR_{it-1}$
$PW_{it} = .82\overline{PR}_{t-1}$	$PW_{it} = PW_{it-1}$	$PW_{it} = PW_{it-1}$
$B_{it} = 104$	$B_{it} = B_{it-1}$	$B_{it} = B_{it-1}$

If Marketed by a Private Brander:

One Year Old:	Two Years Old:	Three or Four Years Old:
$A_{it} = .25\overline{A}_{t-1}$	$A_{it} = .25\overline{A}_{t-1}$	$A_{it} = .25\overline{A}_{t-1}$
$CP_{it} = .25\overline{CP}_{t-1}$	$CP_{it} = .25\overline{CP}_{t-1}$	$CP_{it} = .25\overline{CP}_{t-1}$
$DP_{it} = \overline{DP}_{t-1}$	$DP_{it} = \overline{DP}_{t-1}$	$DP_{it} = \overline{DP}_{t-1}$

Table 3-3. (cont.)

One Year Old:	Two Years Old:	Three or Four Years Old:
$SC_{it} = \overline{SC}_{t-1}$	$SC_{it} = \overline{SC}_{t-1}$	$SC_{it} = \overline{SC}_{t-1}$
$PR_{it} = .70\overline{PR}_{t-1}$	$PR_{it} = PR_{it-1}$	$PR_{it} = PR_{it-1}$
$PW_{it} = .50PR_{t-1}$	$PW_{it} = PW_{it-1}$	$PW_{it} = PW_{it-1}$
$B_{it} = 95$	$B_{it} = B_{it-1}$	$B_{it} = B_{it-1}$

*Variables are defined in Table 3-1.
Bars denote industry average of the decision variable.

wholesale prices charged by these brands leave room for rather large retailer margins, which could also be needed to get effective distribution.

In the second year of a brand's existence, the established companies are conjectured to keep using the same rules for determining a brand's marketing expenditures as they used in its first year. Prices and brand quality, however, are expected to be set at the same levels that were arrived at in a brand's first year. Furthermore, three- and four-year old brands are conjectured to follow rules that set *all* marketing expenditures at past year's industry average levels, but that again set prices and quality at levels identical to the previous year.

The manager of a brand that does not belong to an established company can be presumed to think that his brand enters the market at a disadvantage. Such a manager can be expected to feel that he must employ a somewhat different marketing strategy in entering the market than an established company might use. Brand managers are therefore assumed to conjecture that new rivals from major, nonestablished, consumer products firms will employ a strategy that includes larger than average marketing expenditures in all four areas and the production of a higher quality product. These large expenditures are also expected to persist through a second year.

The strategy a private brander is conjectured to use to break into the industry is quite different from the strategies the other two types of brands are conjectured to employ. The brand managers in the model believe that private branders will enter with slightly lower quality brands that have significantly lower prices and that are supported by rather small advertising and consumer-directed promotion budgets. This type of strategy is expected to be followed for four years.

Unfortunately, the conjectures that brand managers in the model make about *new* rivals have the same weakness as the conjectures they make about *established* rivals. In both cases, rivals are conjectured to have little ingenuity and competitive spirit. Although new and established rivals do not *actually* behave this way in the model—all rivals go through the decision procedure in Figure 3-1–brand managers were allowed to *think* that their rivals will always act this way to help keep the model relatively simple. However, this compromise could not be accepted in one exceptional case that is described below.

Conjectures made about existing rivals in the year a control has just been introduced. In a year when a control on advertising expenditures has just been introduced, it is unlikely that a brand manager would make the conjectures found in Tables 3-2 and 3-3. The manager would probably conjecture that his rivals will try to figure out new marketing strategies to help them mitigate the effects of the control. It is therefore assumed that, in this year only, each brand manager conjectures that his rivals will go through a search procedure, to determine their marketing strategies, that is basically identical to the one he normally goes through. In other words, the brand manager assumes that, in this year, his rivals will turn around and conjecture that he will follow the decision rules found in Tables 3-2 and 3-3 and that they will then search (see below) for marketing mixes that will prove satisfactory.

Search Procedure of the Brand Manager. The search procedures, as shown in Figure 3-1, that brand managers normally employ and rivals are conjectured to use (in the year a control has been introduced) are described in the following sections.

Established brand search procedure. After making conjectures about what his rivals will do over the next four years, the manager of an established brand must determine what marketing strategy to use himself over those years. The manager attempts to locate a strategy that will achieve the objectives he has set for his brand.

There are many different types of objectives that a brand manager could be assumed to possess. One could assume that a brand manager attempts to maximize his brand's contribution to corporate profits, as might be done if a conventional economic model of industry behavior were being built. Or one could adopt Baumol's sales-maximization hypothesis[12] or a utility-maximization hypothesis.[13] Another alternative would be to assume that the manager is a "satisficer" in accordance with the beliefs of people such as Simon, Cyert, March, and others.[14] Managers could be assumed to not have the time, money, knowledge, or information necessary to locate a strategy that will yield optimum profits, sales, market share, or whatever. Instead, managers could be assumed to be satisfied with achieving certain minimum levels of criterion variables.

The brand managers in the model described here are assumed to be satisficers. They are assumed to be content with achieving a reasonable growth rate in the contribution their brand makes to corporate profits. This assumption was made for three reasons. First, several empirical studies have shown business managers to behave more like satisficers than maximizers.[15] Second, it was felt that the opportunity costs associated with spending long hours searching for a profit-maximizing strategy would preclude brand managers of grocery products, who are usually kept very busy dealing with day-to-day crises, from behaving like maximizers when planning their annual strategies.[16] Third, it was felt that a lack of adequate data might prevent brand managers from being maximizers.

Consequently, each brand manager in the model is assumed to strive for the following goal: *The manager seeks to earn a stream of after-tax profits over the next four years that will grow at a rate of 5 percent per year from the highest after-tax profits earned by his brand during the past four years. If his brand has not earned after-tax profits during the past four years that are greater than 5 percent of the dollar sales achieved in the previous year, the manager would want his stream of future profits to grow from 5 percent of his last year's dollar sales.*

Each year the brand manager computes the present value of this desired stream of profits using a discount rate of 10 percent. This computation produces a figure PVO, which is used as a benchmark against which the expected results of various marketing strategies are tested. The brand manager searches for a strategy that will yield a discounted four-year stream of expected profits (PV̂) that is greater than or equal to PVO.

A diagram of the search procedure each manager of an established brand employs is found in Figure 3-3. In this search, the manager attempts to find settings for decision parameters of given decision rules that will produce a PV̂ greater than or equal to PVO. The decision rules that all brand managers are assumed to follow are found in the lower right-hand corner of Figure 3-3. These rules are almost identical in form to the ones all brand managers conjecture that their established rivals will use. Empirical evidence supporting the assumption that managers use rules that set marketing expenditures at constant percentages of past sales can be found in several studies that show a strong relationship between advertising expenditures and past sales.[17] The other rules were assumed to be used because it was felt that managers in an oligopolistic industry would look to what their rivals were doing before setting prices[i] and would also look to past brand quality before making any changes in quality.

The manager begins his search by putting the decision parameters (P1 to P7) of the seven decision rules at their last year's settings (except for P7, which is set at 1.00). This means that the manager of an established brand first tries to see what will happen if he utilizes the same marketing strategy that all his rivals expect him to use. The manager forecasts what his future profits will be using this old strategy *if* (1) existing rivals do what they are conjectured to do; (2) potential rivals enter when he thinks they will enter (see below); and (3) all

---

[i]This belief was tested during the interviews that were conducted as part of this study (see Chapter Five). For existing empirical evidence of this type of behavior see John A. Howard and William Morgenroth, "Information Processing Model of Executive Decision," *Management Science: Theory* (March 1968), pp. 416-28.

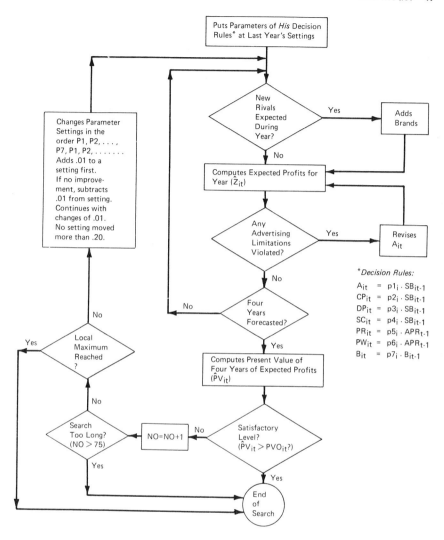

Figure 3-3. Search Procedure of the Manager of an Established Brand.

controls on advertising expenditures are obeyed. If the last year's parameters produce a $\hat{PV}$ that is satisfactory (greater than or equal to PVO), then the search will end. The manager will continue to use exactly the same rules as he used in the past. However, if a $\hat{PV}$ is computed which is less than PVO, the search will continue and a new set of decision parameters will be tested.

Decision parameters are changed in the following way: *The manager changes only one decision parameter per iteration. The parameter P1 is changed first. It is increased by the amount .01 to see if a satisfactory P̂V can be achieved. If this proves successful, then the search stops. If a .01 upward change in P1 does not produce a satisfactory P̂V, but does produce an improved P̂V, then another .01 upward change will be tried. If the first .01 upward change produces neither a satisfactory nor improved P̂V, then a .01 downward change will be tried. When upward or downward changes in P1 produce no more improvements in P̂V, or when P1 has already been changed .20 from its last year's setting, or when P1 falls below .01 or above 1.50, the same manipulations will be tried with P2. After P2, P3 will be tried; and so on down to P7, which is followed by a retrial of P1. The process stops when either (1) a satisfactory P̂V is reached, (2) a local maximum is reached (i.e., no .01 parameter change can lead to an improved P̂V), or (3) 75 interactions have occurred and no improvement in P̂V was achieved by the last change.*

Justification for making each change a relatively "round" number can be found in the "theory of focal points."[18] The order for testing changes in the first three decision parameters was selected to be consistent with information provided by the National Commission on Food Marketing. Its report on the breakfast cereal industry stated that:

> Grocery manufacturers generally prefer to employ: (1) media advertising; (2) consumer-directed promotions such as coupons, free samples, cents-off deals; and (3) dealer-directed promotions such as trade allowances, in that order.[19]

In addition, the sales call parameter was put ahead of the price parameters because it was felt that managers in a differentiated oligopoly would be more reluctant to turn to price changes as a means of improving profits than to changes in sales-call frequency. Finally, changes in the quality parameter were given last priority because real-world cereal brands very rarely change their contents.

The search procedure is cut off the first time no improvement occurs after 75 iterations basically to save computer time. However, this cut off, along with the .20 limit on individual parameter changes and the stopping rule for when a local maximum is reached, could represent the equivalent of a higher management restriction against major changes in marketing strategy.

Once a set of decision parameters have been determined, the brand manager will carry out his marketing strategy. He will use the decision rules to compute his spending levels, prices, and brand quality for the following year and will plan on continuing to use these rules for three more years. Of course, the manager will go through the search procedure again one year later and, at that time, may decide to revise his strategy.

New brand search procedure. The search procedure employed by the manager of a new brand in the model will depend on the age of his brand. The manager of a brand that is in its first or second year can be presumed to be interested, first, in his brand's immediate survival and, second, in its long-run welfare. Thus, it is assumed that such a manager has as his objective the achievement of merely positive profits in the first two years of his brand's life. Moreover, since the manager of a one- or two-year old brand is assumed to have only a one-year planning horizon, he does not have to determine decision rules that will dictate his strategy past the current year. The search procedure for this manager therefore involves the location of settings for the seven marketing decision variables themselves—not settings of seven decision parameters—that will produce positive expected profits in the coming year.

The diagram in Figure 3-3 would need to be changed slightly to portray the search procedure of the manager of a one- or two-year old brand. This manager starts his search by considering the profit consequences of actually using the same marketing mix (strategy) that all his rivals think he is going to use in that year. He forecasts one year's profits if he were to follow the decision rules found in Table 3-3 to determine his marketing expenditures, prices, and brand quality. If this marketing mix produces positive expected profits, he will use it. Otherwise, he will test out each of the seven decision variables in the same order as they are presented in the tables (advertising first, brand quality seventh) in an effort to find mixes that will diminish expected losses and eventually produce positive expected profits. The size of the changes he tries in each variable in one iteration are:

> Advertising: $100,000;
> Consumer-Directed Promotion: $10,000;
> Dealer-Directed Promotion: $10,000;
> Sales Calls: $10,000;
> Retail Price: $.01;
> Wholesale Price: $.01;
> Brand Quality: .01.

No variable is permitted to be changed more than five times in the same direction without first testing the effects of changing all the other variables. This restriction forces the manager of a new brand to experiment with all the marketing variables rather than concentrate on a few. As with the other search procedure, search is cut off when either a local maximum or 75 iterations are reached.

The manager of a brand that is three or four years old utilizes a search procedure identical to that found in Figure 3-3, with one major difference. This manager does not start out his search by putting the decision parameters at their last year's settings. Instead, he first puts the parameters at settings that will produce values for the decision variables that equal the spending levels, prices, and brand quality that other rivals think he will be using in the upcoming year. This allows him to start his search procedure with parameter settings that are not overly large. A three- or four-year old brand will typically have just made a large initial investment in marketing. A starting parameter setting based on previous year's spending, and sales from a year before that, will most likely be an impractical place to start a search routine.

Conjectures Made about Potential Rivals. Brand managers in the model conjecture that new rival brands will enter the market in the future when total after-tax profits for all brands reach significantly high levels. This conjecture is described in Table 3-4. It is assumed that brand managers know who is going to enter in the current year. However, to predict what will happen in years $t+1$ to $t+3$, a manager, first, divides total actual profits in the industry during the previous year by a conjectured satisfactory profit level for a brand ($1,000,000) and, second, subtracts from this figure the number of brands in the market during the previous year. He expects one entrant if the difference between the two figures is greater than one, two entrants if the difference is greater than two, and three entrants if the difference is greater than three. The first brand that he would expect to enter in a given year would belong to an established company *(a company already in the market or in markets that are extremely similar)*, the second to a consumer products marketer, and the third to a private brander. Entering established company brands are expected to be brought out first by established companies that do not already have brands in this particular market, and then by the other established companies according to which firm brought out its last new brand in the market at the earliest point in time. Consumer products marketers and private branders are expected to become established companies after their brands have survived for four years.

When a new brand is conjectured to enter, the managers assume that it will behave like a first-year brand right from the start. New entrants are not conjectured to test market their brand prior to full-scale entry. As will be shown below, the submodel of potential entrants' *actual* behavior always has them putting their brands into test market before full-scale entry, and, furthermore, does not have them basing their entry decisions on past industry profits.

Several economic theorists have stressed the importance of considering how the decisions of managers are influenced by the threat of potential entry.[j] These theorists have developed a number of analytical models in which managers conjecture that potential rivals will enter when either prices or profits become high.[20] In using these models, results have been obtained in which managers of dominant firms "limit price" (i.e., keep their price lower than they

---

[j]Baron has stated: "A major advance in the theory of imperfect competition has been the recognition that established firms must take into account possible actions by potential as well as by existing competitors." See David P. Baron, "Limit Pricing, Potential Entry, and Barriers to Entry," *American Economic Review* (September 1973), pp. 666-74.

Table 3-4. Conjectures Made by the Brand Manager About the Behavior of Potential Rivals

---

About Year t:

The brand manager *knows* that the brands that will enter in the current year will be those that were in test market during the previous year and acquired a 10 percent share of their test market.

About Years $t+1, \ldots, t+3$:

The brand manager *conjectures* that in future years new brands will enter as follows:

If $0 < \dfrac{TZ_{t-1}}{SAT} - N_{t-1} < 1$, no new brands will enter in year t.

If $1 \leqslant \dfrac{TZ_{t-1}}{SAT} - N_{t-1} < 2$, an established firm will enter with a new brand in year t.

If $2 \leqslant \dfrac{TZ_{t-1}}{SAT} - N_{t-1} < 3$, an established firm and a consumer products firm will enter with new brands in year t.

If $3 \leqslant \dfrac{TZ_{t-1}}{SAT} - N_{t-1}$, an established firm, a consumer products firms, and a private brander will enter with new brands in year t.*

Where:

TZ = Total industry after-tax profits

SAT = A conjectured satisfactory profit level for a brand

N = Number of brands in the industry

---

*Different corporate image indexes (CI) are assigned to the brands of different types of firms.

would if they were maximizing short-run profits) to retard entry.[21] Although empirical evidence of limit pricing behavior is scanty,[22] the assumption that managers expect rivals to enter when prices or profits become high still has a great deal of intuitive appeal. For this reason, the managers in the model conjecture that rivals will enter when profits become high.[k] Profits were selected rather than prices because it was felt that managers in a grocery manufacturing industry would believe that potential entrants would be more attracted by the existence of supernormal profits than they would be by high prices on a differentiated product.

---

[k]This assumption was tested during the interviews that were conducted as part of this study (see Chapter Five).

Abandonment Decision. The last thing a brand manager in the model does in his annual decision procedure is decide whether to continue marketing his brand for another year. The rules all brand managers use to make this decision are displayed in Table 3-5. If their brand is under four years old, managers will stop marketing the brand if certain levels of market share have not been reached. These levels are assumed to be used because it was felt that they represent a reasonable growth rate for a brand's share. In addition, brands that are four years old or greater are abandoned if a 7 percent share has not been achieved *or* if positive after-tax profits have not been earned by the brand for four straight years. The 7 percent cut off was selected for use in the model because a share lower than this would prevent a manager from taking advantage of economies of scale in manufacturing and transportation (unless the entire market were to become considerably larger). The four-year limit on losses is used because it was felt that a brand manager would not tolerate losses for any longer than this no matter what his share of the market might be.

Potential Rival Manufacturers' Submodel

The *actual* behavior of potential rival manufacturers in the model differs considerably from what existing rivals think it will be. Each year, managers of three potential rival brands (an established company brand, a consumer products marketer brand, and a private brand) are assumed to look into the market and to go through the decision procedure found in Figure 3-4 in deciding whether they should enter. They employ a straightforward capital-budgeting approach in reaching their entry decision. After estimating their profit equation, each potential rival makes conjectures about how existing rivals will behave during the next ten years. These conjectures are essentially the same as

Table 3-5. The Abandonment Decision of the Brand Manager

The brand manager uses the following rules to decide whether to continue marketing his brand:

Age of Brand
in Year Just
Completed:

In test market	If $SHARE_{it-1} < .001$, then drop
1 year old	If $SHARE_{it-1} < .03$, then drop
2 years old	If $SHARE_{it-1} < .05$, then drop
3 years old	If $SHARE_{it-1} < .07$, then drop
4 years old and up	If $SHARE_{it-1} < .07$, then drop
	If all $Z_{it-1}, \ldots, Z_{it-4} < 0$, then drop

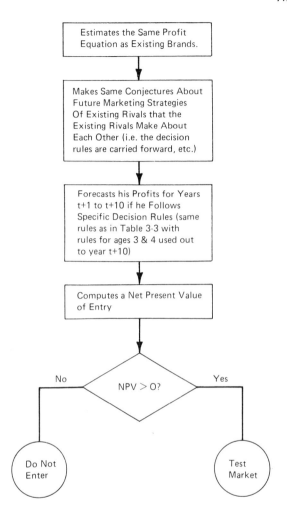

Figure 3-4. Actual Behavior of a Potential Rival.

the ones existing rivals make about each other (i.e., the decision rules are carried forward). Next, he forecasts what his profits will be for ten years if he and no one else were to enter the market. This forecast assumes that he would utilize a specific marketing strategy over the ten years. This strategy can be found in the decision rules in Table 3-3 with the rules for three- and four-year old brands being carried out, in this case, to year ten. In other words, the potential rival forecasts what his profits would be if he behaved, for at least the first four years, the way existing rivals think new rivals behave.

After forecasting ten years of profits, the potential rival then computes what his cash flow would be in each of the ten years (i.e., he adds back depreciation to after-tax profits). The cash flow estimates are discounted to the present and the cash outlay required for an initial investment in plant and equipment is subtracted from this figure to give a "Net Present Value of Entry" (NPV). If NPV is positive, entry will occur because an adequate (higher than the discount rate) rate of return on investment can be earned.

The discount rate employed by potential rivals that are consumer products marketers or private branders is 20 percent. The discount rate employed by potential rivals that are established companies is 10 percent. The difference in discount rates is assumed because a company that is not already in the industry would most likely desire a higher expected rate of return to make up for the risks to which it would be exposed if it entered the market.

The cash outlay for an initial investment in plant and equipment is assumed to be $4,000,000 for a new established company brand and $5,000,000 for new brands belonging to consumer products marketers or private branders. The difference occurs because established companies are assumed to shift fixed assets worth $1,000,000 from their other operations to the production of the new brand. All brands are assumed to use ten-year, straight-line depreciation on fixed assets for reporting purposes.

Recent history in the cereal industry has generally seen existing firms enter the nutritional market and the "natural" market one after the other until all firms had marketed a representative. The model therefore assigns entering established company brands first to established companies that do not have brands in this particular market, and then to the other established companies according to which firm had brought out its last new brand in the market at the earliest point in time. Thus, the model works in such a way that a potential rival manufacturer can also be a manufacturer of an existing brand that has been in the market for several years. It should also be noted that consumer products marketers and private branders are assumed to become established companies when their brands survive for four years.

In the first year after actually entering, all brands are assumed to go into test market. The test market is assumed to be 1 percent of the size of the national market. The strategy used by the brand manager in test market can be computed using the decision rules in Table 3-3. The manager is assumed to use the rules for first-year brands found in the exhibit, except that in the four marketing spending areas he only spends 1 percent of the level dictated by the rules.

Clearly, the submodel of potential rival manufacturers has several weaknesses. For example, potential rivals conjecture that existing rivals will not react sharply to the entry of a new competitor but will continue to use past decisions rules. Also, a potential rival assumes that he will be the only one to enter over the next ten years. And, most importantly, potential rivals do not forecast the consequences of using a variety of different postentry marketing strategies in assessing the feasibility of entry. Ideally, a model could be built in which potential rivals would go through a search procedure similar to the one existing rivals go through in this model. One could also add a reaction conjecture and a conjecture about the entry of other new rivals. However, adding any of these things to the potential rival submodel described here would add substantial amounts of computer time to each run of the overall model. It was therefore decided to keep this submodel somewhat simpler than the existing manufacturers' submodel.

Retailers' Submodel

The equations that describe the behavior of retailers in the model have already appeared in Table 3-1. These equations are presented again in Table 3-6. For purposes of clarity, the parameter values that were actually used in the benchmark run of the model are included in these equations rather than the symbols found in Table 3-1.

The equations in Table 3-6 show that the effectiveness of a brand's distribution effort is assumed to be a complex function of the corporate image possessed by the firm marketing the brand, the total sales in the market, and the past and current marketing strategies employed by all existing brand managers.

Manufacturers are assumed to deal directly with chain stores and

Table 3-6. The Distribution Effectiveness Response Function

$$D_{it} = \left[\frac{CI_{it}}{200}\right]\left[\frac{DREV_{it}}{250,000}\right]^{.15}\left[\frac{SC_{it}}{ASC_t}\right]^{.05}$$

Where:

$$CI_{it} = CI_{it-1} + 10\,(FSH_{kt-1} - FSH_{kt-2})$$

$$DREV_{it} = SI_t \cdot S\hat{H}ARE_{it}(PR_{it} - PW_{it} - .10) + DP_{it}$$

$$S\hat{H}ARE_{it} = \frac{PR_{it}^{-2.0} \cdot D_{it-1}^{1.6} \cdot AG_{it}^{.5} \cdot CI_{it}^{.06} \cdot B_{it}^{.06} \cdot CP_{it}^{.05}}{\Sigma_j PR_{jt}^{-2.0} \cdot D_{jt-1}^{1.6} \cdot AG_{jt}^{.5} \cdot CI_{jt}^{.06} \cdot B_{jt}^{.06} \cdot CP_{jt}^{.05}}$$

$$D_{it-1} = \frac{CI_{it}}{200} \text{ if } NAGE_{it} \leqslant 1$$

Variables are defined in Table 3-1.

other retailers in this model. No brokers or wholesalers are assumed to be used by the manufacturers in distributing their brands. This tends to be the situation that actually exists in the cereal industry today.[23] Thus, the retailers' submodel consists of an aggregate response function that represents how all retailers react to the efforts of the brand managers to get effective distribution for their brands.

The endogenous variable, D_{it}, is defined as the distribution effectiveness index of brand i in year t. This index can be viewed as an expression of the availability of brand i in year t and of the reseller support it receives in that year. The values the index takes can be considered the equivalent of the proportion of national retail grocery volume held by the outlets that carry the brand, *adjusted for* the amount of shelf locations, retail advertising, cooperation with consumer-directed promotion efforts, or other forms of reseller support the brand receives. A brand that achieves a D_{it} equal to .60 can be viewed as having attained very low availability (his brand can be found in outlets which hold, say, 85 percent of national retail grocery volume) and poor retailer support. A brand which achieves a D_{it} of 1.00 can be viewed as having attained the maximum possible availability (about a 95 percent figure) plus a significant amount of reseller support.

A major determinant of a brand's distribution effectiveness index is assumed to be the corporate image index of the firm to which the brand belongs. A firm's corporate image index represents the goodwill the firm has created by successfully operating in a market or a group of related markets over a number of years. The three original firms in the model are assigned corporate image indices that equal the percentage of the entire ready-to-eat cereal market, plus the number 100, held by Kellogg, Quaker Oats, and General Mills in the early 1960s. Thus, Firms 1, 2, and 3 are assigned indices of 139, 106, and 122, respectively. In addition, it is assumed that other established firms enter the market with an index of 105; consumer products marketers enter with an index of 100; and private branders enter with an index of 90. Brand managers in the model can improve their firm's corporate image index by increasing their brand's market share.

A brand is assumed to attain a certain amount of distribution effectiveness based solely on its firm's corporate image. The first term in the response function divides the corporate image by a constant, and the resultant figure becomes a base upon which adjustments are made. Corporate image is assumed to be an important determinant of distribution effectiveness in the model because evidence collected by Montgomery has shown chain-store buyers to be quite sensitive to the variable "company reputation" in deciding whether to stock a new product or not.[24]

The corporate image term of the distribution effectiveness response function is adjusted by two factors. First, if retailers expect to earn more than a moderate level of gross profits from a brand in a year, then an upward adjustment is made. The small exponent in the second term of the function indicates, however, that higher expected retail gross profits have a rapidly diminishing upward effect on distribution effectiveness. A brand can get only a finite amount of availability and support. The equations found in Table 3-6 show that expected retail gross profits from a brand in a year is computed by (1) taking industry sales in pounds for that year; (2) multiplying it times the share a brand would receive in that year if it only were to attain its previous year's distribution effectiveness (SHARE)[1]; (3) multiplying that figure by the retailer's margin per pound for the brand, less ten cents per pound to cover costs; and (4) adding dealer-directed promotion for the brand to the prior sum to get a final figure.

The second adjustment factor in the distribution effectiveness response function is relative sales call expenditures. If a brand spends more than the average brand does on sales calls, an upward adjustment in its distribution effectiveness index is made. However, rapidly diminishing returns from higher sales call expenditures are also assumed to exist.

The retailers submodel represents another aspect of the model that can be criticized for being overly simple or unrealistic. The most glaring weakness of this submodel is that it is based only partially on empirical evidence. Unfortunately, data on how chain stores make decisions is extremely rare since very few studies have been done on this subject. Although the equations used for this submodel are felt to be a reasonable expression of how retailers react to the marketing strategies of manufacturers, the availability of more data would allow this submodel to be improved considerably.[m]

Consumers' Submodel

The consumers' submodel consists of two basic response functions: a function that determines the total sales in pounds of the industry (market), and a function that determines the market share of each brand in the industry. These response functions are presented again in Table 3-7, with the parameter values from the benchmark run included rather than the appropriate symbols.

The industry sales response function makes pound sales in one year equal to total U.S. population times the previous year's per capita sales, adjusted for changes in (1) the total goodwill built up by industry advertising; (2) the total industry spending on consumer-directed promotion; and (3) the industry's average retail price. The use of this type of function amounts to assuming that

---

[1]The form of the equation used to compute the share of a brand, if it only were to attain the previous year's distribution effectiveness level, is the same as the form of the equation used to compute a brand's actual market share. This equation is discussed in the next section of this chapter. It should also be noted that when a brand is in test market or in its first year, D_{it-1} is set equal to CI/200 rather than to a nonexistent previous year's distribution effectiveness level in making the necessary computations.

[m]A question about the behavior of chain stores was asked in the interviews that were done as part of this study. See Chapter Five for a discussion of the responses.

Table 3-7. The Industry Sales Response Function and the Market-Share Response Function

$$SI_t = POP_t \cdot PCAP_{t-1} \cdot \left[\frac{TAG_t}{TAG_{t-1}}\right]^{ETA_t} \left[\frac{TCP_t}{TCP_{t-1}}\right]^{.05} \left[\frac{APR_t}{APR_{t-1}}\right]^{-1.5}$$

$$SHARE_{it} = \frac{PR_{it}^{-2.0} \cdot D_{it}^{1.6} \cdot AG_{it}^{.5} \cdot CI_{it}^{.06} \cdot B_{it}^{.06} \cdot CP_{it}^{.05}}{\sum_j PR_{jt}^{-2.0} \cdot D_{jt}^{1.6} \cdot AG_{jt}^{.5} \cdot CI_{jt}^{.06} \cdot B_{jt}^{.06} \cdot CP_{jt}^{.05}}$$

Where:

$$ETA_t = .85 - .00000001 TAG_t$$

$$AG_{it} = .4A_{it} + .3A_{it-1} + .2A_{it-2} + .1A_{it-3}$$

Variables are defined in Table 3.1.

consumers are rather loyal to the product category (for example, nutritional cereals) and are shifted to other product categories only when advertising goodwill diminishes, consumer-directed promotion spending decreases, or prices increase. Also, new customers are assumed to be attracted to the product category by increases in advertising goodwill, increases in consumer-directed promotion, and declines in price.

Changes in price are assumed to have the most pronounced effect on industry sales and thus the price term is awarded the largest sensitivity parameter. (Since no changes in price levels throughout the economy are assumed to occur during the time period being simulated, changes in average price from one year to the next can be assumed to have a significant effect on sales.) The price elasticity of demand equals 1.5. Changes in consumer-directed promotion expenditures are assumed to have a small effect on industry sales, and thus the consumer promotion term is awarded a very small sensitivity parameter. The sensitivity parameter for the advertising goodwill term is assumed to decline from a large value as total goodwill in the industry grows larger.[n] This is done to account for the existence of diminishing returns to advertising.[o] A per capita income variable was not included in this response function because it was felt that the effect of changes in per capita income on cereal sales is probably

[n]Comanor and Wilson have found cereal sales to be strongly related to advertising. See William S. Comanor and Thomas A. Wilson, "Advertising and the Distribution of Consumer Demand," Research paper #160, Stanford University Graduate School and Business, May 1973.

[o]For a survey of evidence on diminishing returns to advertising, see Julian L. Simon, *Issues in the Economics of Advertising* (Urbana, Ill.: University of Illinois Press, 1970).

negligible. Higher income could produce a shift to more expensive breakfast items like eggs or bacon rather than produce more cereal sales.

The advertising goodwill variable is included in the industry sales response function and in the market share function discussed below to allow *carryover effects* from advertising to operate in the model. Although there are many other ways to model the carryover effects of advertising,[25] the goodwill approach was used because of its simplicity. The goodwill function used in the model is designed to let the current year's spending on advertising have a greater influence on current industry sales and market share than the previous year's advertising, and so on.

The form of the market share response function used in the model was probably first suggested by Kotler,[26] and this type of function has since been found to fit real-world data reasonably well in work done by Urban,[27] Lambin,[28] and Nakanishi.[29] The function puts a brand's market share equal to its share of the total industry *marketing effort.* A brand's effort in a year is equal to the numerator of the market share equation found in Table 3-7. The sensitivity parameters indicate that market share is assumed to be most sensitive to changes in price, distribution effectiveness, advertising goodwill,[P] corporate image and brand quality, and consumer-directed promotion, in that order. This type of market share model has the advantage of being *interactive* and of allowing the sum of all the shares in an industry to equal one.

If better and more complete data has been available and had been used to estimate these two response functions, one might have more confidence in the entire model. As mentioned at the beginning of this chapter, an attempt *was* made to estimate the parameters of the market share response function by using an artificial data base. However, the inadequacies of the data base and the fact that the parameter estimates, when used in the model, produced unreasonable behavior on the part of brand managers (i.e., overly large spending in certain areas, and so forth) led to a decision to utilize other parameter values.

Starting Conditions for the Model

Each run of the model starts out with three brands in the industry that belong to three different firms. (Six established firms are assumed to exist at the beginning of a run, including the three already marketing brands.) These brands can be viewed to be the equivalent of "Special K," "Life," and "Total"—the three brands that made up the nutritional cereal market during the early 1960s.[30] A portion of the artificial data base discussed earlier, covering four years (1961 to 1964) of these brand's operations, is read into the computer at the start of the program. The last two years of this data base can be found in the output of the benchmark run displayed in Appendix B (under the data for

---

[P]The sensitivity parameters associated with the advertising goodwill variables in both the industry sales and market share response functions create a situation where there are nonincreasing returns to advertising for all managers in the model.

Brands 1, 2, and 3, years 3 and 4). This data is needed to compute the advertising goodwill values, corporate image indexes, and so on for the brands during year 5. All the runs of the model start from year 5, which can be considered the equivalent of 1965. Details on the different variations of the model that were tested are found in the next chapter.

SUMMARY

In this study, a model was built of a hypothetical, oligopolistic, grocery manufacturing industry. This model is patterned after the nutritional submarket of the ready-to-eat breakfast cereal industry. The assumptions that are made in this model were drawn from economic theory, marketing theory, and empirical evidence. The model contains four submodels that interact in a yearly cycle: (1) a manufacturers' submodel, (2) a potential rival manufacturers' submodel, (3) a retailers' submodel, and (4) a consumers' submodel.

The manufacturers' submodel consists of several brand managers competing with one another in an n-person, nonzero-sum game. The managers of established brands (over four years old) are assumed to be "satisficers" who choose marketing strategies that they expect will yield a satisfactory stream of after-tax profits over a four-year period. They select their marketing strategies after making conjectures about the behavior of existing rivals (they are conjectured to behave like they have in the past) and potential rivals (they are conjectured to enter when industry profits are high), and after going through a search procedure in which they test out alternative marketing strategies starting with the strategy they used in the previous year. The actual and conjectured behavior of the managers of new brands (less than five years old) in the manufacturers' submodel differs somewhat from that of managers of established brands.

The potential rival manufacturers' submodel consists of three potential entrants who look into the industry each year and decide whether to enter. One potential entrant is a brand of a firm already established in the industry; another is a brand belonging to a consumer products marketer not already in the market; and the third is a private brand. These brands will enter if their calculations show the net present value of entry to be positive. All new entrants to the industry spend a year in test market before being marketed on a full-scale basis.

The retailers' submodel depicts how retailers respond to the marketing strategies of the manufacturers. Retailers will provide a brand with effective distribution (high availability and reseller support), if the firm that markets the brand has a good corporate image, if the brand is expected to have a high market share, if the retailer's margin of the brand is adequate, and if dealer-directed promotion and sales calls expenditures for the brand are at competitive levels.

The consumers' submodel determines the total sales in the industry and the market share earned by each brand. Industry sales are assumed to be most sensitive to changes in price, population, advertising goodwill, and consumer-directed promotion expenditures, in that order. A brand's market share is assumed to be most sensitive to changes in its price, distribution effectiveness, advertising goodwill, corporate image, brand quality, and consumer-directed promotion, in that order. The advertising goodwill variable is used to account for carryover effects from advertising.

The industry is assumed to have three brands belonging to three firms at the start of each run of the model. The experiments that are performed in the different runs of the model are discussed in Chapter Four.

NOTES TO CHAPTER THREE

1. Milton P. Brown et al., "The Quaker Oats Life Cereal Case," in *Problems in Marketing* (New York: McGraw-Hill, 1968), pp. 161-95.

2. National Commission on Food Marketing, *Studies of Organization and Competition in Grocery Manufacturing, Technical Study No. 6* (Washington, D.C.: U.S. Government Printing Office, 1966).

3. National Commission, *Studies*; Robert D. Buzzell and Robert E.M. Nourse, *Product Innovation in Food Processing: 1954-1964* (Boston: Harvard Business School, 1967); Robert D. Buzzell, Walter J. Salmon, and Richard F. Vancil, *Product Profitability Measurement and Merchandising Decisions* (Boston: Harvard Business School, 1965); and Gary A. Marple and Harry B. Wissman, *Grocery Manufacturing in the United States* (New York: Praeger, 1968).

4. See the "Life Cereal Case" in Brown et al., *Problems*, pp. 161-95; and the "General Foods-Post Division Case" in Brown et al., *Problems*, pp. 720-840.

5. The first approximation of the model can be found in Paul N. Bloom, "Pretesting Government Controls on Advertising Expenditures: A Simulation Approach," *Proceedings of the Third Annual Albert Haring Symposium* (Bloomington, Ind.: Indiana University, 1973).

6. *National Advertising Investments* (New York: Leading National Advertisers, 1965-1972).

7. See, for example, John C. Maxwell, "Cold Cereals Industry Goes Through Growth Year," *Advertising Age* (March 26, 1973), p. 3. Another source that was used was *The Cereal Industry: An Economic, Marketing and Financial Investigation* (Bellmore, N.Y.: Morton Research Corporation, 1972).

8. For further discussion of the distinction between strategic and tactical decisions, see Philip Kotler, *Marketing Management: Analysis, Planning, and Control* (Englewood Cliffs, N.J.: Prentice-Hall, 1972); and Stanton G. Cort and Luis V. Dominguez, "Plan-It: Simulation Applied to a Marketing Decision System," working paper, Indiana University School of Business, November 1973.

9. National Commission, *Studies*; and Brown et al., "Life Cereal."

10. Augustin Cournot, *Researches Into the Mathematical Principles*

of the Theory of Wealth, translated by N.T. Bacon (Homewood, Ill.: Richard D. Irwin, 1963).

11. Walter Taplin, "Advertising Appropriation Policy," *Economica* (August 1959), pp. 227-39; Donald C. Marschner, "Theory Versus Practice in Allocating Advertising Money," *Journal of Business* (July 1967), pp. 282-302; Richard Schmalensee, *The Economics of Advertising* (Amsterdam: North-Holland Publishing, 1972). An article that shows a practitioner's (vice president of Quaker Oats Co.) belief that advertising budgets are based on past sales is Kenneth Mason, "How Much Do You Spend on Advertising? Product is Key," *Advertising Age* (June 12, 1972), p. 41.

12. William J. Baumol, *Business Behavior, Value and Growth* (New York: Harcourt, Brace and World, 1967).

13. See, for example, Oliver E. Williamson, *Corporate Control and Business Behavior* (Englewood Cliffs, N.J.: Prentice-Hall, 1970).

14. See Herbert Simon, "Theories of Decision-Making in Economics and Behavioral Science," *American Economic Review* (June 1959), pp. 253-83; Richard M. Cyert and James G. March, *A Behavioral Theory of the Firm* (Englewood Cliffs, N.J.: Prentice-Hall, 1963); Richard M. Cyert and Herbert A. Simon, "Theory of the Firm: Behavioralism and Marginalism," working paper, Carnegie-Mellon University, 1972; Armen A. Alchian, "Uncertainty, Evolution, and Economic Theory," *Journal of Political Economy* (June 1950), pp. 211-22; and P.W.S. Andrews and Elizabeth Brunner, "Business Profits and the Quiet Life," *Journal of Industrial Economics* (November 1962), pp. 72-78.

15. See Cyert and March, *A Behavioral Theory*. Other evidence that can be interpreted as providing support for a satisficing assumption are Joseph L. Bower, *Managing the Resource Allocation Process: A Study of Corporate Planning and Investment* (Cambridge, Mass.: Harvard Business School, 1970); John A. Howard and William Morgenroth, "Information Processing Model of Executive Decision," *Management Science: Theory* (March 1968), pp. 416-28; Marschner, "Theory Versus Practice"; and R.L. Hall and C.J. Hitch, "Price Theory and Business Behavior," *Oxford Economic Papers* (May 1939), pp. 12-45.

16. For a discussion of the time constraints on brand managers, see Bower, *Managing*, p. 55.

17. Same references as note 11.

18. See Thomas C. Schelling, *The Strategy of Conflict* (Cambridge, Mass.: Harvard University Press, 1960); and F.M. Scherer, *Industrial Market Structure and Economic Performance* (Chicago: Rand McNally, 1970), p. 179.

19. National Commission, *Studies*, p. 17.

20. Works that treat high prices as the signal that managers feel attracts entry are Joe S. Bain, *Barriers to New Competition* (Cambridge, Mass.: Harvard University Press, 1956); Paolo Sylos-Labini, *Oligopoly and Technical Progress* (Milan, Italy: Guiffre, 1957); Franco Modigliani, "New Developments on the Oligopoly Front," *Journal of Political Economy* (June 1958), pp. 215-32; and Morton I. Kamien and Nancy L. Schwartz, "Limit Pricing and Uncertain Entry," *Econometrica* (May 1971), pp. 441-54. Works that treat high profits as the signal are G. Pyatt, "Profit Maximization and the Threat of New Entry,"

Economic Journal (1971), pp. 242-55; and F.H. Hahn, "Excess Capacity and Imperfect Competition," *Oxford Economic Papers* (1955), pp. 229-40.

21. Same references as note 20.

22. For a review of empirical evidence on this subject, see Louis W. Stern, "Limit Pricing and Other Issues in Potential Competition Theory," working paper, Northwestern University Graduate School of Management, 1974.

23. National Commission, *Studies*, p. 139.

24. David B. Montgomery, "New Product Distribution: An Analysis of Supermarket Buyer Decisions," paper presented at the 1973 American Marketing Association Doctoral Consortium, Michigan State University, 1973. For similar findings, see Neil H. Borden, *Acceptance of Food Products by Supermarkets* (Cambridge, Mass.: Harvard Business School, 1968), pp. 206-11.

25. See Philip Kotler, *Marketing Decision Making: A Model Building Approach* (New York: Holt, Rinehart and Winston, 1971), Ch. 5.

26. Philip Kotler, "Competitive Strategies for New Product Marketing Over the Life Cycle," *Management Science* (December 1965), pp. 104-19.

27. Glen L. Urban, "A Mathematical Modeling Approach to Product Line Decisions," *Journal of Marketing Research* (February 1969), pp. 40-47.

28. Jean-Jacques Lambin, "A Computer On-Line Marketing Mix Model," *Journal of Marketing Research* (May 1972), pp. 119-26.

29. Masao Nakanishi, "Measurement of Sales Promotion Effect at the Retail Level—A New Approach," in Bonis W. Becken and Helmut Becken, eds. *Marketing Education and the Real World* (Chicago: American Marketing Association, 1973), pp. 338-43.

30. Brown, et al., "Life Cereal."

Chapter Four

Tests of Controls

A group of experiments were performed with the simulation model described in the previous chapter. These experiments were conducted to test the competitive effects of controls on advertising expenditures and to evaluate the sensitivity of the model. The results of these experiments are analyzed in this chapter. Before presenting this analysis, however, the measures of competition that were monitored during each experiment, or computer run, must be described.

MONITORED MEASURES OF COMPETITION

Industrial organization economists typically measure the extent of competition in a market by looking at several measures of the structure and performance of that market. The measures of competition that were monitored during each computer run of this study are similar to those that an industrial organization economist might monitor. These measures are discussed below.

Number of Firms and Brands

Economists often look at the number of firms in an industry to give them an indication of competitive conditions. It is hypothesized that the more firms there are in an industry, the more difficult it becomes for collusion (either explicit or tacit) to take place. Thus, *independent* behavior is more likely to occur in industries with large numbers of firms. Also, the existence of a large number of firms in an industry may indicate that barriers to entry are not overly difficult to surmount.

The existence of a large number of *brands* in an industry can also indicate that independent behavior is present and that barriers to entry are not insurmountable. Even if several brands belonging to the same firm make up a major portion of the available brands, it is possible, though not probable, that vigorous intrafirm competition might occur. It must be kept in mind, however, that many individuals feel that *brand proliferation* by large firms can be used as an anticompetitive tactic. These people claim that some large firms use "satellite" or secondary brands to drive out smaller firms, or use a continuous parade of new brands to help frighten away potential competitors. For example, the large gasoline companies have been accused of trying to drive out smaller competitors,[1] and the large ready-to-eat breakfast cereal manufacturers have been accused of trying to frighten away competitors,[2] through the use of brand proliferation. Thus, it is questionable whether the number of brands in an industry should be used as an indicator of competition. Nevertheless, both the number of firms and the number of brands were monitored in this study.

The number of firms (or brands) in an industry does not reveal anything about the *size distribution* of these firms. There could be one huge firm and numerous little ones, which would indicate that a different type of competition were occurring than if all firms were relatively close in size. Therefore, another measure—the concentration ratio—must be examined to get information on the size distribution of firms in an industry.

Market Concentration

There are many different types of concentration ratios. These ratios can reveal the percentage of total market sales, assets, employees, or something else held by the two, three, four or more firms (or brands) that have the most of these variables in a market. In this study, two- and three-firm concentration ratios were monitored, which indicated the share of total market sales *in pounds* held by the two or three firms with the largest shares. Two- and three-brand concentration ratios were also monitored.

Observation of concentration ratios in conjunction with figures on the number of firms and brands in an industry can disclose important information about competitive conditions in a market. A market with numerous, equal-size firms is generally believed to be more likely to have vigorous competition than one dominated by a few large firms.

Of course, there are some people who feel that a few, large firms can compete just as vigorously as numerous smaller firms. These people argue that only large firms can afford to take the risks and commit the capital necessary to be innovative in certain industries.[3] This is a persuasive line of reasoning that cannot be ignored. To acquire a true feeling for the extent of competition in an industry, therefore, one must look beyond its number and size distribution of firms to other measures of its competitiveness.

Market Advertising Expenditures

The presence of *product differentiation* is considered to be an important structural characteristic of a market. Markets characterized by product differentiation are believed by many to be more difficult to enter because large advertising outlays are felt to be needed to convince consumers that a new brand differs from existing brands. It is also argued that product differentiation makes markets less competitive by allowing firms to avoid competing on a price basis. Of course, this latter argument tends to equate competition with *price* competition, which is somewhat shortsighted. Nonprice competition can be just as vigorous as price competition and can lead to more *variety* for consumers. Moreover, product differentiation can actually lead to *more* price competition by making it more difficult for firms to agree (overtly or tacitly) on prices.[4]

In spite of the difficulties one can have in interpreting what the presence or absence of product differentiation indicates about the *extent* of competition in an industry, it is still useful to try to measure the amount of product differentiation in order to acquire a feeling for the *character* of competition in that industry. Unfortunately, a valid, reliable measure of product differentiation has not been developed. Economists have been forced to use industry advertising expenditures as a crude indicator of the extent of product differentiation in an industry. This same indicator was monitored during each computer run of this study. The logic behind using advertising expenditures as a measure is that, in theory, the presence of nonprice competition is associated closely with the presence of product differentiation. It must be remembered, however, that this logic fails to account for the fact that differentiation can exist only if consumers actually perceive brands to be different.

The three measures of competition that have been discussed to this point are measures that say something about the *structure* of a market. The remaining measures indicate something about the *performance* of a market.

Profits

Persistent high (supernormal) profits in an industry are usually taken to be a sign of allocative inefficiency or of monopoly power. High rates of return on owner's equity are viewed as evidence of the former, while high rates of return on sales are viewed as evidence of the latter. If rates of return on owner's equity in an industry remain high for a long period of time, it is usually assumed that something is blockading a shift in society's resources to this profitable endeavor. If rates of return on sales in an industry remain high also, it is usually assumed that firms are extracting monopoly (higher than competitive) prices from consumers.

The value of each firm's and each brand's after-tax profits were monitored during each run of the model. In addition, rates of return on sales were monitored. No computation of return on owner's equity was made because an owner's equity figure was not included in the model. However, some indication of *relative* allocative efficiency was obtained by comparing profits from year to year and from run to run.

Profit rates are not a perfect measure of allocative efficiency and monopoly power or, for that matter, of competition. Profit rates could be kept high by continuous innovation, marketing and production expertise, and other factors. Even when competition is reasonably vigorous, some firms may be able to achieve persistent high profits by continually employing superior competitive tactics.

Selling Costs

Many economists believe that selling costs will be lower in competitive markets. Although no one has been able to define what would be an acceptable level of selling costs, the feeling persists that competitive firms will try to keep their advertising, promotion, and sales call expenditures to a minimum. Of course, those who have adopted this viewpoint have failed to recognize that firms in certain industries often compete in a manner that brings about an escalation of selling costs. Consequently, shifts in the volume of selling costs can really only reveal information about changes in the *character* of competition, not the *extent* of it. Thus, the spending by all brands on advertising, consumer-directed promotion, dealer-directed promotion, and sales calls was monitored during each run of the model to detect changes in the character of competition only.

Prices

Competitive markets are widely believed to produce lower prices than noncompetitive ones. Thus, a decline in prices throughout an industry is generally viewed as a sign that more vigorous competition is taking place. In this study, the wholesale and retail prices of all the brands in the simulated industry were monitored to give an indication of competitive activity.

Brand Quality

Competitive markets presumably have sellers trying to outdo one another by creating higher quality products. An index of brand quality was therefore monitored during each run of the model for all brands. It should be noted, however, that it is possible that firms will make the investments needed to improve the quality of products only if they feel *insulated* from competition.

EXPERIMENTAL DESIGN

Table 4-1 shows the characteristics of each of the 21 runs that were performed in this study after the model was put into its finalized form. The runs represent the partial completion of an 8x2x2 factorial design in which the three factors controlled were (1) type of control on advertising expenditures (8 types); (2) degree of sensitivity (high or moderate) of the industry sales response function to changes in total advertising goodwill in the industry; and (3) type of objectives managers would be satisfied to reach (profit stream or cash-flow stream). A full factorial design of 32 runs was not employed because of limits on

Table 4-1. Experimental Design

| | | Type of Assumptions: | | |
Type of Control:[a]	No Assumption Changes	Assumption Change 1: SI *Less* Sensitive to (TAG_t/TAG_{t-1})	Assumption Change 2: Cash-Flow Objectives	Assumption Changes 1&2: SI *Less* Sensitive and Cash-Flow Obj.
No Control	Run #1[b] (Benchmark)	Run #2	Run #3	Run #4
Control A: 5% Straight Tax	Run #5			Run #6
Control B: Progressive Tax	Run #7	Run #8	Run #9	
Control C: 10% Limit on A/S	Run #10	Run #11	Run #12	
Control D: 20% Limit on A/S	Run #13	Run #14		
Control E: $3 million Limit	Run #15	Run #16		
Control F: Depreciation (.6+.15+.15+.1)	Run #17	Run #18	Run #19	
Control G: Depreciation (.3+.3+.2+.2)	Run #20		Run #21	

[a]Controls are all introduced in the first year of a run.

[b]All runs last for eight years.

A/S = Advertising-Sales Ratio.

TAG = Total Industry Advertising Goodwill.

SI = Industry Sales in Pounds.

computer time.[a] Furthermore, a standard fractional factorial design, such as the one used by Bonini in his classic simulation study,[5] was not employed because a design that tested the interactions that were of most interest to the author could not be located.[b] Instead, the 21 runs that were executed were those judged to be of greatest relevance of this study.

Each of the 21 runs simulated eight years of the industry's behavior. The benchmark run of the model (see Appendix B) can be thought of as an attempt to simulate the actual behavior of the nutritional submarket of the

[a]Because of the lengthy search routines in the model, an eight-year run of the model cost anywhere from $20.00 to $30.00.

[b]The designs that were examined included those found in National Bureau of Standards, "Fractional Factorial Designs for Factors at Two Levels," *Applied Mathematics Series 48* (Washington, D.C.: U.S. Government Printing Office, 1957).

ready-to-eat breakfast cereal industry during the years 1965 to 1972. The other 20 runs can be viewed as simulations of what the market would have been like *if* controls on advertising expenditures had been introduced *in 1965* and/or *if* the industry sales response function or objectives of the managers had been different than what is assumed in the benchmark run.

Because the model is deterministic, it was not necessary to *replicate* each of the runs to get a large sample upon which to base estimates of the means and variances of the dependent measures of each run. This is often done with stochastic simulation models.[6] If starting conditions, parameter values, response functions and other assumptions are held the same for two runs of this model, identical output will result.

The seven controls that were tested and two assumptions that were varied are described below. The reasons why these particular changes were tested and the methods used to implement these changes are also discussed.

Control A: 5 Percent Straight
Tax on Advertising

None of the proposals that were discussed in Chapter One called for a straight tax to be imposed on advertising to encourage competition. Instead, progressive taxes and other measures were endorsed for this purpose. However, straight taxes *have* been suggested by many people as a means of raising revenue for governments or of reducing the quantity of advertising for reasons other than to encourage competition. It was therefore decided that it would be interesting to see how the imposition of a straight tax on the simulated industry would affect competition. It was considered possible that a straight tax could alter the nature of competition in an industry even if it were not introduced for this purpose.

A 5 percent straight tax was introduced into the model by changing the profit equation used to compute a brand's expected and actual profits. Five percent of each brand's current-year advertising expenditures was subtracted from its after-tax profits. It was thereby assumed that the individual brand manager, and not the entire firm for which he worked, was held accountable for the tax liability incurred through spending funds on advertising for his brand.

Control B: Progressive Tax on
Advertising of 2 Percent
Per Million

Since progressive taxes have been proposed by several people as a means to encourage competition in certain industries (see Chapter One), this type of measure was tested by using the model. A progressive tax rate that grows continuously as *brand* advertising expenditures grow was used to compute each brand manager's tax burden. This rate was computed using the following formula:

Rate = .02 · (Brand Advertising Expenditures/1,000,000).

Thus, a brand manager who spent $5 million on advertising for his brand was considered responsible for paying a tax of 10 percent of this expenditure, or $500,000, *in addition to* his regular corporate income taxes.

The tax rate and tax burden under a progressive tax on advertising was assumed to be imposed on a *per brand* rather than *per firm* basis primarily because the model does not portray a decision process for determining a *firm's* total advertising budget, only a brand's budget. In addition, there is some reason to believe that if a progressive tax were tried, it would actually be introduced on a per brand basis. Policy makers might want to avoid situations where firms would spend all of their advertising budget on one or two brands or where innovative, improved brands would not be brought out by established firms because of the high marginal tax rate even a small introductory advertising campaign would incur. Policy makers might also want to allow moderate spending on advertising for all brands in order to provide consumers with adequate information on product alternatives.

Control C: 10 Percent Limit on
the Advertising-Sales Ratio

Control D: 20 Percent Limit on
the Advertising-Sales Ratio

Several people have suggested that competition could be encouraged in some industries by placing a limit on the percent of sales revenue that a firm could spend on advertising. A Nader study group has, in effect, endorsed this type of measure by recommending that any spending over a percentage of sales deemed appropriate by the FTC should be taxed at a 100 percent rate.[7] Two percentage limits—10 and 20 percent—were tested by using the model, and both were introduced in the way endorsed by the Nader group. The profit equation in the model was adjusted to subtract 100 percent of any *brand's* spending on advertising that exceeded 10 or 20 percent of its sales from the brand's after-tax profits. A limit on each brand's spending rather than on each firm's spending was tested for essentially the same reasons that a per brand progressive tax was tested. It should also be noted that brands that were three years old or less were exempted from these two controls.

Control E: $3 Million Limit on
Advertising Per Brand

Because a limit on the advertising-sales ratio allows larger-selling brands to spend more on advertising than smaller-selling brands, it is conceivable that an absolute dollar limit on advertising expenditures might be imposed instead. Therefore, a $3 million limit *per brand* was tested using the model. It was felt that $3 million represented a reasonable limit since it exceeds what the smaller brands in the submarket spent during the simulated time period, but is less than what the larger brands spent. Once again, the limit was tested on a per pound basis for essentially the same reasons that a progressive tax was tested in this way.

Control F: Depreciation Requirement
(Current Advertising Expense =
$$.6A_t + .15A_{t-1} + .15A_{t-2} + .1A_{t-3})$$

Control G: Depreciation Requirement
(Current Advertising Expense =
$$.3A_t + .3A_{t-1} + .2A_{t-2} + .2A_{t-3})$$

Several people have suggested that requiring firms to depreciate their advertising expenditures for tax purposes would encourage them to spend less on advertising. Two types of depreciation requirements were tested using the model to see whether they actually reduced advertising expenditures and whether they encouraged other forms of competition. The first type of requirement that was tested allowed brand managers to write off advertising expenditures at a fast rate (see schedule above). The second requirement that was tested allowed the brand manager a slower write-off of advertising outlays (see schedule above).

The two depreciation schedules that were tested were chosen because they allowed the brand manager to deduct an amount that was either greater than or smaller than the amount of advertising goodwill his brand held in a year. It was felt that a manager might react differently to these two write-off rates.

Assumption Change 1: Industry
Sales Made Less Sensitive to Changes
in Total Industry Advertising Goodwill

As indicated in Chapter Three, the benchmark run of the model utilized an industry sales response function that made industry sales quite sensitive to changes in total industry advertising goodwill; although as quantities of goodwill were built up, this sensitivity declined. It was felt reasonable to make advertising such an important determinant of industry sales because, among other reasons, during the 1960s the nutritional submarket experienced a "growth" stage in its life cycle—a stage when advertising *can* be very effective.

However, it was also felt that controls on advertising expenditures should be tested by using a model that made advertising a somewhat less important determinant of industry sales. Thus, the effect of making ETA (the sensitivity parameter) always equal to a smaller number was tested. The alterations found in brackets below were made to the industry sales response function:

$$SI_t = [1.05] \cdot POP_t \cdot PCAP_{t-1} \cdot \left(\frac{TAG_t}{TAG_{t-1}}\right)^{ETA_t} \left(\frac{TCP_t}{TCP_{t-1}}\right)^{.05}$$
$$\left(\frac{APR_t}{APR_{t-1}}\right)^{-1.5}$$

where $ETA_t = [-.20] + .85 - .00000001 \cdot TAG_t$.

This assumption change made it possible to explore how an industry might behave during a growth stage where advertising was less responsible for changes in sales.

Assumption Change 2: Managers Given Cash-Flow Objectives

The established brand managers in the benchmark run of the model are always satisfied with utilizing a marketing strategy that will yield a rising stream of after-tax expected profits. However, it is conceivable that managers might desire, instead, to have a rising stream of cash flowing into their firms. This second type of objective might become prevalent after a depreciation requirement on advertising has been introduced, since managers might be made more conscious of their cash flows as a result of this type of policy change. It was therefore decided that the effect of giving managers cash-flow objectives should be tested using the model. Managers were assumed to strive for a stream of *net* cash inflow that grew at a 5 percent rate from the best cash inflow they achieved during the previous four years. (A minimum acceptable starting level for the cash-flow stream was considered to be 5 percent of previous year's dollar sales plus $500,000 [depreciation].)

A manager's cash flow was computed by identifying a portion of his brand's fixed costs as depreciation ($500,000 per year) and adding this amount back to after-tax profits. If a depreciation requirement for advertising was being tested, the following computation was made to get a yearly *net* cash flow figure for a brand:

$$Cash\ Flow_{it} = Z_{it} + 500,000 - (d_1 + d_2 + d_3)A_{it}$$
$$+ (d_1 A_{it-1} + d_2 A_{it-2} + d_3 A_{it-3}).$$

Where Z_{it} = After-tax profits of brand i in year t;

A_{it} = Advertising expenditures of brand i in year t;

d_1, d_2, d_3 = Proportions of advertising expenditures from years $t-1$, $t-2$, and $t-3$ charged off in year t.

ANALYSIS OF RUNS

Because of the weaknesses associated with the measures of competition discussed earlier, it is difficult to rely on a single number, or even a set of numbers, to measure objectively how much competition has changed in an industry. It is necessary to also do a *qualitative* evaluation of the differences in competitive activity that occur in an industry under various conditions. Thus, the following analyses of the 21 computer runs include both quantitative and qualitative evaluations of the competitive effects of making various changes in the benchmark model.

Run #1: The Benchmark Run

Run #1 served as a benchmark to the other 20 runs. It was the run in which no controls were tested and no assumption changes were tried. It attempted to simulate as closely as possible the real-world activity of the nutritional cereal market. In this section, only a short description is provided of what happened during this run. A copy of the computer output of this run can be found in Appendix B, and a comparison of this output to real-world data can be found in Chapter Five.

The run starts out in year 5 with three brands in the industry. Brand 1—the equivalent of "Special K"—is the dominant brand and holds a rather large share of the market. It is Brand 1's tenth year in existence, and it has started to earn a rather large (12.4 percent) after-tax return on sales by taking advantage of the goodwill it has built up with retailers and consumers and by charging relatively high prices. Brand 2—"Life"—is a young brand that is barely earning a profit. It has managed to acquire a rather large share of the market through charging low prices and spending heavily on consumer-directed promotion. But Brand 2 has not been able to achieve very effective distribution primarily because of the relatively weak corporate image of its parent firm, and also because it has not been spending very much on dealer-directed promotion and sales calls. Brand 3—"Total"—is a newcomer to the industry that seems to have a bright future. It has already acquired a large share of the market and it has a firm with a strong corporate image behind it, which has helped it to attain more effective distribution than Brand 2.

In the early years (5 to 7) of the run, Brands 1 and 3 sit back and enjoy their good fortune and do not make any changes in their marketing strategy (i.e., they do not search for other strategies). They continue to earn good profits and to enjoy improving sales. On the other hand, Brand 2 switches to a strategy of larger advertising expenditures, somewhat higher prices, and lower quality, which manages to improve its profits and distribution effectiveness, but not its sales. During this time period, three new brands are also brought out by cereal companies not already in the nutritional market. The industry is in a growth stage, and it clearly can support these new brands at this time. Thus, only the market shares of the three original brands, not their sales, are negatively affected by the entry.

In year 8, the manager of Brand 1 concludes that he is no longer satisfied with his old marketing strategy and decides to search for a marketing mix that will yield a larger stream of expected profits. His search leads him to the decision to spend substantially more on advertising, consumer-directed promotion, and dealer-directed promotion, and this results in larger sales for his brand. Firm 1, the owner of Brand 1, also goes into test market with a secondary brand (Brand 7) during year 8. This brand will become a big success as it takes advantage of the excellent corporate image of Firm 1.

Brand 3 reacts to Brand 1's strategy change in year 9. It cuts its advertising expenditures, increases its dealer-directed promotion, and improves its retailer's margin (retail price minus wholesale price) in order to achieve considerably more effective distribution. At the same time, Brand 1 makes a readjustment in its strategy by raising its prices and lowering its dealer-directed promotion and quality. Brand 7 enters on a full-scale basis and immediately acquires the third largest market share through a strategy of low price, very large dealer-directed promotion expenditures, and reasonably large expenditures in the other spending categories.

The last three years of the run (years 10 to 12) see industry sales leveling off, Brands 1, 3 and 7 growing stronger, and the rest of the industry struggling for survival. No new entrants come into the industry during the last years, although the existing brands expect some entry by cereal company brands in future years. In short, the industry has reached maturity by this time and little growth can be anticipated in the future.

Run #2: No Controls, Assumption Change 1

Before analyzing the output of Run #2, some explanation must be provided of the format of the tables used throughout the remainder of this chapter to summarize the similarities and differences between pairs of computer runs. The first of these tables is Table 4-2. It displays a comparison of Run #2 and Run #1. As indicated in Table 4-2, all the tables first present a comparison of the structural characteristics of the simulated industry in two different runs. In addition, the top half of each table also includes a comparison of the size of industry sales (in pounds) in the two runs. The bottom half of each table contains a summary of the results of a comparison, on a *per brand basis*, of the

Table 4-2.   Analysis of Run #2—Type of Control: None; Assumption Change: 1—Compared to Run #1

Measures of Competition:	Run #	Year							
		5	6	7	8	9	10	11	12
Structural:									
(Pound Sales) (x10⁶)	2	83.7	101.0	122.6	146.5	166.3	170.3	183.4	198.0
	1	84.7	102.6	124.0	149.3	163.2	170.9	174.2	180.0
No. of Firms	2	4	5	6	6	6	5	5	5
	1	4	5	6	6	6	6	6	6
No. of Brands	2	4	5	6	7	7	6	7	7
	1	4	5	6	7	7	7	7	7
2-Firm C.R.	2	.77	.67	.58	.52	.58	.70	.71	.74
	1	.77	.66	.56	.52	.60	.64	.65	.68
2-Brand C.R.	2	.77	.67	.58	.52	.46	.53	.54	.56
	1	.77	.66	.56	.52	.47	.49	.49	.51
3-Firm C.R.	2	1.00	.88	.76	.66	.71	.82	.83	.84
	1	1.00	.88	.75	.67	.70	.74	.75	.77
3-Brand C.R.	2	1.00	.88	.76	.66	.59	.70	.71	.74
	1	1.00	.88	.75	.67	.60	.64	.65	.68
Mkt. Adv. Exps. (x10⁶)	2	9.2	13.0	16.7	20.0	23.2	21.3	21.3	24.1
	1	9.7	13.5	17.1	21.7	22.9	24.2	24.0	26.4

	Brand Number-Firm Number										
	1-1	2-2	3-3	4-4	5-5	6-6	7-1	8-2	9-3	10-4	11-5
Performance: (Supp. Info.)											
After-Tax Profits	+	−	+	d	+	?	+	0d	0		
· Return on Sales	+	+	+	−	+	?	+				

Adv. Exps.	−	−	+	−	+	+
A/S	−	−	+	−	−	−
C.-D. Promotion	?	?	?	?	?	?
CP/S	?	+	?	?	+	?
D.-D. Promotion	+	+	+	?	+	+
DP/S	+	+	+	−	−	?
Sales Calls Exps.	+	?	+	?	+	?
SC/S	+	+	+	?	+	+
Retail Prices	−	?	?	−	?	?
Wholesale Prices	−	?	?	−	−	?
Brand Quality	−	?	−	−	?	?

Code:

0	=	Brand does not appear in run to which it is being compared.
∅	=	Brand does not appear in this run but appears in run to which it is being compared.
e	=	Brand appears *earlier* in this run than in run to which it is being compared.
l	=	Brand appears *later* in this run than in run to which it is being compared.
d	=	Brand *dies* earlier in this run than in run to which it is being compared.
s	=	Brand *survives* longer in this run than in run to which it is being compared.
+	=	*Higher* values than in run to which it is being compared.
−	=	*Lower* values than in run to which it is being compared.
?	=	*Unclear difference* in values between runs.

values of the performance variables generated by the two runs. Some supplemental information is also provided in the bottom half of each table which tells whether brands entered or left the industry at different points in time during the two runs.

The values of the performance variables generated by one run were judged to be "significantly" different than the values generated by another (baseline) run if certain conditions were met. The figures on profits, return on sales, selling costs, selling costs as a percentage of sales, retail and wholesale prices, and brand quality generated by a first run for a particular brand for a particular year were compared to the figures generated by a baseline run for the same brand and the same year. If a brand entered or left at different times during the two runs—as was the case with Brand 1 of Firm 4 in the comparison of Runs #2 and #1—then the comparison was made between the performance figures for a brand at identical *age* levels rather than at identical years. For a given brand in a given year (or at a given age), the following amounts were judged to represent "significant" differences between two runs in the values of the thirteen performance variables:

Profits: A \$200,000 difference;
Return on Sales: A 1 percent difference;
Selling Costs (Advertising, Consumer-Directed Promotion, Dealer-Directed Promotion, and Sales Calls): A \$200,000 difference;
Selling Costs as a Percentage of Sales (A/S,CP/S,DP/S, and SC/S): A 1 percent difference;
Retail Price and Wholesale Price: A \$.01 difference;
Brand Quality: A 2.0 difference.

Thus, if Brand 1 of Firm 1 had at least \$200,000 less in advertising expenditures in all eight years of one run than it did in all eight years of a baseline run, a minus sign would have been placed in the appropriate cell of the table comparing the runs. Likewise, if at least \$200,000 more were spent on consumer-directed promotion by Brand 2 of Firm 2 in all eight years of one run than was spent by the brand in the corresponding years of a baseline run, a plus sign would have been placed in the appropriate cell of the table comparing these two runs.

In cases where the differences between runs were not significant in all years and/or were not all in the same direction, the following rule was used in awarding plus signs, minus signs, or question marks to cells: *Let V_{ijkm} equal the value generated for performance variable i of brand j in year k (or at age k) during Run #m. In comparing Run #a to Run #b, if ($V_{ijka} - V_{ijkb}$) was positive (negative) at least as often as it was negative (positive) in the years being compared, and if a majority of the subset of the ($V_{ijka} - V_{ijkb}$)'s that represented significant differences were positive (negative), then a plus sign (minus sign) was awarded to the cell for performance variable i of brand j in the table of Run #a. A question mark was placed in this cell if a plus sign or minus* *sign could not be awarded*. Thus, a plus sign was awarded in Table 4-2 to the advertising expenditures of Brand 6 because in its first year (year 8) the brand had insignificantly lower advertising expenditures in Run #2 than it had in Run #1,[c] in its second year it had significantly lower expenditures, and in its last three years it had significantly higher expenditures. On the other hand, a minus sign had to be awarded to the advertising-sales ratio of Brand 6 because this ratio was significantly lower in Run #2 than in Run #1 during the brand's first two years, significantly higher during its third year, insignificantly lower during its fourth year, and exactly the same in its fifth year.

The term "significant," used here to describe differences between runs, should not be confused with the term "statistically significant." The deterministic nature of the model made it meaningless to test for the statistical significance of differences between runs using analysis of variance or other statistical tests. These tests are used to compute the probability that a change in a dependent measure of an experiment could be caused by chance rather than by some experimental variation. But since there are no stochastic elements in the model, any change in the output of the model *must* have been caused by experimental variations of the model's assumptions or makeup and not by chance occurrences.

With the explanation of the format of the tables completed, an analysis of Run #2 can now be presented. The purpose of executing this run was to see how sensitive the model was to Assumption Change 1 (industry sales made less sensitive to advertising) and, also, to provide a baseline run against which Runs #8, #11, #14, #16, and #18 could be compared. As shown in Table 4-2, the model proved to be somewhat sensitive to this assumption change, though the nature of competition in the simulated industry did not change dramatically in Run #2.

In fact, the effects of making the industry sales response function less sensitive to changes in industry advertising goodwill were reasonably predictable. Without the need to keep industry advertising expenditures increasing rapidly to produce some growth in industry sales, the brand managers generally spent less on advertising. This resulted in slightly lower industry sales at the beginning of the run. However, at the end of the run, slightly higher industry sales were generated because the growth term of 1.05 that was added to the response function for this run prevented the industry sales figure from tapering off as it did in Run #1.

The growth term also caused the brand managers in this run to expect a relatively greater number of future entrants to the industry as sales continued to move upward. This expectation of new entrants was apparently responsible for the somewhat lower prices charged by the managers in Run #2.

---

[c]Comparisons between runs were not made for a brand's test-market year. Thus, although Brand 6 went into test market in both Runs #2 and #1 in year 7, comparisons of the values of the performance variables of the brand started in year 8.

A "limit pricing" strategy seems to have been used by the managers to deter entry. It should also be noted that the lower prices seem to have caused lower quality brands to have been produced in efforts to cut costs.

One unpredictable event that occurred in Run #2 was the death of Brand 4 after year 9. This death resulted in higher market concentration, higher profits, and a few shifts in marketing strategy during the last three years of the run. Brand 4's demise was caused by the fact that it had much larger expenditures on advertising and sales calls for years 8 and 9 during this run. The manager of Brand 4 apparently felt a need to react to the larger *dollar* spending on advertising and sales calls by Brand 1 during years 5, 6 and 7. Brand 1 spent more on a dollar basis during these years because its sales were higher. A less aggressive strategy with lower advertising expenditures on the part of Brand 2 seems to have allowed Brand 1 to attain higher sales in those years.

One more thing should be mentioned about Run #2. Two additional brands tried to enter the industry during this run. A new brand (Brand 8) was put into test market by Firm 2 during year 11, but it failed to acquire a high enough market share to allow full-scale entry. Firm 3, however, successfully test marketed a brand (Brand 9) during year 12, and it replaced Brand 4 as the seventh brand in the market.

Run #3: No Controls,
Assumption Change 2

Run #3 was executed to test how sensitive the model was to Assumption Change 2 and, also, to provide a baseline run against which Runs #9, #12, #19, and #21 could be compared. Table 4-3 shows that the effects of this assumption change were relatively minor. In fact, the first three years of Run #3 were identical to Run #1. Giving the brand managers in the model cash-flow objectives rather than profit objectives had little influence on the industry's structure or performance.

Substantial differences between Runs #3 and #1 were not really expected. The same depreciation figure ($500,000 per year) was added back to the after-tax profits of all brands to get yearly cash-flow figures, and this action could not, by itself, be expected to change the model's output very much. However, Run #3 *was* expected to be different from Runs #19 and #21 and, possibly, from Runs #9 and #12. These runs were compared to Run #3 to test whether four of the advertising controls had a different impact upon competition when cash-flow objectives were assumed to exist than they did when profit objectives were assumed. These comparisons are discussed later in this chapter.

Run #4: No Controls, Assumption
Changes 1 and 2

A determination of the magnitude of the interaction between Assumption Changes 1 and 2 was made possible by the execution of Run #4.

This run was also used as a baseline run against which Run #6 was compared. A comparison between Run #4 and Run #1 is shown in Table 4-4. As with Run #2, this run's output was somewhat different than Run #1.

Most of the differences between Runs #4 and #1 can be attributed to the effects of Assumption Change 1, since Assumption Change 2 was found to have only a slight effect on the model's output. However, the interaction of the two assumption changes seems to have had some influence on the figures produced by Run #4. In particular, the interaction apparently allowed Brand 4 to survive through all of Run #4—something that did not occur during Run #2. Brand 4 survived past year 9 in Run #4 because it cut back its advertising and sales call expenditures in year 9 and managed to earn a profit in its fourth year of existence. Brand 4 made this cut in spending because it went through a longer search procedure during Run #4. The longer search procedure was made necessary for Brand 4 by strategy changes of Brands 1 and 3 that occurred in this run during years 7 and 8, but did not occur in Run #2. The survival of Brand 4 caused Run #4 to have higher market sales and advertising expenditures, lower concentration, and somewhat different marketing strategies on the part of the other brands than Run #2.

Run #5: 5 Percent Straight Tax

A comparison between Run #5 and Run #1 is presented in Table 4-5. This comparison indicates that a 5 percent straight tax on advertising did little to encourage competition in the simulated industry over the eight-year period. Moreover, if the simulation had been run out a few more years, it appears as though competition in the industry would have diminished substantially. The industry had already lost Brand 5 after year 10, and it would have also lost Brand 2 after year 12 (Brand 2 failed to earn a profit during the last four years of the run).

The primary effect that the tax had on the industry was to make the advertising expenditures of all brands lower than they were in Run #1. No general increases or decreases were detected in selling costs other than advertising, in prices, or in brand quality during Run #5. Because industry sales were quite sensitive to changes in industry advertising goodwill in this run, the smaller advertising expenditures caused by the tax led to relatively lower industry sales. The lower sales, along with the substantial tax payments, produced lower profits and lower returns on sales throughout the industry. As a result, Brand 5 was forced out of the industry after year 10, since it had taken losses for four straight years. With Brand 5 out of the picture, concentration rose substantially during the last two years of the run.

Thus, although the tax produced smaller advertising expenditures (and possibly less product differentiation), no new entrants were attracted to the industry. Entry actually looked less attractive to potential entrants because of the advertising tax and because the industry's growth rate was slower. Further-

Table 4-3.   Analysis of Run #3—Type of Control: None; Assumption Change: 2—Compared to Run #1

Measures of Competition:	Run #		Year							
		5	6	7	8	9	10	11	12
Structural:									
(Pound Sales) (x 10^6)	3	84.7	102.6	124.0	149.3	164.0	172.0	175.2	177.0
	1	84.7	102.6	124.0	149.3	163.2	170.9	174.2	180.0
No. of Firms	3	4	5	6	6	6	6	6	6
	1	4	5	6	6	6	6	6	6
No. of Brands	3	4	5	6	7	7	7	7	7
	1	4	5	6	7	7	7	7	7
2-Firm C.R.	3	.77	.66	.56	.52	.60	.63	.65	.66
	1	.77	.66	.56	.52	.60	.64	.65	.68
2-Brand C.R.	3	.77	.66	.56	.52	.47	.48	.50	.51
	1	.77	.66	.56	.52	.47	.49	.49	.51
3-Firm C.R.	3	1.00	.88	.75	.68	.70	.73	.74	.75
	1	1.00	.88	.75	.67	.70	.74	.75	.77
3-Brand C.R.	3	1.00	.88	.75	.67	.60	.63	.65	.66
	1	1.00	.88	.75	.67	.60	.64	.65	.68
Mkt. Adv. Exps. (x 10^6)	3	9.7	13.5	17.1	21.7	22.6	23.5	23.6	24.6
	1	9.7	13.5	17.1	21.7	22.9	24.2	24.0	26.4

		Brand Number-Firm Number									
		1-1	2-2	3-3	4-4	5-5	6-6	7-1	8-2	9-3	10-4	11-5
Performance: (Supp. Info.)											
After-Tax Profits		?	?	+	?	?	?	—				
Return on Sales		?	?	+	?	?	?	—				

Table 4-4.   Analysis of Run #4—Type of Control: None; Assumption Change: 1 and 2—Compared to Run #1

Measures of Competition:	Run #	Year							
		5	6	7	8	9	10	11	12
Structural:									
(Pound Sales) (x 10⁶)	4	83.7	101.0	123.1	149.7	166.5	181.2	192.3	205.7
	1	84.7	102.6	124.0	149.3	163.2	170.9	174.2	180.0
No. of Firms	4	4	5	6	6	6	6	6	6
	1	4	5	6	6	6	6	6	6
No. of Brands	4	4	5	6	7	7	8	8	9
	1	4	5	6	7	7	7	7	7
2-Firms C.R.	4	.77	.67	.58	.53	.59	.61	.62	.66
	1	.77	.66	.56	.52	.60	.64	.65	.68
2-Brand C.R.	4	.77	.67	.58	.53	.47	.46	.46	.44
	1	.77	.66	.56	.52	.47	.49	.49	.51
3-Firm C.R.	4	1.00	.88	.76	.69	.70	.73	.74	.76
	1	1.00	.88	.75	.67	.70	.74	.75	.77
3-Brand C.R.	4	1.00	.88	.76	.67	.59	.61	.62	.58
	1	1.00	.88	.75	.67	.60	.64	.65	.68
Mkt. Adv. Exps. (x 10⁶)	4	9.2	13.0	16.7	21.1	22.2	24.2	24.5	26.3
	1	9.7	13.5	17.1	21.7	22.9	24.2	24.0	26.4

	Brand Number-Firm Number										
	1-1	2-2	3-3	4-4	5-5	6-6	7-1	8-2	9-3	10-4	11-5
Performance: (Supp. Info.)											
After-Tax Profits	+	−	+	+	+	?	?	0d	0	0d	
Return on Sales	+	−	+	+	?	?	+				

Adv. Exps.	—	+	—	+	+	+	—
A/S	—	+	—	+	+	+	+
C.-D. Promotion	?	?	?	?	?	?	? ?
CP/S	?	?	?	?	?	?	? ?
D.-D. Promotion	?	?	?	?	?	—	? ?
DP/S	?	?	—	?	—	—	+
Sales Calls Exps.	?	?	?	?	?	?	? ?
SC/S	?	?	—	?	—	?	? ?
Retail Prices	—	?	—	?	?	+	—
Wholesale Prices	—	?	—	?	—	—	?
Brand Quality	?	—	?	—	—	+	?

Code:

0 = Brand does not appear in run to which it is being compared.

∅ = Brand does not appear in this run but appears in run to which it is being compared.

e = Brand appears *earlier* in this run than in run to which it is being compared.

1 = Brand appears *later* in this run than in run to which it is being compared.

d = Brand *dies* earlier in this run than in run to which it is being compared.

s = Brand *survives* longer in this run than in run to which it is being compared.

+ = *Higher* values than in run to which it is being compared.

— = *Lower* values than in run to which it is being compared.

? = *Unclear difference* in values between runs.

Adv. Exps.	—	—	—	+	+	+	—
A/S	—	—	?	?	?	?	—
C.-D. Promotion	?	?	?	?	?	?	?
CP/S	?	+	?	?	?	?	?
D.-D. Promotion	?	?	?	?	?	?	?
DP/S	?	?	—	—	+	+	+
Sales Calls Exps.	?	?	?	?	?	?	?
SC/S	+	+	+	+	+	+	+
Retail Prices	?	—	—	+	+	—	?
Wholesale Prices	?	—	—	+	+	—	?
Brand Quality	?	?	?	—	—	—	?

Code:

0	=	Brand does not appear in run to which it is being compared.
∅	=	Brand does not appear in this run but appears in run to which it is being compared.
e	=	Brand appears *earlier* in this run than in run to which it is being compared.
l	=	Brand appears *later* in this run than in run to which it is being compared.
d	=	Brand *dies* earlier in this run than in run to which it is being compared.
s	=	Brand *survives* longer in this run than in run to which it is being compared.
+	=	*Higher* values than in run to which it is being compared.
—	=	*Lower* values than in run to which it is being compared.
?	=	*Unclear difference* in values between runs.

Table 4-5.   Analysis of Run #5—Type of Control: 5 Percent Straight Tax; Assumption Change: None—Compared to Run #1

Measures of Competition:	Run #	Year							
		5	6	7	8	9	10	11	12
Structural:									
(Pound Sales) (x 10^6)	5	83.4	99.3	118.5	141.3	155.5	159.8	150.0	155.0
	1	84.7	102.6	124.0	149.3	163.2	170.9	174.2	180.0
No. of Firms	5	4	5	6	6	6	6	5	5
	1	4	5	6	6	6	6	6	6
No. of Brands	5	4	5	6	7	7	7	6	6
	1	4	5	6	7	7	7	7	7
2-Firm C.R.	5	.76	.67	.58	.50	.57	.63	.71	.74
	1	.77	.66	.56	.52	.60	.64	.65	.68
2-Brand C.R.	5	.76	.67	.58	.50	.45	.47	.54	.56
	1	.77	.66	.56	.52	.47	.49	.49	.51
3-Firm C.R.	5	1.00	.88	.75	.65	.69	.73	.82	.83
	1	1.00	.88	.75	.67	.70	.74	.75	.77
3-Brand C.R.	5	1.00	.88	.75	.65	.57	.63	.71	.74
	1	1.00	.88	.75	.67	.60	.64	.65	.68
Mkt. Adv. Exps. (x 10^6)	5	9.2	12.6	15.9	19.4	20.9	21.0	18.9	21.1
	1	9.7	13.5	17.1	21.7	22.9	24.2	24.0	26.4

	Brand Number-Firm Number										
	1-1	2-2	3-3	4-4	5-5	6-6	7-1	8-2	9-3	10-4	11-5
Performance: (Supp. Info.)					d						
After-Tax Profits	—	—	?	—	?	?	?				
Return on Sales	?	—	—	—	—	—	?				

Adv. Exps. A/S	−	−	−	−	−	−
C.-D. Promotion	−	?	?	?	?	−
CP/S	?	+	?	?	?	?
D.-D. Promotion	−	?	?	?	−	−
DP/S	?	?	+	?	?	−
Sales Calls Exps.	?	?	?	?	?	−
SC/S	?	?	+	?	?	−
Retail Prices	+	?	?	−	−	+
Wholesale Prices	+	?	+	−	−	?
Brand Quality	?	?	?	−	+	?

Code:

0 = Brand does not appear in run to which it is being compared.

∅ = Brand does not appear in this run but appears in run to which it is being compared.

e = Brand appears *earlier* in this run than in run to which it is being compared.

1 = Brand appears *later* in this run than in run to which it is being compared.

d = Brand *dies* earlier in this run than in run to which it is being compared.

s = Brand *survives* longer in this run than in run to which it is being compared.

+ = *Higher* values than in run to which it is being compared.

− = *Lower* values than in run to which it is being compared.

? = *Unclear difference* in values between runs.

more, lower prices for consumers did not appear. In fact, two of the leading brands (Brands 1 and 3) had relatively higher prices at the end of Run #5 and this trend would have probably led to relatively higher profits for these brands had the run been extended beyond year 12.

Run #6: 5 Percent Straight Tax, Assumption Changes 1 and 2

A 5 percent straight tax on advertising had about the same effect on the industry in Run #6 as it did in Run #5. Imposing the tax on a model with a different industry sales response function and different managerial objectives still produced relatively lower advertising expenditures, lower industry sales, lower profits, more exits, higher concentration, and no general lowering of prices. The tax probably did more to discourage competition than to encourage it. Table 4-6 contains a summary of the effects of the tax in Run #6.

It should also be noted that a slight tendency to spend more on dealer-directed promotion and sales calls appeared in Run #6. However, the magnitude of this increased spending was not very large.

Run #7: Progressive Tax

A progressive tax of 2 percent per million dollars spent on advertising definitely encouraged brand managers to spend less on advertising in Run #7 (see Table 4-7). This, in turn, led to relatively lower industry sales. The tax and the smaller industry sales forced a delay of three years in the entry of Brands 6 and 7, and this resulted in higher market concentration during the early years of the run. However, the delayed entry of Brands 6 and 7 also allowed Brands 2, 4, and 5 to grow relatively stronger during the interim and, thus, at the end of Run #7, market concentration was lower than it was in Run #1.

The delayed entry of Brands 6 and 7 also had another interesting effect. Even though they earned slightly lower profits early in Run #7 because of the tax, Brands 1 and 3 waited two years longer in this run to search for new marketing strategies to use to improve their expected profits. Without Brands 6 and 7 in the industry, Brands 1 and 3 could afford to be more complacent. This complacency delayed price increases by these brands and also led to relatively lower spending on dealer-directed promotion.

In conclusion, it is difficult to say that a progressive tax would encourage competition based on the results of Run #7. The tax did eventually lead to lower concentration, but this may have been a temporary situation since Brands 2, 4, and 5 did not end up being that much stronger in Run #7 than they were in Run #1. In addition, entry did not look any more attractive to potential entrants, in spite of the lower industry advertising expenditures, because new entrants would also have to bear the burden of the tax. Finally, the relatively lower prices that were charged in Run #7 were not the result of what could be called price competition. Instead, they came about because Brands 1 and 3 failed to raise their prices as soon as they did in Run #1.

Run #8: Progressive Tax, Assumption Change 1

In an industry where sales were less sensitive to changes in advertising goodwill, the effect of a progressive tax was slightly different. However, the tax did not appear to encourage vigorous competition in this situation. As shown in Table 4-8, there were some signs that competition increased in Run #8, but it did not increase in any pronounced way.

As in Run #7, the tax caused the brand managers in Run #8 to spend less on advertising. The reduction in advertising expenditures did not result, however, in lower industry sales in this case. Instead, industry sales in Run #8 stayed reasonably close to the figures for Run #2. Moreover, without a lowering of industry sales, the tax by itself was not capable of delaying the entry of any new brands as it did in Run #7. In fact, the entry of Brand 8 and 9 occurred earlier in Run #8 than in Run #2, and Brand 4 also survived until the end of Run #8. A tenth brand even tried unsuccessfully to enter the industry during year 12 of this run. All of the above resulted in lower concentration ratios in the last four years of Run #8 than were generated by Run #2.

The tax also led to a similar occurrence in Run #8 as occurred in Run #7 with respect to the search procedures of Brands 1 and 3. The search procedures of these brands were begun one year later and were somewhat shorter (in Run #8) than in Run #2. But rather than being caused by the delayed entry of rival brands, as was the case in Run #7, the complacency of Brands 1 and 3 seems to have been caused by the fact that they *expected* fewer new rivals to enter the industry because of the tax. Regardless of the cause, the delayed and shorter research procedures of Brands 1 and 2 led, once again, to a failure to raise prices and dealer-directed promotion expenditures.

In summary, one could say that the progressive tax produced a slightly greater increase in competition in Run #8 than it did in Run #7. In Run #8, the tax seemed to help rather than hinder entry by established company brands (though not by other types). It also led to relatively larger drops in concentration. However, the weaker brands in the industry (Brands 2, 4, 5, and 6) did not become very much stronger as a result of the tax, and the relatively lower prices that were charged were an outgrowth of complacency.

Run #9: Progressive Tax, Assumption Change 2

When managers were given cash-flow objectives and a progressive tax was tested, the tax again had a mixed effect on competition. In a similar fashion to Run #7, entry by Brands 4, 5, 6 and 7 was delayed for several years. But like Run #7, the industry ended Run #9 with relatively lower concentration (see Table 4-9).

One pro-competitive effect of the tax at the end of Run #9 was the encouragement of a certain amount of competition in brand quality. However, the tax also was responsible for the higher prices and higher consumer-directed

Table 4-6. Analysis of Run #6—Type of Control: 5 Percent Straight Tax; Assumption Change: 1 and 2—Compared to Run #4

Measures of Competition:	Run #	Year							
		5	6	7	8	9	10	11	12
Structural:									
(Pound Sales) (x 10⁶)	6	83.4	100.5	120.2	142.7	158.6	172.8	170.7	174.2
	4	83.7	101.0	123.1	149.7	166.5	181.2	192.3	205.7
No. of Firms	6	4	5	6	6	6	6	5	4
	4	4	5	6	6	6	6	6	6
No. of Brands	6	4	5	6	7	7	7	7	6
	4	4	5	6	7	7	8	8	9
2-Firm C.R.	6	.76	.68	.61	.53	.60	.63	.71	.79
	4	.77	.67	.58	.53	.59	.61	.62	.66
2-Brand C.R.	6	.76	.68	.61	.53	.48	.48	.53	.59
	4	.77	.67	.58	.53	.47	.46	.46	.44
3-Firm C.R.	6	1.00	.88	.76	.68	.71	.73	.82	.90
	4	1.00	.88	.76	.69	.70	.73	.74	.76
3-Brand C.R.	6	1.00	.68	.76	.67	.60	.63	.71	.79
	4	1.00	.88	.76	.67	.59	.61	.62	.58
Mkt. Adv. Exps. (x 10⁶)	6	9.1	12.4	15.6	19.4	19.7	21.4	18.3	19.8
	4	9.2	13.0	16.7	21.1	22.2	24.2	24.5	26.3

	Brand Number-Firm Number										
	1-1	2-2	3-3	4-4	5-5	6-6	7-1	8-2	9-3	10-4	11-5
Performance:											
(Supp. Info.)		d			d			1	1	Ø	
After-Tax Profits	—	—	—	?	?	—	+				
Return on Sales	—	—	—	—	—	—	—				

Adv. Exps. A/S	–	–	–	–	–	–
	–	–	–	–	–	–
C.-D. Promotion CP/S	–	?	?	?	?	?
	?	?	?	?	?	?
D.-D. Promotion DP/S	+	+	+	+	+	+
	+	+	+	+	+	+
Sales Calls Exps. SC/S	?	?	?	?	?	?
	?	+	+	+	+	+
Retail Prices	–	?	+	+	+	?
Wholesale Prices	?	?	+	+	+	?
Brand Quality	?	?	–	–	+	?

Code:

0 = Brand does not appear in run to which it is being compared.

∅ = Brand does not appear in this run but appears in run to which it is being compared.

e = Brand appears *earlier* in this run than in run to which it is being compared.

l = Brand appears *later* in this run than in run to which it is being compared.

d = Brand *dies* earlier in this run than in run to which it is being compared.

s = Brand *survives* longer in this run than in run to which it is being compared.

+ = *Higher* values than in run to which it is being compared.

– = *Lower* values than in run to which it is being compared.

? = *Unclear difference* in values between runs.

Table 4-7. Analysis of Run #7—Type of Control: Progressive Tax; Assumption Change: None—Compared to Run #1

Measures of Competition:	Run #	Year							
		5	6	7	8	9	10	11	12
Structural:									
(Pound Sales) (x 10⁶)	7	82.7	97.5	115.6	129.4	135.7	140.0	149.5	153.0
	1	84.7	102.6	124.0	149.3	163.2	170.9	174.2	180.0
No. of Firms	7	4	5	5	5	5	6	6	6
	1	4	5	6	6	6	6	6	6
No. of Brands	7	4	5	5	5	5	6	7	7
	1	4	5	6	7	7	7	7	7
2-Firm C.R.	7	.76	.68	.57	.56	.56	.57	.54	.60
	1	.77	.66	.56	.52	.60	.64	.65	.68
2-Brand C.R.	7	.76	.68	.57	.56	.56	.57	.54	.48
	1	.77	.66	.56	.52	.47	.49	.49	.51
3-Firm C.R.	7	1.00	.88	.74	.72	.71	.72	.67	.70
	1	1.00	.88	.75	.67	.70	.74	.75	.77
3-Brand C.R.	7	1.00	.88	.74	.72	.71	.72	.67	.60
	1	1.00	.88	.75	.67	.60	.64	.65	.68
Mkt. Adv. Exps. (x 10⁶)	7	9.0	12.3	15.2	16.2	16.3	16.9	19.8	19.2
	1	9.7	13.5	17.1	21.7	22.9	24.2	24.0	26.4

	Brand Number-Firm Number										
	1-1	2-2	3-3	4-4	5-5	6-6	7-1	8-2	9-3	10-4	11-5
Performance: (Supp. Info.)							1	1			
After-Tax Profits	—	?	—	+	+	?	?				
Return on Sales	—	?	—	?	+	?	?				

Adv. Exps.	—	—	?	?	—	—
A/S	—	—	—	—	—	?
C.-D. Promotion	?	?	?	?	?	?
CP/S	?	?	?	?	+	?
D.-D. Promotion	?	—	+	+	—	?
DP/S	+	+	+	+	—	+
Sales Calls Exps.	?	?	?	?	?	?
SC/S	?	+	?	?	?	+
Retail Prices	—	—	—	—	+	+
Wholesale Prices	—	?	?	+	?	+
Brand Quality	—	?	—	—	?	?

Code:

0 = Brand does not appear in run to which it is being compared.

∅ = Brand does not appear in this run but appears in run to which it is being compared.

e = Brand appears *earlier* in this run than in run to which it is being compared.

1 = Brand appears *later* in this run than in run to which it is being compared.

d = Brand *dies* earlier in this run than in run to which it is being compared.

s = Brand *survives* longer in this run than in run to which it is being compared.

+ = *Higher* values than in run to which it is being compared.

— = *Lower* values than in run to which it is being compared.

? = *Unclear difference* in values between runs.

Table 4-8.   Analysis of Run #8—Type of Control: Progressive Tax; Assumption Change: 1—Compared to Run #2

Measures of Competition:	Run #	5	6	7	8	9	10	11	12
Structural:									
(Pound Sales) ($\times 10^6$)	8	83.2	99.4	119.7	144.0	158.5	168.8	176.2	193.1
	2	83.7	101.0	122.6	146.5	166.3	170.3	183.4	198.0
No. of Firms	8	4	5	6	6	6	6	6	6
	2	4	5	6	6	6	5	5	5
No. of Brands	8	4	5	6	7	7	8	8	9
	2	4	5	6	7	7	6	7	7
2-Firm C.R.	8	.76	.69	.60	.53	.57	.59	.60	.65
	2	.77	.67	.58	.52	.58	.70	.71	.74
2-Brand C.R.	8	.76	.69	.60	.52	.45	.47	.47	.47
	2	.77	.67	.58	.52	.46	.53	.54	.56
3-Firm C.R.	8	1.00	.88	.76	.67	.69	.70	.70	.74
	2	1.00	.88	.76	.66	.71	.82	.83	.84
3-Brand C.R.	8	1.00	.88	.76	.67	.57	.59	.59	.58
	2	1.00	.88	.76	.66	.59	.70	.71	.74
Mkt. Adv. Exps. ($\times 10^6$)	8	9.0	12.4	15.7	19.5	18.1	18.3	17.7	21.7
	2	9.2	13.0	16.7	20.0	23.2	21.3	21.3	24.1

Brand Number-Firm Number

	Run #	1-1	2-2	3-3	4-4	5-5	6-6	7-1	8-2	9-3	10-4	11-5
Performance: (Supp. Info.)					s				ed	e	0	
After-Tax Profits	8	—	?	—	?	?	?	—				
Return on Sales	2	—	?	—	?	+	?	?				

Adv. Exps.						
A/S	−	−	−	−	−	−
C.-D. Promotion						
CP/S	?	?	?	?	?	?
D.-D. Promotion						
DP/S	?	?	−	+	?	−
Sales Calls Exps.						
SC/S	+	+	+	−	?	−
Retail Prices	−	?	−	−	−	+
Wholesale Prices	+	+	?	−	?	+
Brand Quality	+	?	+	+	−	+

Code:

0	=	Brand does not appear in run to which it is being compared.
∅	=	Brand does not appear in this run but appears in run to which it is being compared.
e	=	Brand appears *earlier* in this run than in run to which it is being compared.
1	=	Brand appears *later* in this run than in run to which it is being compared.
d	=	Brand *dies* earlier in this run than in run to which it is being compared.
s	=	Brand *survives* longer in this run than in run to which it is being compared.
+	=	*Higher* values than in run to which it is being compared.
−	=	*Lower* values than in run to which it is being compared.
?	=	*Unclear difference* in values between runs.

Table 4-9. Analysis of Run #9—Type of Control: Progressive Tax; Assumption Change: 2—Compared to Run #3

Measures of Competition:	Run #	5	6	7	8	9	10	11	12
Structural:									
(Pound Sales) (x 10⁶)	9	82.9	87.7	91.4	105.8	122.3	133.5	139.3	145.6
	3	84.7	102.6	124.0	149.3	164.0	172.0	175.2	177.0
No. of Firms	9	3	3	4	5	5	6	6	6
	3	4	5	6	6	6	6	6	6
No. of Brands	9	3	3	4	5	5	6	7	7
	3	4	5	6	7	7	7	7	7
2-Firm C.R.	9	.76	.78	.79	.70	.60	.56	.51	.56
	3	.77	.66	.56	.52	.60	.63	.65	.66
2-Brand C.R.	9	.76	.78	.79	.70	.60	.56	.50	.45
	3	.77	.66	.56	.52	.47	.48	.50	.51
3-Firm C.R.	9	1.00	1.00	1.00	.88	.75	.73	.66	.68
	3	1.00	.88	.75	.68	.70	.73	.74	.75
3-Brand C.R.	9	1.00	1.00	1.00	.88	.75	.73	.66	.57
	3	1.00	.88	.75	.67	.60	.63	.65	.66
Mkt. Adv. Exps. (x 10⁶)	9	9.6	10.1	10.8	15.1	17.8	18.0	17.7	19.4
	3	9.7	13.5	17.1	21.7	22.6	23.5	23.6	24.6

	1-1	2-2	3-3	4-4	5-5	6-6	7-1	8-2	9-3	10-4	11-5
							Brand Number-Firm Number				
Performance:											
(Supp. Info.)				1	1	1	1				
After-Tax Profits	+	+	+	?	?	+	?				
Return on Sales	+	+	?	?	?	+	?				

Adv. Exps.	−	?	?	+	+	−
A/S	−	−	−	+	−	−
C.-D. Promotion	?	+	?	+	+	+
CP/S	?	+	+	+	?	+
D.-D. Promotion	?	?	+	+	−	?
DP/S	?	?	?	?	−	?
Sales Calls Exps.	?	?	?	+	?	−
SC/S	?	−	−	?	−	−
Retail Prices	+	+	+	+	+	+
Wholesale Prices	+	+	+	+	+	+
Brand Quality	?	?	?	+	?	?

Code:

0 = Brand does not appear in run to which it is being compared.
∅ = Brand does not appear in this run but appears in run to which it is being compared.
e = Brand appears *earlier* in this run than in run to which it is being compared.
1 = Brand appears *later* in this run than in run to which it is being compared.
d = Brand *dies* earlier in this run than in run to which it is being compared.
s = Brand *survives* longer in this run than in run to which it is being compared.
+ = *Higher* values than in run to which it is being compared.
− = *Lower* values than in run to which it is being compared.
? = *Unclear difference* in values between runs.

promotion expenditures that appeared in this run. On balance, it must be said that the progressive tax did very little to encourage competition in Run #9.

Run #10: 10 Percent Limit on
the Advertising-Sales Ratio

The effect of requiring brand managers to pay a 100 percent tax on their advertising expenditures that exceeded 10 percent of sales was to suppress competition severely rather than to encourage it (see Table 4-10). Even though new brands were exempted from this limit for their first three years, all entry to the industry was blockaded by this control. Potential rivals were thwarted by the existence of the spending limit and by the fact that industry sales would be much smaller given the requirement of lower advertising expenditures.

Besides cutting off entry to the industry, the limit also contributed to the earlier death of Brand 2 in Run #10. Brands 1 and 3 discovered that it was necessary for them to exceed the 10 percent limit to keep their sales up. But Brand 2 could not afford to pay the stiff penalty for exceeding the limit and suffered as a result. Also, Brand 2 was hurt because it could not cover its costs during a small amount of price competition that occurred during the middle of Run #10.

The price competition that occurred also hurt Brand 3. In addition, Brand 3 could not afford to pay penalties as large as those paid by Brand 1 for exceeding the advertising limit. Furthermore, Brand 3 had lower sales than Brand 1, which gave it a lower advertising limit. Thus, Run #10 ended with Brand 1 growing stronger at the expense of Brand 3, and prices rising rapidly following the death of Brand 2 (a relatively low-price brand that had kept down the average price in the industry). The industry was clearly headed toward becoming a monopoly.

Run #11: 10 Percent Limit,
Assumption Change 1

A 10 percent limit on the advertising-sales ratio had a different effect on an industry whose industry sales response function was less sensitive to changes in advertising goodwill. Examination of Table 4-11 will reveal that the limit did not suppress competition in Run #11 as it did in Run #10. However, the limit could not be said to have encouraged vigorous competition either. At best, the limit could be said to have inspired a temporary competitive skirmish that could not be expected to continue in the long-run.

The limit caused a rather large reduction in advertising expenditures by all brands, and this resulted in lower industry sales than in Run #2. But the limit was not restrictive enough (the three-year exemption existed), nor was the industry sales growth rate slowed down enough to cause entry to be stopped. In fact, Brands 8 and 9 entered a year earlier in Run #1 than they did in Run #2, and Brand 8 even survived test marketing in the former run. Furthermore, an additional brand (Brand 10) went through a successful test market during year 12 of Run #11. The net present values of entry for potential rivals that were not established company brands were also higher (but still negative) for this run. Thus, the relatively lower concentration ratios at the end of Run #11 were the result of what were apparently lowered product differentiation barriers to entry.

Besides creating easier entry, the limit also caused some of the competitive behavior that appeared in Run #10 to appear in Run #11. But, as in Run #10, this competitive behavior did not have positive long-run consequences for the industry. Price and quality competition among Brands 2 through 9 developed, but this competition only seemed to hurt most of these brands. In particular, retail prices were kept so low by some brands that huge sums had to be spent on dealer-directed promotion to get retailers to accept brands with very small retailer margins. On top of this, the weaker brands found that they could not afford to pay the enormous penalties being paid by Brand 1 for exceeding the advertising limit; nor were they allowed to spend as much as Brand 1 on advertising in the first place. The combination of lower prices, higher dealer-directed promotion expenditures, costly improvements in quality, and small advertising expenditures (relative to Brand 1) was enough to drive Brand 2 out of the industry at an early age; to drive Brand 4 out at the same age it left the industry in Run #2; and to put Brands 3, 5, 6, 8, and 9 in rather weak positions. In the meantime, Brand 1 and its sister brand, Brand 7, earned good profits with steady or increasing prices. They were in a strong enough position at the end of Run #11 to eventually take over the entire industry.

Run #12: 10 Percent Limit, Assumption Change 2

Table 4-12 shows that the 10 percent limit had practically the same effect in this run as it did in Run #10. The limit managed to suppress competition severely by cutting off entry, by driving out Brand 2, and by putting Brand 3 in a weak position relative to Brand 1. Thus, Assumption Change 2 (giving managers cash-flow objectives) had a negligible effect on the impact of a 10 percent limit.

Run #13: 20 Percent Limit on the Advertising-Sales Ratio

A 20 percent limit on the advertising-sales ratio had a slight, suppressing effect on competition in Run #13. As shown in Table 4-13, although the limit led to lower advertising expenditures, lower prices, and higher brand quality—outcomes that should indicate a higher level of competition—it also led to one less brand (and firm), little change in concentration, and higher returns on sales for two of the stronger brands in the industry (Brands 1 and 3). These latter outcomes indicate that the competition that was inspired by the limit only served to hurt some of the weaker brands and to help some of the stronger ones.

Table 4-10. Analysis of Run #10—Type of Control: 10 Percent Limit on A/S; Assumption Change: None—Compared to Run #1

Measures of Competition:	Run #	Year							
		5	6	7	8	9	10	11	12
Structural:									
(Pound Sales) (x 10^6)	10	81.7	72.7	75.6	75.0	75.7	67.4	63.7	63.5
	1	84.7	102.6	124.0	149.3	163.2	170.9	174.2	180.0
No. of Firms	10	3	3	3	3	3	2	2	2
	1	4	5	6	6	6	6	6	6
No. of Brands	10	3	3	3	3	3	2	2	2
	1	4	5	6	7	7	7	7	7
2-Firm C.R.	10	.77	.81	.85	.87	.89	1.00	1.00	1.00
	1	.77	.66	.56	.52	.60	.64	.65	.68
2-Brand C.R.	10	.77	.81	.85	.87	.89	1.00	1.00	1.00
	1	.77	.66	.56	.52	.47	.49	.49	.51
3-Firm C.R.	10	1.00	1.00	1.00	1.00	1.00	1.00	1.00	1.00
	1	1.00	.88	.75	.67	.70	.74	.75	.77
3-Brand C.R.	10	1.00	1.00	1.00	1.00	1.00	1.00	1.00	1.00
	1	1.00	.88	.75	.67	.60	.64	.65	.68
Mkt. Adv. Exps. (x 10^6)	10	8.8	4.6	7.7	6.5	6.5	6.0	6.5	7.3
	1	9.7	13.5	17.1	21.7	22.9	24.2	24.0	26.4

Brand Number-Firm Number

	1-1	2-2	3-3	4-4	5-5	6-6	7-1	8-2	9-3	10-4	11-5
		d		∅	∅	∅	∅				

Performance: (Supp. Info.)

		1-1	2-2	3-3
After-Tax Profits		—	—	—
Return on Sales		—	—	—

Adv. Exps. A/S	—	—	—
C.-D. Promotion CP/S	+	—	?
	+	+	?
D.-D. Promotion DP/S	—	?	+
		+	+
Sales Calls Exps. SC/S	—	?	—
Retail Prices	+	—	—
Wholesale Prices	?	—	—
Brand Quality	—	+	—

Code:

0	=	Brand does not appear in run to which it is being compared.
∅	=	Brand does not appear in this run but appears in run to which it is being compared.
e	=	Brand appears *earlier* in this run than in run to which it is being compared.
l	=	Brand appears *later* in this run than in run to which it is being compared.
d	=	Brand *dies* earlier in this run than in run to which it is being compared.
s	=	Brand *survives* longer in this run than in run to which it is being compared.
+	=	*Higher* values than in run to which it is being compared.
—	=	*Lower* values than in run to which it is being compared.
?	=	*Unclear difference* in values between runs.

Table 4-11. Analysis of Run #11—Type of Control: 10 Percent Limit on A/S; Assumption Change: 1—Compared to Run #2

Measures of Competition:	Run #	Year							
		5	6	7	8	9	10	11	12
Structural:									
(Pound Sales) (x 10^6)	11	75.4	80.5	92.3	112.6	131.3	128.1	148.1	170.5
	2	83.7	101.0	122.6	146.5	166.3	170.3	183.4	198.0
No. of Firms	11	4	5	6	6	6	5	5	6
	2	4	5	6	6	6	5	5	5
No. of Brands	11	4	5	6	7	7	6	7	8
	2	4	5	6	7	7	6	7	7
2-Firm C.R.	11	.74	.68	.64	.57	.62	.75	.67	.73
	2	.77	.67	.58	.52	.58	.70	.71	.74
2-Brand C.R.	11	.74	.68	.64	.57	.48	.60	.55	.49
	2	.77	.67	.58	.52	.46	.53	.54	.56
3-Firm C.R.	11	1.00	.88	.78	.69	.74	.87	.79	.82
	2	1.00	.88	.76	.66	.71	.82	.83	.84
3-Brand C.R.	11	1.00	.88	.78	.69	.62	.75	.67	.61
	2	1.00	.88	.76	.66	.59	.70	.71	.74
Mkt. Adv. Exps. (x 10^6)	11	5.9	6.5	8.5	11.3	12.3	10.5	13.2	14.2
	2	9.2	13.0	16.7	20.0	23.2	21.3	21.3	24.1

Performance:	Brand Number-Firm Number										
	1-1	2-2	3-3	4-4	5-5	6-6	7-1	8-2	9-3	10-4	11-5
(Supp. Info.)		d						es	e	0	
After-Tax Profits	—	—	—	—	?	?	+				
Return on Sales	—	—	—	—	—	?	+				

Adv. Exps. A/S	—	—	—	—	—	—
C.-D. Promotion CP/S	+	?	?	+	?	?
D.-D. Promotion DP/S	+	+	+	+	+	+
Sales Calls Exps. SC/S	+	?	+	—	—	—
Retail Prices	+	—	+	+	—	—
Wholesale Prices	?	—	+	+	+	—
Brand Quality	+	+	+	+	—	?

Code:

0	=	Brand does not appear in run to which it is being compared.
∅	=	Brand does not appear in this run but appears in run to which it is being compared.
e	=	Brand appears *earlier* in this run than in run to which it is being compared.
l	=	Brand appears *later* in this run than in run to which it is being compared.
d	=	Brand *dies* earlier in this run than in run to which it is being compared.
s	=	Brand *survives* longer in this run than in run to which it is being compared.
+	=	*Higher* values than in run to which it is being compared.
—	=	*Lower* values than in run to which it is being compared.
?	=	*Unclear difference* in values between runs.

Table 4-12. Analysis of Run #12—Type of Control: 10 Percent Limit on A/S; Assumption Change: 2—Compared to Run #3

Measures of Competition:	Run #	Year							
		5	6	7	8	9	10	11	12
Structural:									
(Pound Sales) (x 10⁶)	12	82.1	74.3	77.3	77.8	78.5	70.4	65.0	61.5
	3	84.7	102.6	124.0	149.3	164.0	172.0	175.2	177.0
No. of Firms	12	3	3	3	3	3	2	2	2
	3	4	5	6	6	6	6	6	6
No. of Brands	12	3	3	3	3	3	2	2	2
	3	4	5	6	7	7	7	7	7
2-Firm C.R.	12	.77	.81	.85	.88	.90	1.00	1.00	1.00
	3	.77	.66	.56	.52	.47	.48	.50	.51
2-Brand C.R.	12	.77	.81	.85	.88	.90	1.00	1.00	1.00
	3	.77	.66	.56	.52	.47	.48	.50	.51
3-Firm C.R.	12	1.00	1.00	1.00	1.00	1.00	1.00	1.00	1.00
	3	1.00	.88	.75	.68	.70	.73	.74	.75
3-Brand C.R.	12	1.00	1.00	1.00	1.00	1.00	1.00	1.00	1.00
	3	1.00	.88	.75	.67	.60	.63	.65	.66
Mkt. Adv. Exps. (x 10⁶)	12	8.9	4.9	7.8	6.7	6.7	6.3	6.2	6.1
	3	9.7	13.5	17.1	21.7	22.6	23.5	23.6	24.6

	Brand Number-Firm Number										
	1-1	2-2	3-3	4-4	5-5	6-6	7-1	8-2	9-3	10-4	11-5
Performance:											
(Supp. Info.)		ø		ø	ø	ø	ø				
'After-Tax Profits	—	—	—								
Return on Sales	—	—	—								

Adv. Exps.	—	—	—
A/S	—	—	—
C.-D. Promotion	+	?	?
CP/S	+	+	?
D.-D. Promotion		?	+
DP/S	?	+	+
Sales Calls Exps.	—	—	—
SC/S	—	+	—
Retail Prices	+	—	—
Wholesale Prices	+	—	—
Brand Quality	—	+	—

Code:

0 = Brand *does not appear* in run to which it is being compared.

∅ = Brand *does not appear* in this run but appears in run to which it is being compared.

e = Brand appears *earlier* in this run than in run to which it is being compared.

1 = Brand appears *later* in this run than in run to which it is being compared.

d = Brand *dies* earlier in this run than in run to which it is being compared.

s = Brand *survives* longer in this run than in run to which it is being compared.

+ = *Higher* values than in run to which it is being compared.

— = *Lower* values than in run to which it is being compared.

? = *Unclear difference* in values between runs.

Table 4-13. Analysis of Run #13—Type of Control: 20 Percent Limit on A/S; Assumption Change: None—Compared to Run #1

Measures of Competition:	Run #	Year							
		5	*6*	*7*	*8*	*9*	*10*	*11*	*12*
Structural:									
(Pound Sales) (x 10⁶)	13	83.7	98.4	115.2	138.0	159.1	165.3	162.1	136.9
	1	84.7	102.6	124.0	149.3	163.2	170.9	174.2	180.0
No. of Firms	13	4	5	6	6	6	6	6	5
	1	4	5	6	6	6	6	6	6
No. of Brands	13	4	5	6	7	7	7	7	6
	1	4	5	6	7	7	7	7	7
2-Firm C.R.	13	.76	.67	.58	.52	.56	.57	.57	.65
	1	.77	.66	.56	.52	.60	.64	.65	.68
2-Brand C.R.	13	.76	.67	.58	.51	.44	.44	.43	.50
	1	.77	.66	.56	.52	.47	.49	.49	.51
3-Firm C.R.	13	1.00	.88	.76	.67	.68	.70	.71	.80
	1	1.00	.88	.75	.67	.70	.74	.75	.77
3-Brand C.R.	13	1.00	.88	.76	.67	.56	.57	.57	.65
	1	1.00	.88	.75	.67	.60	.64	.64	.68
Mkt. Adv. Exps. (x 10⁶)	13	9.3	12.1	14.5	18.4	22.0	21.1	18.7	14.1
	1	9.7	13.5	17.1	21.7	22.9	24.2	24.0	26.4

	Brand Number-Firm Number									
1-1	*2-2*	*3-3*	*4-4*	*5-5*	*6-6*	*7-1*	*8-2*	*9-3*	*10-4*	*11-5*
					d					

Performance:
(Supp. Info.)

	1-1	*2-2*	*3-3*	*4-4*	*5-5*	*6-6*	*7-1*
After-Tax Profits	–	–	?	?	?	–	–
Return on Sales	+	–	+	?	–	–	–

Adv. Exps. A/S	—	—	—	—	+	?	— ?
C.-D. Promotion CP/S	? ?	? ?	? ?	? ?	? ?	? ?	—
D.C. Promotion DP/S	? +	?	? ?	+ +	+ +	— ?	+ +
Sales Calls Exps. SC/S	— ?	? —	?	?	? ?	? ?	— ? ?
Retail Prices	—	—	—	—	—	—	—
Wholesale Prices	—	—	—	—	—	—	?
Brand Quality	+	+	+	+	+	+	? ?

Code:

0 = Brand does not appear in run to which it is being compared.

∅ = Brand does not appear in this run but appears in run to which it is being compared.

e = Brand appears *earlier* in this run than in run to which it is being compared.

l = Brand appears *later* in this run than in run to which it is being compared.

d = Brand *dies* earlier in this run than in run to which it is being compared.

s = Brand *survives* longer in this run than in run to which it is being compared.

+ = *Higher* values than in run to which it is being compared.

— = *Lower* values than in run to which it is being compared.

? = *Unclear difference* in values between runs.

The most direct effect of the 20 percent limit was to lower advertising expenditures throughout the industry, which led, in turn, to lower industry sales. The lower sales and the existence of the limit did not delay the entry of any new brands, but things were made more difficult for some of these brands *after* entry. The manager of Brand 6, for example, found that he needed to spend large sums on advertising in order to raise his sales. He was able to do this with moderate success in year 10, when his brand was only three years old, because he was exempt from the limit. But in year 11, he went over the limit just enough to cause him to pay a penalty that reduced his profits to a negative value for a fourth straight year, which forced him to remove his brand from the market. This manager was also not helped by the small amount of price and quality competition that occurred during Run #13.

Thus, with a 20 percent limit, smaller brands still could not afford to pay the penalties for exceeding the limit, while larger brands found that they did not need to exceed the limit (as they were forced to do with a 10 percent limit). Moreover, since larger brands were given larger dollar limits because of their larger sales, the competitive disadvantage of smaller brands became quite serious. Brand 2, like Brand 6, was about to become a victim of this disadvantage at the end of Run #13 since it experienced its fourth straight year of negative profits in year 12. In addition, Brands 4 and 5 would assuredly fall victim to this disadvantage in later years, despite their somewhat better profit performance in Run #13.

Run #14: 20 Percent Limit,
Assumption Change 1

In Run #14, with industry sales made less sensitive to advertising, the 20 percent limit had an unclear effect on competition in the simulated industry. A few of the occurrences in this run suggest that competition was increased by the limit. However, a few other occurrences suggest an opposite conclusion.

The data found in Table 4-14 reveal that the limit encouraged more spending on advertising by Brands 5, 6, and 7. These brands spent relatively more on advertising at three years of age, before they were subjected to the limit, to get a competitive edge on their rivals. The increased sales that resulted from this strategy led to the relatively higher advertising budgets (which were set at fixed percentages of past sales) in subsequent years.

The higher advertising budgets produced relatively higher industry sales in Run #14. This tended to make the industry more attractive to entry by established company brands. Brand 8 and 9 entered two years earlier (Brand 8 still failed in a test market), and two additional brands were test marketed, though without success. Brand 4 also survived through the end of the run because, in part, of the higher sales. The improved sales of Brands 4, 5, and 6, and the earlier entry by Brand 9, produced somewhat lower concentration in this run.

One might want to view the lower concentration as a sign that competition increased during Run #14. One might also want to view the higher quality of industry brands and the lower dealer-directed promotion and sales calls expenditures as providing support for this position. But the absence of price competition, the earlier death of Brand 2, and the failure of Firms 2, 4, and 5 to bring out secondary brands that could survive a test-market period does not allow one to be very optimistic about the future of competition in this industry. Firms 1 and 2 were deeply entrenched with excellent distribution for their brands at the end of Run #14. The competitive advantage they had for their brands of being allowed higher dollar limits on advertising expenditures was also starting to hurt Brands 4, 5, and 6 at the end of the run. Clearly, competition could be expected to diminish.

Run #15: Limit of $3 Million
on Advertising

A $3 million limit on how much each brand could spend on advertising tended to hurt competition rather than help it in Run #15. Examination of Table 4-15 will reveal that the limit produced fewer brands and firms, higher concentration, and higher returns on sales for the stronger brands. The limit did not encourage price competition, quality competition, or lower selling costs. At first glance, about the only pro-competitive effect of the limit was lower industry advertising expenditures. But even this effect turned out to have anticompetitive consequences.

The lower industry advertising expenditures led to lower industry sales in Run #15. Sales were not small enough, nor was the limit restrictive enough, to discourage Brands 4, 5, 6, and 7 from entering at the same time they did in Run #1. However, once these brands were in the industry, the lower sales helped to force these brands into a different behavior pattern during their first four years. While these brands were three and four years old, their brand managers discovered that since Brands 1, 2, and 3 were locked into spending relatively small amounts on advertising, Brands 4, 5, 6, and 7 would have to spend more on advertising than they did at equivalent ages in Run #1 to keep industry sales at a reasonable level in future years. They also found that this strategy could improve their market shares. Although this strategy generated higher sales for each of these brands at four years of age than they had during Run #1, it also produced larger expenses for these brands. The higher expenses put Brands 4, 5, and 6 into negative profit positions for each of their first four years, and thus all three were forced out of the industry in Run #15. Without these brands, the industry became highly concentrated.

Run #16: Limit of $3 Million,
Assumption Change 1

If one favors concentration as an indicator of competition, then one would conclude that a $3 million limit on advertising expenditures had a

Table 4-14. Analysis of Run #14—Type of Control: 20 Percent Limit on A/S; Assumption Change: 1—Compared to Run #2

Measures of Competition:	Run #	Year 5	6	7	8	9	10	11	12
Structural:									
(Pound Sales) (x 10⁶)	14	82.7	98.4	117.4	141.6	164.7	182.7	198.1	203.8
	2	83.7	101.0	122.6	146.5	166.3	170.3	183.4	198.0
No. of Firms	14	4	5	6	6	6	6	6	5
	2	4	5	6	6	6	5	5	5
No. of Brands	14	4	5	6	7	8	8	9	8
	2	4	5	6	7	7	6	7	7
2-Firm C.R.	14	.76	.67	.59	.51	.55	.57	.61	.69
	2	.77	.67	.58	.52	.58	.70	.71	.74
2-Brand C.R.	14	.76	.67	.59	.51	.43	.43	.41	.43
	2	.77	.67	.58	.52	.46	.53	.54	.56
3-Firm C.R.	14	1.00	.88	.76	.67	.68	.70	.73	.81
	2	1.00	.88	.76	.66	.71	.82	.83	.84
3-Brand C.R.	14	1.00	.88	.76	.67	.55	.56	.54	.57
	2	1.00	.88	.76	.66	.59	.70	.71	.74
Mkt. Adv. Exps. (x 10⁶)	14	9.2	12.2	15.1	20.2	24.4	25.2	24.8	24.0
	2	9.2	13.0	16.7	20.0	23.2	21.3	21.3	24.1

	Brand Number-Firm Number										
	1-1	2-2	3-3	4-4	5-5	6-6	7-1	8-2	9-3	10-4	11-5
Performance: (Supp. Info.)		d		s				ed	e	0d	0d
After-Tax Profits	?	?	—	+	+	+	?				
Return on Sales	+	?	+	?	+	?	+				

Adv. Exps. A/S	+	—	—	+	+	?	?
C.-D. Promotion CP/S	?	?	?	?	?	?	?
D.-D. Promotion DP/S	—	?	?	+	+	—	—
Sales Calls Exps. SC/S	?	?	—	?	?	?	?
Retail Prices	+	+	+	—	—	?	+
Wholesale Prices	+	+	?	—	?	?	?
Brand Quality	+	+	+	+	+	+	?

Code:

0 = Brand does not appear in run to which it is being compared.
∅ = Brand does not appear in this run but appears in run to which it is being compared.
e = Brand appears *earlier* in this run than in run to which it is being compared.
l = Brand appears *later* in this run than in run to which it is being compared.
d = Brand *dies* earlier in this run than in run to which it is being compared.
s = Brand *survives* longer in this run than in run to which it is being compared.
+ = *Higher* values than in run to which it is being compared.
— = *Lower* values than in run to which it is being compared.
? = *Unclear difference* in values between runs.

Table 4-15.   Analysis of Run #15—Type of Control: Limit of $3 Million; Assumption Change: None—Compared to Run #1

Measures of Competition:	Run #	Year							
		5	6	7	8	9	10	11	12
Structural:									
(Pound Sales) (x 10⁶)	15	81.7	90.1	100.9	115.9	133.4	128.6	117.5	101.0
	1	84.7	102.6	124.0	149.3	163.2	170.9	174.2	180.0
No. of Firms	15	4	5	6	6	6	5	4	3
	1	4	5	6	6	6	6	6	6
No. of Brands	15	4	5	6	7	7	6	5	4
	1	4	5	6	7	7	7	7	7
2-Firm C.R.	15	.76	.66	.56	.48	.52	.60	.69	.81
	1	.77	.66	.56	.52	.60	.64	.65	.68
2-Brand C.R.	15	.76	.66	.56	.48	.39	.43	.49	.58
	1	.77	.66	.56	.52	.47	.49	.49	.51
3-Firm C.R.	15	1.00	.90	.79	.68	.67	.75	.85	1.00
	1	1.00	.88	.75	.67	.70	.74	.75	.77
3-Brand C.R.	15	1.00	.90	.79	.68	.54	.60	.69	.81
	1	1.00	.88	.75	.67	.60	.64	.65	.68
Mkt. Adv. Exps. (x 10⁶)	15	8.6	10.4	12.0	15.0	19.1	17.4	14.5	11.9
	1	9.7	13.5	17.1	21.7	22.9	24.2	24.0	26.4

	Brand Number-Firm Number										
	1-1	2-2	3-3	4-4	5-5	6-6	7-1	8-2	9-3	10-4	11-5
Performance: (Supp. Info.)											
After-Tax Profits	−	+	+	d	d	d	+				
Return on Sales	+	+	+	−	−	−	+				

Adv. Exps.	—	+	—	?	?	—
A/S	—	+	—	?	?	—
C.-D. Promotion	—	?	?	?	?	?
CP/S	+	?	+	+	+	?
D.-D. Promotion	?	?	—	+	—	—
DP/S	?	?	—	+	—	—
Sales Calls Exps.	—	?	?	?	?	?
SC/S	+	—	+	+	—	?
Retail Prices	+	+	—	?	+	+
Wholesale Prices	+	?	?	?	—	+
Brand Quality	+	—	—	—	?	?

Code:

0 = Brand does not appear in run to which it is being compared.

∅ = Brand does not appear in this run but appears in run to which it is being compared.

e = Brand appears *earlier* in this run than in run to which it is being compared.

l = Brand appears *later* in this run than in run to which it is being compared.

d = Brand *dies* earlier in this run than in run to which it is being compared.

s = Brand *survives* longer in this run than in run to which it is being compared.

+ = *Higher* values than in run to which it is being compared.

— = *Lower* values than in run to which it is being compared.

? = *Unclear differences* in values between runs.

favorable effect on competition in Run #16. On the other hand, if one prefers measures of competition such as prices and selling expenses, the opposite conclusion would be reached. The limit clearly strengthened the position of some of the weaker brands in the industry, but it also produced no price competition, little quality competition, and no pronounced downward movement in selling expenses other than advertising (see Table 4-16).

Because of the different industry sales response function that was used in Run #16 (less sensitive to advertising), industry sales were not restricted by the limit as severely as they were in Run #15. Thus, unlike Run #15, Brands 5 and 6 were able to survive until the end of Run #16 (Brand 4 died as it did in Run #2). The relatively higher spending on advertising by these brands, and by Brand 2, came more out of a desire to improve market share than to raise industry sales. These brands found that an extra dollar spent on advertising did more for their profits than it would have without the spending limit because Brands 1, 3, and 7 were spending less.

The limit therefore helped Brands 2, 5, and 6 to finish Run #16 in rather good shape. The existence of the limit also made entry appear relatively more attractive to all types of brands in Run #16. This resulted in an earlier, unsuccessful test-market attempt by Brand 8; an earlier, very successful introduction of Brand 9; and two unsuccessful test-market attempts by Brands 10 and 11. The improved health of Brands 2, 5, and 6 and the earlier entry of Brand 9 led to much lower concentration ratios at the end of Run #16.

Perhaps, in time, the more equitable size distribution brought about by the $3 million limit would lead to some vigorous price and quality competition in the simulated industry. But competition of this type might also drive the weaker brands out of the market. Firms 1 and 3 still had their strong corporate images at the end of Run #16, and their brands were enjoying more effective distribution than the others. Vigorous price and quality competition would therefore probably work to the advantage of these larger firms.

Run #17: Depreciation Requirement
for Advertising (.6+.15+.15+.10)

The best way to describe what occurred in Run #17 is to say that the depreciation requirement backfired. The requirement *did* inspire one form of competition in the simulated industry—an advertising war—which was exactly what it was trying to prevent. The advertising war resulted in higher concentration, higher profits and returns on sales, higher selling costs, and much higher prices (see Table 4-17).

Why did the depreciation requirement encourage more rather than less spending on advertising? The answer is somewhat complex. A depreciation requirement allows a brand manager to defer writing off a portion of current advertising outlays, while it forces him to write off a portion of past outlays instead. If a manager would find it advantageous to spend more on advertising in one year than he had in past years, regardless of whether a depreciation requirement is being enforced, such a requirement would allow him to report higher after-tax profits in that year. The manager in this situation would therefore find that by spending more on advertising, he could still earn higher profits than he would have without the requirement and he could also take advantage of the favorable current and carryover effects of advertising. Moreover, he would find that it pays for him, in most situations, to keep advertising expenditures at a steady level or moving upward in order to avoid having to report lower after-tax profits than he would have to report without the requirement (if advertising drops, outlays from past years must still be deducted). Since the managers in Run #17 are assumed to seek a rising stream of after-tax profits, the depreciation requirement would encourage a manager in the above situation to spend relatively more on advertising.

The managers of Brands 2 and 4 found themselves in the situation described above at the start of Run #17. They therefore decided to spend substantially more on advertising than they would have without the depreciation requirement, and this strategy produced excellent results for them. While these managers were executing this strategy change, the managers of Brands 1 and 3 found that, at first, they did not need to react to the depreciation requirement. Initially, the requirement produced higher after-tax profits for Brands 1 and 3 than they had in Run #1, and their managers saw no need to search for other strategies. But as Brands 2 and 4 grew stronger, Brands 1 and 3 were forced to react, and they, too, discovered that raising their advertising expenditures was a wise strategy.

The depreciation requirement also had an inhibiting effect on entry. Potential entrants (except for Brand 4) were frightened away by the advertising war and by the fact that their cash outflows in each year would be greater with the requirement. The higher taxes on profits (if advertising expenditures were rising) and higher advertising outlays that would be inspired by the requirement were not to the liking of potential entrants who looked to a discounted cash flow figure to tell them the desirability of entry. Less entry produced higher profits, higher concentration, and, to some extent, higher prices.

Run #18: Depreciation Requirement
(.6+.15+.15+.10), Assumption Change 1

In Run #18, the depreciation requirement had a similar impact on the simulated industry as it did in Run #17. An advertising war was started and entry was also made less attractive to potential rivals. However, the short-run overall effect on competition was more favorable in Run #18. As shown in Table 4-18, the requirement even caused a slight drop in concentration, a decline in profits and returns on sales for the two leading brands, some lower prices, and some higher quality products.

The depreciation requirement had a different effect in Run #18 than

Table 4-16. Analysis of Run #16—Type of Control: Limit of $3 Million; Assumption Change: 1—Compared to Run #2

Measures of Competition:	Run #	Year 5	6	7	8	9	10	11	12
Structural:									
(Pound Sales) (x 10⁶)	16	82.2	92.9	106.1	124.2	145.6	150.7	169.4	185.3
	2	83.7	101.0	122.6	146.5	166.3	170.3	183.4	198.0
No. of Firms	16	4	5	6	6	6	5	6	5
	2	4	5	6	6	6	5	5	5
No. of Brands	16	4	5	6	7	8	7	8	8
	2	4	5	6	7	7	6	7	7
2-Firm C.R.	16	.76	.67	.58	.49	.51	.59	.63	.55
	2	.77	.67	.58	.52	.58	.70	.71	.74
2-Brand C.R.	16	.76	.67	.58	.94	.37	.42	.39	.38
	2	.77	.67	.58	.52	.46	.53	.54	.56
3-Firm C.R.	16	1.00	.90	.78	.67	.67	.76	.77	.68
	2	1.00	.88	.76	.66	.71	.82	.83	.84
3-Brand C.R.	16	1.00	.90	.78	.67	.53	.59	.54	.53
	2	1.00	.88	.76	.66	.59	.70	.71	.74
Mkt. Adv. Exps. (x 10⁶)	16	8.6	10.4	12.0	14.8	19.5	17.8	20.2	20.9
	2	9.2	13.0	16.7	20.0	23.2	21.3	21.3	24.1

Brand Number-Firm Number

Performance: (Supp. Info.)	1-1	2-2	3-3	4-4	5-5	6-6	7-1	8-2	9-3	10-4	11-5
After-Tax Profits	−	+	?	?	?	?	+	ed	e	0d	0d
Return on Sales	+	+	+	−	−	?	+				

Adv. Exps.	—	+	—	—	—
A/S	+	+	+	+	—
C.-D. Promotion	—	?	?	?	—
CP/S	+	?	+	? ?	?
D.-D. Promotion	—	?	?	+	—
DP/S	—	?	+	+	—
Sales Calls Exps.	—	?	—	? ?	?
SC/S	—	+	—	—	—
Retail Prices	+	?	—	+	+
Wholesale Prices	+	+	—	+	?
Brand Quality	+	?	+	+	?

Code:

0 = Brand does not appear in run to which it is being compared.

∅ = Brand does not appear in this run but appears in run to which it is being compared.

e = Brand appears *earlier* in this run than in run to which it is being compared.

l = Brand appears *later* in this run than in run to which it is being compared.

d = Brand *dies* earlier in this run than in run to which it is being compared.

s = Brand *survives* longer in this run than in run to which it is being compared.

+ = *Higher* values than in run to which it is being compared.

— = *Lower* values than in run to which it is being compared.

? = *Unclear difference* in values between runs.

Table 4-17. Analysis of Run #17—Type of Control: .6+.15+.15+.1 Depreciation; Assumption Change: None—Compared to Run #1

Measures of Competition:	Run #	Year							
		5	*6*	*7*	*8*	*9*	*10*	*11*	*12*
Structural:									
(Pound Sales) (x 10^6)	17	88.7	124.5	152.0	155.5	160.6	162.6	164.3	167.0
	1	84.7	102.6	124.0	149.3	163.2	170.9	174.2	180.0
No. of Firms	17	4	4	4	4	4	4	4	4
	1	4	5	6	6	6	6	6	6
No. of Brands	17	4	4	4	4	4	4	4	4
	1	4	5	6	7	7	7	7	7
2-Firm C.R.	17	.78	.65	.60	.63	.65	.67	.69	.70
	1	.77	.66	.56	.52	.60	.64	.65	.68
2-Brand C.R.	17	.78	.65	.60	.63	.65	.67	.69	.70
	1	.77	.66	.56	.52	.47	.49	.49	.51
3-Firm C.R.	17	1.00	.84	.80	.83	.85	.85	.86	.86
	1	1.00	.88	.75	.67	.70	.74	.75	.77
3-Brand C.R.	17	1.00	.84	.80	.83	.85	.85	.86	.86
	1	1.00	.88	.75	.67	.60	.64	.65	.68
Mkt. Adv. Exps. (x 10^6)	17	11.3	21.1	25.0	24.1	28.8	30.0	32.5	32.6
	1	9.7	13.5	17.1	21.7	22.9	24.2	24.0	26.4

	Brand Number-Firm Number										
	1-1	*2-2*	*3-3*	*4-4*	*5-5*	*6-6*	*7-1*	*8-2*	*9-3*	*10-4*	*11-5*
					∅	∅	∅				
Performance: (Supp. Info.)											
After-Tax Profits	+	+	+	+							
Return on Sales	+	+	+	+							

Adv. Exps.	+	+	+	+
A/S	+	+	+	+
C.-D. Promotion	+	+	+	+
CP/S	+	?	?	?
D.-D. Promotion	?	?	?	?
DP/S	–	–	–	–
Sales Calls Exps.	+	+	+	+
SC/S	–	?	–	–
Retail Prices	+	+	+	+
Wholesale Prices	+	+	+	+
Brand Quality	+	+	+	+

Code:

0 = Brand does not appear in run to which it is being compared.

∅ = Brand does not appear in this run but appears in run to which it is being compared.

e = Brand appears *earlier* in this run than in run to which it is being compared.

l = Brand appears *later* in this run than in run to which it is being compared.

d = Brand *dies* earlier in this run than in run to which it is being compared.

s = Brand *survives* longer in this run than in run to which it is being compared.

+ = *Higher* values than in run to which it is being compared.

– = *Lower* values than in run to which it is being compared.

? = *Unclear difference* in values between runs.

Table 4-18.   Analysis of Run #18—Type of Control: .6+.15+.15+.10 Depreciation; Assumption Change: 1—Compared to Run #2

Measures of Competition:	Run #	Year							
		5	6	7	8	9	10	11	12
Structural:									
(Pound Sales) (x 10^6)	18	86.1	110.5	130.5	159.4	185.9	208.0	222.4	221.5
	2	83.7	101.0	122.6	146.5	166.3	170.3	183.4	198.0
No. of Firms	18	4	4	5	6	6	6	6	5
	2	4	5	6	6	6	5	5	5
No. of Brands	18	4	4	5	6	7	7	7	6
	2	4	5	6	7	7	6	7	7
2-Firm C.R.	18	.78	.65	.60	.54	.49	.58	.61	.71
	2	.77	.67	.58	.52	.58	.70	.71	.74
2-Brand C.R.	18	.78	.65	.60	.54	.49	.42	.47	.54
	2	.77	.67	.58	.52	.46	.53	.54	.56
3-Firm C.R.	18	1.00	.85	.81	.71	.64	.69	.73	.82
	2	1.00	.88	.76	.66	.71	.82	.83	.84
3-Brand C.R.	18	1.00	.85	.81	.71	.64	.58	.61	.71
	2	1.00	.88	.76	.66	.59	.70	.71	.74
Mkt. Adv. Exps. (x 10^6)	18	10.3	16.9	18.1	26.8	31.6	35.8	34.0	29.0
	2	9.2	13.2	16.7	20.0	23.2	21.3	21.3	24.1

	1-1	2-2	3-3	4-4	5-5	6-6	7-1	8-2	9-3	10-4	11-5
Brand Number-Firm Number				S	ld	1	1	Ø	Ø		
Performance: (Supp. Info.)			?								
After-Tax Profits	—	?		+	+	+	+				
Return on Sales	—	?	—	+	+	+	+				

Adv. Exps.	+	+	+	+	+	+	+	+
A/S	+	+	+	+	+	+	+	+
C.-D. Promotion	?	?	?	?	+	?	?	?
CP/S	?	?	?	?	−	?	?	?
D.-D. Promotion	+	?	−	+	+	+	+	+
DP/S	?	?	+	−	−	−	?	?
Sales Calls Exps.	−	?	?	?	+	+	?	+
SC/S	−	?	?	−	−	−	−	−
Retail Prices	?	−	+	+	+	+	+	+
Wholesale Prices	?	−	?	?	?	+	+	?
Brand Quality	+	?	+	+	?	?	?	?

Code:

0 = Brand does not appear in run to which it is being compared.

∅ = Brand does not appear in this run but appears in run to which it is being compared.

e = Brand appears *earlier* in this run than in run to which it is being compared.

l = Brand appears *later* in this run than in run to which it is being compared.

d = Brand *dies* earlier in this run than in run to which it is being compared.

s = Brand *survives* longer in this run than in run to which it is being compared.

+ = *Higher* values than in run to which it is being compared.

− = *Lower* values than in run to which it is being compared.

? = *Unclear difference* in values between runs.

it did in Run #17 because of the different industry sales response functions used in the two runs. With industry sales being less sensitive to changes in advertising goodwill, as it was in Run #18, there was not quite as great an incentive for brands to escalate their advertising expenditures. As a result, entry by Brands 5, 6, and 7 was only delayed, and not completely cut off, by fears of entering the advertising war. However, Brands 8 and 9 did not attempt entry in Run #18, and Brand 5, after a good start, was forced out of the market. Furthermore, Brands 2, 4, and 6 ended the run in rather weak conditions. In the long-run, the industry could be expected to become less competitive than it would have had the depreciation requirement not been introduced.

Run #19: Depreciation Requirement
(.6+.5+.5+.1), Assumption Change 2

A brand manager who seeks a rising stream of cash flowing into his firm could be expected to react differently to an advertising depreciation requirement than one who is concerned about his after-tax profits. The output of Run #19 indicates that imposing a depreciation requirement on an industry with cash-flow objectives did not backfire in the same way it did in Runs #17 and #18 (see Table 4-19). However, the requirement still did not encourage vigorous competition in Run #19.

In most cases, the managers in Run #19 spent less on advertising than they did in Run #3. There was an incentive to spend less because a manager with *increasing* advertising expenditures was penalized with a higher cash outflow for taxes than another manager with identical profit figures but *decreasing* advertising expenditures. However, there were several situations where the depreciation requirement encouraged managers to spend more on advertising. Brand 1, for example, spent more on advertising in the first three years of Run #18 in what appeared to be a reaction to the threat of entry. Brand 1 expected more new entrants at this point of the run because of the increase in *reported* after-tax profits throughout the industry that came about as a result of the depreciation requirement. Brands 4, 5, 6, and 7 also spent more on advertising during their first two years of existence because they were not forced to write off all of their outlays as a current expense and they had no past outlays to deduct.

The reduced advertising expenditures that *did* occur led to lower industry sales. The lower sales and Brand 1's early advertising barrage were responsible for the delayed entry of Brands 4 to 7. The delayed entry, along with the earlier death of Brand 2 (it did not spend enough on advertising), produced slightly higher concentration in the industry at the end of Run #19. The depreciation requirement also did not inspire lower profits and returns on sales, lower prices, higher quality, or lower selling costs other than advertising.

It is possible that if both Assumption Change 1 and Assumption Change 2 had been tried together with a depreciation requirement, a more competitive industry might have resulted. The depreciation requirement did not encourage more competition in Run #19 because, in part, of the high sensitivity of industry sales to changes in advertising goodwill. However, it seems likely that the smaller brands would have been hurt (or helped) just as much by the depreciation requirement as the larger brands if this interaction had been tested, and competition in the industry would not have been altered in any major way.

Run #20: Depreciation Requirement
for Advertising (.3+.3+.2+.2)
Changing the depreciation schedule to require a "slower" write-off of advertising outlays did not really change the way a depreciation requirement affected competition in the simulated industry. The results of Run #20 were quite similar to those of Run #17. In both runs, the requirements produced advertising wars, less entry, and several other noncompetitive outcomes. The major difference between the runs was that the slower write-off rate delayed the entry of Brand 4 for six years. This brand's entry was delayed because it could not afford to pay the higher taxes associated with a slower write-off rate (see Table 4-20).

Run #21: Depreciation Requirement
(.3+.3+.2+.2), Assumption Change 2
The alternative depreciation schedule also did not substantially change the way a depreciation requirement affected competition when the brand managers were assumed to have cash-flow objectives. The requirement still brought about lower advertising outlays (in most situations), lower industry sales, and higher concentration (see Table 4-21). Although the different depreciation schedule allowed Brands 4 to 7 to enter the industry earlier in Run #21 than they did in Run #19, this did not lead to more vigorous competition. These brands could enter earlier in Run #21 because Brand 1 did not utilize an entry-thwarting strategy of large advertising expenditures at the start of this run (as it did in Run #19). However, Brands 4, 5, and 6 were in rather poor shape at the end of Run #21 because they were not spending enough on advertising.

CONCLUSIONS

A summary of how competition was affected in each of the seventeen computer runs that tested a control on advertising expenditures is found in Table 4-22. A five-point scale is used to indicate the direction and intensity of the change in competition produced by a control. A +2 indicates that a control encouraged much more competition in the simulated industry, while a -2 indicates the opposite result.

As the table shows, none of the controls that were tested produced vigorous competition. The controls either (1) inhibited entry (straight tax, 10

Table 4-19. Analysis of Run #19—Type of Control: .6+.15+.15+.1 Depreciation; Assumption Change:2—Compared to Run #3

Measures of Competition:	Run #	5	6	7	8	9	10	11	12
Structural:									
(Pound Sales) (x 10⁶)	19	82.3	87.7	93.1	111.1	135.4	155.1	168.5	155.4
	3	84.7	102.6	124.0	149.3	164.0	172.0	175.2	177.0
No. of Firms	19	3	3	4	5	6	6	6	5
	3	4	5	6	6	6	6	6	6
No. of Brands	19	3	3	4	5	6	7	7	6
	3	4	5	6	7	7	7	7	7
2-Firm C.R.	19	.77	.80	.82	.71	.58	.49	.57	.66
	3	.77	.66	.56	.52	.47	.48	.50	.51
2-Brand C.R.	19	.77	.80	.82	.71	.58	.49	.43	.51
	3	.77	.66	.56	.52	.47	.48	.50	.51
3-Firm C.R.	19	1.00	1.00	1.00	.87	.77	.65	.70	.78
	3	1.00	.88	.75	.68	.70	.73	.74	.75
3-Brand C.R.	19	1.00	1.00	1.00	.87	.77	.65	.57	.66
	3	1.00	.88	.75	.67	.60	.63	.65	.66
Mkt. Adv. Exps. (x 10⁶)	19	9.6	9.9	11.0	16.7	21.5	22.2	23.4	17.6
	3	9.7	13.5	17.1	21.7	22.6	23.5	23.6	24.6

Performance: (Supp. Info.)	1-1	2-2	3-3	4-4	5-5	6-6	7-1	8-2	9-3	10-4	11-5
Brand Number-Firm Number			1	1	1	1	1				
After-Tax Profits	+	d	+	+	+	+	+				
Return on Sales	+	—	+	+	+	+	+				

Adv. Exps.	−	−	?	?	+	+
A/S	−	−	−	?	+	?
C.-D. Promotion	+	?	+	?	+	?
CP/S	?	?	−	?	?	?
D.-D. Promotion	?	?	+	+	+	+
DP/S	?	?	+	+	+	+
Sales Calls Exps.	−	−	?	?	?	?
SC/S	−	−	−	−	−	−
Retail Prices	+	+	?	+	+	+
Wholesale Prices	+	+	+	+	+	+
Brand Quality	−	?	−	?	?	?

Code:

0 = Brand does not appear in run to which it is being compared.

∅ = Brand does not appear in this run but appears in run to which it is being compared.

e = Brand appears *earlier* in this run than in run to which it is being compared.

l = Brand appears *later* in this run than in run to which it is being compared.

d = Brand *dies* earlier in this run than in run to which it is being compared.

s = Brand *survives* longer in this run than in run to which it is being compared.

+ = *Higher* values than in run to which it is being compared.

− = *Lower* values than in run to which it is being compared.

? = *Unclear difference* in values between runs.

Table 4-20. Analysis of Run #20—Type of Control: .3+.3+.2+.2 Depreciation; Assumption Change: None—Compared to Run #1

Measures of Competition:	Run #	5	6	7	8	9	10	11	12
Structural:									
(Pound Sales) (x 10⁶)	20	87.6	105.5	129.8	158.2	162.9	160.5	161.1	180.0
	1	84.7	102.6	124.0	149.3	163.2	170.9	174.2	180.0
No. of Firms	20	3	3	3	3	3	3	4	4
	1	4	5	6	6	6	6	6	6
No. of Brands	20	3	3	3	3	3	3	4	4
	1	4	5	6	7	7	7	7	7
2-Firm C.R.	20	.78	.78	.78	.75	.76	.79	.80	.70
	1	.77	.66	.56	.52	.60	.64	.65	.68
2-Brand C.R.	20	.78	.78	.78	.75	.76	.79	.80	.70
	1	.77	.66	.56	.52	.47	.49	.49	.51
3-Firm C.R.	20	1.00	1.00	1.00	1.00	1.00	1.00	1.00	.87
	1	1.00	.88	.75	.67	.70	.74	.75	.77
3-Brand C.R.	20	1.00	1.00	1.00	1.00	1.00	1.00	1.00	.87
	1	1.00	.88	.75	.67	.60	.64	.65	.68
Mkt. Adv. Exps. (x 10⁶)	20	10.6	13.8	17.6	25.3	26.1	25.9	29.7	44.1
	1	9.7	13.5	17.1	21.7	22.9	24.2	24.0	26.4

Year

	1-1	2-2	3-3	4-4	5-5	6-6	7-1	8-2	9-3	10-4	11-5
Performance: (Supp. Info.)											
After-Tax Profits	+	+	+	1	∅	∅	∅				
Return on Sales	+	+	+	+							

Brand Number-Firm Number

Adv. Exps.	+	+	+	+
A/S	+	+	+	+
C.-D. Promotion	+	+	+	+
CP/S	?	−	?	+
D.-D. Promotion	+	?	−	+
DP/S	?	?	−	−
Sales Calls Exps.	+	+	+	+
SC/S	?	−	−	?
Retail Prices	+	−	+	+
Wholesale Prices	+	−	+	+
Brand Quality	+	+	+	?

Code:

0 = Brand does not appear in run to which it is being compared.
∅ = Brand does not appear in this run but appears in run to which it is being compared.
e = Brand appears *earlier* in this run than in run to which it is being compared.
l = Brand appears *later* in this run than in run to which it is being compared.
d = Brand *dies* earlier in this run than in run to which it is being compared.
s = Brand *survives* longer in this run than in run to which it is being compared.
+ = *Higher* values than in run to which it is being compared.
− = *Lower* values than in run to which it is being compared.
? = *Unclear difference* in values between runs.

Table 4-21.   Analysis of Run #21—Type of Control: .3+.3+.2+.2 Depreciation; Assumption Change: 2—Compared to Run #3

Measures of Competition:	Run #	Year							
		5	*6*	*7*	*8*	*9*	*10*	*11*	*12*
Structural:									
(Pound Sales) (x 10⁶)	21	80.0	95.8	117.8	138.1	142.4	125.7	119.5	116.7
	3	84.7	102.6	124.0	149.3	164.0	172.0	175.2	177.0
No. of Firms	21	4	5	6	6	6	5	5	5
	3	4	5	6	6	6	6	6	6
No. of Brands	21	4	5	6	7	7	6	6	6
	3	4	5	6	7	7	7	7	7
2-Firm C.R.	21	.75	.68	.57	.48	.58	.66	.70	.74
	3	.77	.66	.56	.52	.47	.48	.50	.51
2-Brand C.R.	21	.75	.68	.57	.47	.43	.53	.55	.60
	3	.77	.66	.56	.52	.47	.48	.50	.51
3-Firm C.R.	21	1.00	.85	.75	.64	.71	.79	.82	.84
	3	1.00	.88	.75	.68	.70	.73	.74	.75
3-Brand C.R.	21	1.00	.84	.75	.64	.58	.66	.70	.74
	3	1.00	.88	.75	.67	.60	.63	.65	.66
Mkt. Adv. Exps. (x 10⁶)	21	8.2	12.3	16.3	18.6	17.4	13.4	13.3	14.9
	3	9.7	13.5	17.1	21.6	22.6	23.5	23.6	24.6

	Brand Number-Firm Number										
	1-1	*2-2*	*3-3*	*4-4*	*5-5*	*6-6*	*7-1*	*8-2*	*9-3*	*10-4*	*11-5*
Performance: (Supp. Info.)		d									
After-Tax Profits	−	−	−	−	?	?	+				
Return on Sales	+	−	+	−	−	−	+				

Adv. Exps. A/S	—	—	—	—	—	—
C.-D. Promotion CP/S	+	?	?	?	?	+
	?	?	?	?	?	?
D.-D. Promotion DP/S	—	—	?	?	—	—
	?	—	—	—	—	—
Sales Calls Exps. SC/S	—	?	?	?	?	?
	?	?	?	?	?	?
Retail Prices	+	+	+	+	+	+
Wholesale Prices	+	?	+	—	—	—
Brand Quality	+	?	+	+	+	?

Code:

0 = Brand does not appear in run to which it is being compared.

∅ = Brand does not appear in this run but appears in run to which it is being compared.

e = Brand appears *earlier* in this run than in run to which it is being compared.

l = Brand appears *later* in this run than in run to which it is being compared.

d = Brand *dies* earlier in this run than in run to which it is being compared.

s = Brand *survives* longer in this run than in run to which it is being compared.

+ = *Higher* values than in run to which it is being compared.

— = *Lower* values than in run to which it is being compared.

? = *Unclear difference* in values between runs.

Table 4-22. Summary of Competitive Effects of Controls

Type of Control:	No Assumption Changes	Assumption Change 1: SI Less Sensitive to (TAG_t/TAG_{t-1})	Assumption Change 2: Cash-Flow Objectives	Assumption Changes 1&2: SI Less Sensitive and Cash-Flow Obj.
		Type of Assumptions:		
Control A: 5% Straight Tax	Run #5 −1			Run #6 −1
Control B: Progressive Tax	Run #7 0	Run #8 +1	Run #9 0	
Control C: 10% Limit on A/S	Run #10 −2	Run #11 0	Run #12 −2	
Control D: 20% Limit on A/S	Run #13 −1	Run #14 0		
Control E: $3 million Limit	Run #15 −1	Run #16 0		
Control F: Depreciation (.6+.15+.15+.1)	Run #17 −2	Run #18 −1	Run #19 0	
Control G: Depreciation (.3+.3+.2+.2)	Run #20 −2		Run #21 0	

Where:

+2 = Control encouraged much more competition

+1 = Control encouraged more competition

 0 = Control had unclear effect on competition

−1 = Control encouraged less competition

−2 = Control encouraged much less competition

percent limit, depreciation requirements); (2) penalized the weaker, small brands more than the stronger, large brands (straight tax, 10 and 20 percent limits); (3) encouraged the kind of competition in the industry that hurt the small brands and helped the large brands (10 and 20 percent limits, $3 million limit); (4) stimulated more rather than less spending on advertising (depreciation requirements); or (5) did very little (progressive tax). Only the progressive tax seemed to have an overall favorable effect on competition, but this effect came out strongly only when industry sales were made less sensitive to changes in industry advertising goodwill. Moreover, none of the controls that were tested were able to attract entrants from outside the six established companies, to bring about a lowering of prices,[d] or to inspire large improvements in brand quality. In

[d]Prices may have been lower in one run than they were in another as a result of a control, but none of the controls were able to bring prices to lower levels than they were in year 5 of a run.

short, these controls did not manage to seriously hurt the deeply entrenched brands with the strong corporate images. To be successful at encouraging vigorous competition in this model, a control would have to hurt the corporate images of the dominant firms and thereby start to reduce the superiority these firms have in getting effective distribution for their brands. It is questionable whether any control on advertising expenditures could accomplish this task.

Based on these findings, one is tempted to conclude that putting controls on advertising expenditures is not the way for a government to encourage more competition in an oligopolistic industry. However, there are three reasons why caution must be used in generalizing from these findings:

1. Only a small sample of the thousands of possible advertising controls was tested. For example, a progressive tax of a different magnitude or a limit of a different size might have produced different results.
2. The controls were tested in only one type of simulated industry. If models patterned after other industries had been used to test the controls— particularly industries that were not in a growth stage, that had firms (brands) of relatively equal size, or that had increasing returns to advertising[e]–different results might have occurred.
3. The model that was used (or any of its tested variations) may not be a reasonably valid representation of a real-world industry. If this is the case, then a faulty property of the model may have been responsible for the failure of some of the controls to produce greater competition.

Although it was not possible to test other samples of controls or to perform tests with models of other industries, an evaluation *was* made of the validity of the model that was used in this study. The next chapter contains this evaluation.

SUMMARY

The experiments that were performed with the computer simulation model that was built for this study were conducted primarily to test the competitive effects of introducing controls on advertising expenditures. Several measures of competition, such as concentration ratios and prices, which were monitored during each run of the model, gave an indication, but not a complete picture, of how competition was affected by making various changes in the model. A *qualitative* analysis of the activity in each run was also made to gain deeper insight into the competitive effects of changing the model.

---

[e]Increasing returns to advertising, or economies of scale in advertising, could make an industry less competitive by putting smaller advertisers at a cost disadvantage—it would cost them more in advertising to sell one unit than it would cost larger advertisers. It should be noted, however, that there is very little empirical evidence to support the notion that there are increasing returns to advertising. See James M. Ferguson, *Advertising and Competition: Theory, Measurement, Fact* (Cambridge, Mass.: Ballinger Publishing Co., 1974), Ch. 4.

Seven controls on advertising expenditures were tested by using the model: a straight tax, a progressive tax, two limits on the advertising-sales ratio (10 and 20 percent), a $3 million limit, and two depreciation requirements. The effects of making two basic changes in the model's behavioral assumptions were also tested. The first of these assumption changes made the industry sales response function of the model less sensitive to changes in industry advertising goodwill. The second assumption change gave the brand managers in the model cash-flow objectives rather than profit objectives. Twenty-one computer runs, representing the partial completion of a full factorial design of 32 cells, were executed and analyzed during this study.

The results of the 21 computer runs revealed that the 7 controls on advertising expenditures were unable to stimulate vigorous competition in the simulated industry. The controls either (1) inhibited entry by new competitors; (2) penalized small brands more than large brands; (3) encouraged the kind of competition that hurt small brands and helped large brands; (4) stimulated more rather than less spending on advertising; or (5) did very little. The assumption changes had a slight, moderating effect on the impact of some of the controls, but not enough to make any of the controls look highly desirable.

Caution should be used in generalizing from these findings. Only a few controls were tested and only one type of industry was simulated (one in a growth stage with unequal-sized firms and nonincreasing returns to advertising). Furthermore, the model may not be a reasonably valid representation of a real-world industry. An evaluation of the validity of the model is found in the next chapter.

NOTES TO CHAPTER FOUR

1. See Fred C. Allvine and James M. Patterson, *Competition Ltd.: The Marketing of Gasoline* (Bloomington: Indiana University Press, 1972).

2. See "The Cereal Case: Opening Shot in FTC War on 'Structural' Shared-Monopoly or Attack on 'Marketing' Irregularities?" *Antitrust Law and Economics Review* (Fall 1971).

3. See Joseph A. Schumpeter, *Capitalism, Socialism, and Democracy* (New York: Harper and Bros., 1942); and John Kenneth Galbraith, *American Capitalism* (Boston: Houghton-Mifflin, 1952).

4. See F.M. Scherer, *Industrial Market Structure and Economic Performance* (Chicago: Rand McNally, 1970), pp. 186-92.

5. Charles P. Bonini, *Simulation of Information and Decision Systems in the Firm* (Englewood Cliffs, N.J.: Prentice-Hall, 1963).

6. See Thomas H. Naylor, *Computer Simulation Experiments with Models of Economic System* (New York: Wiley, 1971).

7. See Mark J. Green, Beverly C. Moore, and Bruce Wasserstein, *The Closed Enterprise System* (New York: Grossman Publishers, 1972), p. 318.

Chapter Five

Validation of the Model

The findings reported in the previous chapter can be useful to public policy makers only if the simulation model can be shown to have a reasonable amount of external validity. It must be established that, first, the benchmark run of the model represents a reasonably close approximation of how a real-world industry might operate under normal conditions and, second, the runs that test controls represent a reasonably close approximation of how an industry might operate *if* controls on advertising expenditures were in existence. The steps that were taken to validate the model are described in this chapter.

OVERVIEW OF THE VALIDATION PROCEDURE

Validation of a simulation model is not a simple or straightforward task. As Van Horn has pointed out:

> There is no such thing as "the" appropriate validation procedure. Validation is problem-dependent.[1]

As a result, the specific steps of the validation procedure that was utilized had to be tailored to the special needs and characteristics of this study. The *general* procedure that was followed, however, has been suggested by Naylor and Finger.[2] Their three-stage validation approach represents a way to satisfy proponents of the three different philosophical positions—rationalism, empiricism, and positive economics—on validation of economic models.

The first stage of the Naylor-Finger approach requires "the formulation of a set of postulates or hypotheses describing the behavior of the system of interest."[3] These postulates should be developed using all available information, observations, general knowledge, relevant theory, and intuition. Extreme care should be taken in the selection of these postulates because only a portion of them could possibly be subjected to empirical testing in the latter stages of the validation procedure. The rest would have to stand up on their own merits.

The discussion in Chapter Three should reveal, among other things, how the first stage of the Naylor-Finger validation procedure was carried out in this study. It should show that the model's postulates or assumptions were designed to be reasonably consistent with existing theory and empirical evidence. However, the postulates were not well-grounded enough to eliminate the need to carry out the other stages of the Naylor-Finger validation procedure.

It should be noted that many simulation studies do not go beyond this first validation stage. Bonini, for example, stopped at this point in his award-winning simulation study saying:

> We do believe . . . that the model is a reasonable representation of real-world behavior. We cannot, of course, completely validate this kind of belief, but what we can and will do is to set forth the major ingredients of our decision rules for separate examination. We will then attempt to justify these rules by relating them to existing theory in the scientific literature of economics, accounting, or the behavioral sciences, or to the literature on business practice.[4]

The second stage of the Naylor-Finger validation procedure calls for the empirical testing of a model's postulates or assumptions.[5] This typically involves the use of statistical "goodness-of-fit" tests to check whether the response functions, distributions, and parameter values used in a model are "correct." Van Horn has also suggested that sensitivity analysis should be done during this stage of the validation procedure.[6] The less sensitive a model's output is to assumption changes, the more confidence one can have in the insights gained from the model.

Because the data that was available for this study was quite limited, it was not possible to perform statistical goodness-of-fit tests of the model's various assumptions. However, three other steps were taken to empirically test these assumptions. First, a sensitivity analysis was performed on two of the model's major assumptions. The results of this analysis can be found as part of the analysis of the computer runs presented in Chapter Four. Second, a "viability" run of sixteen years was executed. The benchmark run was extended out an additional eight years to see whether any "explosive" or unreasonable behavior was produced by the assumptions.[a] The results of this run are reported in the next section of this chapter. Third, a series of personal interviews were conducted with executives from the breakfast cereal industry. During these interviews, respondents were asked about the decision processes of brand managers and about several other subjects. A summary of the responses that

---

[a]Balderston and Hoggatt have suggested viability as a criterion for evaluating simulation models. See F.E. Balderston and A.C. Hoggatt, *Simulation of Market Processes* (Berkeley: Institute of Business and Economic Research, 1962).

were received to each question that was asked and an assessment of whether these responses provide empirical support for the model's assumptions can be found later in this chapter.

The third stage of the Naylor-Finger validation procedure consists of testing a model's ability to predict the behavior of the system under study.[7] The output of a model should be compared to real-world, historical data, and goodness-of-fit tests should be performed. Van Horn has also suggested that a "Turing-type" test could be conducted during this stage to test the face validity of the output.[8] In this test, experts could be asked whether they can detect the difference between simulated output and real-world data.

The model that was built for this study was used to explore the consequences of putting controls on the advertising expenditures of a single industry. Since controls of this type have yet to be tried in the real world, it was not possible to compare the output of the computer runs that tested controls with data from historical experience. The absence of a real-world experience with advertising controls also made it impossible to perform a "Turing-type" test on the output of the runs that tested controls. The predictive validity of the model was therefore tested in two other ways. First, a question included in the personal interviews asked respondents to predict what would happen in the cereal industry if certain controls on advertising expenditures were introduced. Second, a comparison was made between the output of the benchmark run of the model and available real-world data on the cereal industry. This second step served as a test of the predictive validity of the benchmark run. The results of these two validation steps are found later in this chapter.

In summary, it can be said that the validation procedure used in this study attempted to do all that was possible to validate the model given the circumstances. Without a large amount of real-world data, with only limited available computer time, and with no real-world experience with advertising controls to use as a basis for comparison, it was not possible to follow all of the steps of the Naylor-Finger validation procedure. As a result, a variation of the Naylor-Finger approach had to be employed. In the remainder of this chapter, the results of the validation steps that *were* taken are discussed in some detail. Sections are included on the viability run, the personal interviews, and the comparison that was made between the benchmark run and real-world data. A thorough critique of the model is also presented at the end of the chapter.

THE VIABILITY RUN

A copy of the computer output of the benchmark (no controls) run of this study can be found in Appendix B. A discussion of what occurred during this run was presented in the last chapter. The "viability run" was merely a repetition of the benchmark run that was extended eight years. It was executed to see whether the model's output remained stable and reasonable over a sixteen-year period. The results of this extended run indicated that the model could definitely be considered viable.

At the conclusion of the benchmark run (year 12), the simulated industry appeared to have entered a mature stage in the life cycle of its product. This mature stage persisted until the end of the viability run (year 20). Industry sales remained somewhere between 165 million pounds and 187 million pounds throughout the last eight years of the run (see Figure 5-1). With industry sales at a plateau, the brands of Firm 1 (Brands 1 and 7) and Firm 3 (Brand 3) were able to acquire larger and larger shares of the market as time went on. These firms

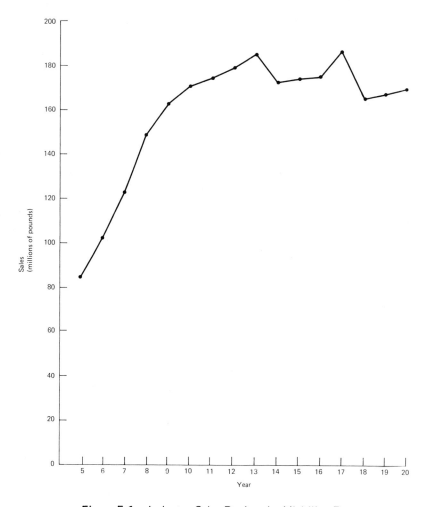

Figure 5-1.   Industry Sales During the Viability Run.

took advantage of their superior corporate images, continued high advertising expenditures, and made certain changes in strategy to help improve their shares. For example, the quality of Brands 1 and 3 was raised to help them gain a larger share. On the other hand, for Brand 7, a strategy of low price and very high dealer-directed promotion expenditures was used to help it to eventually become the largest selling brand in the market by year 20.

As the shares of Brands 1, 3, and 7 grew larger, the shares of Brands 2, 4, 5, and 6 naturally grew smaller. Brand 2 was therefore forced out of the market after year 13, and Brands 4, 5, and 6 left after year 17. In addition, only two attempts were made to enter this mature market during years 13 through 20. Firm 2 failed in an attempt to test market a brand to replace Brand 2 during year 15, while Firm 3 was able to introduce Brand 9 with considerable success during year 16.

Thus the industry developed into a duopoly during the viability run. Each of the two firms ended the run by marketing two highly profitable brands whose prices were rising steadily and whose advertising expenditures were very large (all were spending more than 20 percent of sales). This outcome seems reasonable. There are many grocery products markets that have become dominated by two or three firms during the late-maturity stage of their life cycles. (Examples include detergents, razor blades, and cake mixes.)

The fact that the simulated industry became a duopoly in the viability run should not really alter the interpretation given to the results reported in Chapter Four. It can still be said that vigorous competition was not encouraged by the controls that were tested. What can also be said now, given the results of the viability run, is that during the eight years of Runs #5, #7, #10, #13, #15, #17, and #20, the tested controls were unable to sidetrack the simulated industry's progression toward becoming a duopoly. Moreover, in some cases, these controls were responsible for accelerating this progression.

PERSONAL INTERVIEWS

To help test the face validity and predictive validity of the model, six personal interviews were conducted (during late 1973 and early 1974) with brand (product) managers from four of the largest cereal companies.[b] Each interview took about one hour to complete and was administered by the author. The questions that were asked attempted to acquire information about how brand managers in the cereal industry make decisions and about several other subjects. Because it was necessary to keep the interviews reasonably short, it was not possible to ask questions that tested all of the model's numerous assumptions.

The questionnaire that was utilized was pilot-tested twice before

[b]Because of the sensitive nature of some of the issues explored in this study, two major cereal companies refused to allow their personnel to be interviewed.

actually being used with cereal company brand managers.[c] The questions about brand managers in this questionnaire were designed to elicit responses that described how brand managers *actually* behave, not how they *should* behave. This was done by asking indirect questions about what "most" brand managers in the cereal industry did, rather than by asking respondents to describe what they, themselves, did. In all cases, the respondents described how most brand managers *with their firms* made decisions. They professed to be unfamiliar with how decisions were made within other firms.

It should be pointed out that the answers in three of the interviews may have been biased somewhat by the fact that the respondents had been questioned by investigators from the Federal Trade Commission about one week earlier. Although respondents were *not* told beforehand that this study was investigating some of the same issues the FTC was concerned about,[d] it is possible that they responded differently to questions because of their recent FTC encounter.[e]

The questions that were asked are listed below. Each question is followed by a summary of the answers it received and a discussion of whether the answers provide support for the model.

> Question 1: *To help guide me in my questioning, I first need to know your title and your responsibilities.*

The people that were interviewed were all product managers or former product managers. Two individuals were *senior* product managers for cereal products who had several brand and product managers reporting directly to them. Two other people were group product managers *for new products* who supervised the introduction of all new products including cereals. One of these new-product managers was from a major grocery manufacturing firm that had just brought out its first cereal product. The fifth person interviewed was the product manager for one-half of his firm's cereal line. Finally, the sixth individual was the manager of marketing information services for a major grocery manufacturing firm that produces a line of cereals. This individual had spent five years as a brand manager of a grocery product.

---

[c]One respondent for the pilot test was a brand manager for a major grocery products manufacturer. The other respondent was a university professor who recently completed a large study on brand managers.

[d]Respondents were told only that (1) as part of a research project, a series of personal interviews were being conducted with cereal industry executives; (2) the purpose of the interviews was to accumulate information about how brand managers and others in the industry make decisions; (3) this information would be used to help build a computer simulation model of a segment of the cereal industry; (4) since the questions are rather general, they would not be required to reveal anything of a proprietary nature; and (5) the identity of all respondents would be kept strictly confidential.

[e]One of these respondents seemed quite defensive during the interview, while another seemed extremely candid.

Question 2: *In a case developed by the Harvard Business School called the "Quaker Oats Life Cereal Case," it is stated that in the mid-1960s "the cereal manufacturers tended to group RTE cereals into three somewhat distinguishable categories: presweetened, nutritional, and nonsweetened." Do most people in the industry still tend to categorize RTE cereals in the same or in a similar way today?*

The respondents all agreed that ready-to-eat cereals were no longer viewed as falling within presweetened, nutritional, and nonsweetened categories. However, none of the respondents reported that their firms had abandoned the practice of breaking down ready-to-eat cereals into distinct categories. The current practice seems to be to view ready-to-eat cereals as falling within presweetened (children's), adult (includes nutritional cereals), and natural categories, although the exact breakdown used by a firm depends upon the types of brands it markets and the data services to which it subscribes. (SAMI, a widely used data reporting service, breaks down ready-to-eat cereals into presweetened, all-family, high nutrition, adult, variety pack, natural, and miscellaneous categories. One of the firms that was visited used this categorization.)

Respondents stated that the reason why they did not view nutritional cereals as a major category any more is that in the early 1970s large quantities of nutrients were added to the ingredients of almost all the non-nutritional cereals. This action came in response to complaints about ready-to-eat cereals by consumerists and nutritionists. With almost all brands now having nutrients added, the people in the industry do not feel it is appropriate to make a strong distinction between nutritional and other cereals.

The fact that the respondents still grouped ready-to-eat cereals into separate categories indicates that, to some extent, people in the industry view the ready-to-eat cereal industry as consisting of several distinct markets in which brands compete primarily against other brands in their same category. This finding makes it easier to accept a model that was patterned after only a segment of the cereal industry as a model of a distinct industry. The discovery that nutritional cereals are no longer considered a major category should not make the model less acceptable as a model of an industry. The model was constructed using data on nutritional cereals that was generated long before nutrients were added to most of the non-nutritional cereal brands.

Question 3: *In the National Commission on Food Marketing study of the breakfast cereal industry, the statement is made: "Grocery manufacturers generally prefer to employ: (1) media advertising; (2) consumer-directed promotions such as coupons, free samples, cents-off deals; (3) dealer-directed promotions such as trade allowances, in that order." Do you agree with this statement?*

There was agreement among the respondents that this statement is basically correct. However, all of them stressed that it was difficult to generalize about all grocery manufacturers since certain products may call for different types of strategies. Four of the respondents also pointed out that the quote more accurately describes the preferences of cereal manufacturers than those of other types of grocery manufacturers. Another point that came out in two of the answers was that dealer-directed promotion is not used very heavily by the ready-to-eat cereal manufacturers.

The answers to this question tend to support what is found in the model. The brand managers in the model turn to advertising expenditures first, consumer-directed promotion expenditures second, and dealer-directed promotion expenditures third when they search for strategies to improve their expected profits. It seems fair to assume that managers will test out changes in these three decision variables in the same order as their order of preference for these variables.

> Question 4: *Do you (or "most brand managers" if respondent is not a brand manager) participate in the development of any sort of annual or multi-year plan for your (their) brand? (Probe: Try to ascertain type of plan and whether most other brand managers do the same.)*

All of the respondents stated that every year they participate in the development of both one-year and five-year plans for their brands. The one-year plans are detailed descriptions of the marketing strategies they intend to use in that year. They include statements on how much will be spent on advertising and promotion, what prices will be charged, how the brands will be "positioned," and what sales and profits are expected to be. The five-year plans are put together basically for financial-planning purposes. The information and strategies in the one-year plan are, in most cases, extrapolated out for four more years to provide financial planners with forecasts they can use to determine capital requirements. Only one of the respondents reported that his firm has built mathematical models to help them in this planning process.

The answers to this question provide support for the model. The brand managers in the model go through a planning process similar to the ones reported by the respondents. Like their real-world counterparts, the model's managers plan their strategies for the coming year and forecast what the strategies will do for them if they are also carried out in future years. The only disturbing aspect of the answers to this question is that real-world managers were found to have planning horizons that are one year longer than the four-year horizons of the managers in the model. But this finding should not, by itself, lead one to lose confidence in the model.

> Question 5, Part I: *Could you, in your own words, describe how most brand managers in the cereal industry determine their budgets in these areas? (Probe: Try to ascertain role of percentage of sales figures, role of past budgets, types of forecasts, and so forth.)*

Respondents were then shown a card that described four suggested ways in which brand managers set their advertising, consumer-directed promotion, dealer-directed promotion, and sales call expenditure budgets:

a. *They make a prediction of what sales will be in the coming year, estimate what it will cost them to produce and distribute the predicted demand, determine what a satisfactory level of profits would be given the predicted levels of sales and costs, and then allocate the residual to advertising, promotion, and sales calls.*

b. *They set target levels of sales, market share, or profits, estimate whether spending about the same percentage of sales on advertising, promotion, and sales calls as was spent in the previous year will achieve these target levels, and change the percent of sales spent on each only when it is felt to be needed to hit the target levels.*

c. *They set target levels of sales, market share, or profits and then determine what dollar amounts must be spent on advertising, promotion, and sales calls to reach the target levels, secondarily considering what was spent in past years or what percentage of sales will be spent in each area.*

d. *They simply look at each variable—advertising, consumer promotion, dealer promotion, and sales calls—and see whether increasing or decreasing their budgets for each will improve sales, market share, or profits.*

> Question 5, Part II: *How are decisions on wholesale and retail prices generally made?*

The answers to Part I of this question were varied. The majority of respondents described budgeting procedures that came closest to being like item c in the question. However, the following points also came out in the discussion:

1. One respondent stated that although brand managers try to employ an approach similar to item c, item a comes closest to industry practice. He felt that managers are usually given only a residual figure to work with in determining their marketing expenditures. This individual and another respondent also stressed that product managers spend a great deal of their time managing production and distribution costs.

2. Two of the respondents said that managers usually determine target sales levels by multiplying forecasted industry sales by desired market share levels.

3. One respondent claimed that product managers set target sales levels as low as they possibly can and then set advertising and promotion budgets as high as they can get away with.
4. All of the respondents stated that the percent of sales that was spent on advertising, promotion, and sales calls was of secondary importance to product managers. However, several respondents pointed out that percent of sales figures are probably important to higher management.

The answers to Part II of Question 5 were also varied. The respondents generally agreed that the prices charged by *direct* competitors (e.g., "Post Toasties" is a direct competitor to Kellogg's "Corn Flakes") and the possible reactions of these competitors were important considerations in setting prices. Several of them also stated that the pricing decision was often a "bottom-line" decision in which managers attempted to cover costs while leaving an adequate margin for profits. In addition, two of the respondents stressed that cereal manufacturers have very little control over retail prices.

The answers to Parts I and II of Question 5 suggest that it is necessary to revise the decision procedure employed by the brand managers in the model. Instead of utilizing a decision procedure similar to item b (Part I) of this question, the model should contain a procedure that comes closer to being like items c and a. Based on the limited amount of evidence accumulated in the six interviews, the following procedure would seem to be a closer approximation to real-world behavior than what is found in the model.

First, the brand manager makes a forecast of industry sales in pounds. He then multiplies this figure times what he considers to be a satisfactory market share level in order to get a target level of (pound) sales for the coming year. A forecast of the costs of producing and distributing the target sales level is then made and this step is followed by the determination of a wholesale price that is competitive and that will adequately cover costs. The wholesale price that is selected is used to compute a target *dollar* sales figure and from this figure the manager subtracts (1) his forecasted manufacturing and distribution costs and (2) an amount that represents a satisfactory contribution to corporate profits. The residual amount is left for advertising, promotion, and sales calls.

Second, the manager estimates whether allocating this residual amount to the four spending areas in the same proportions that were used in the previous year can produce the desired sales level. If he does not think this strategy will produce the target sales level (and profits level), he will then estimate whether it is possible to redistribute the residual amount among the four spending areas in a more optimal way. If the redistribution test is not successful, he will then test the effects of spending more than the residual amount on advertising, promotions, and sales calls. He will test the effects of spending more on advertising (than was spent in the redistribution test that scored the best) first, and the effects of spending more on consumer promotions, dealer promotions, and sales calls subsequently. As long as increased spending in any of these areas will bring his expected profits closer to the satisfactory level, he will plan to spend more. However, in no case will he spend very much more on a percentage-of-sales basis than he did in the previous year.

Third, the manager concludes his search as soon as he locates a spending mix that will yield satisfactory expected profits for the coming year. If he cannot find a spending mix that will do this after testing the effects of exceeding the residual amount, he will use the spending mix he has tested that could be expected to perform the best. He will then test the effects of changing his suggested retail price, wholesale price, and brand quality, in that order. If making changes in any of these three variables will improve his expected profits, he will change them. He will also stop his search if he locates a change in price or quality that will yield satisfactory expected profits. However, after changes in brand quality have been tested and an overall mix that can produce satisfactory results has not been located, the manager will settle for the marketing mix that performed the best out of those he has tested.

Fourth, the marketing mix the manager has selected for the coming year is subjected to one final test. The manager checks to see whether the selected strategy will have unfavorable long-run consequences. He will revise his strategy for the coming year if his five-year plan shows that it will produce lower long-run profits than alternative strategies.

Although, on the surface, the decision procedure outlined above appears to be quite different from the procedure used by the brand managers in the model, it is not at all clear that the two procedures would produce different results. Both procedures have managers considering basically the same things; the major differences seem to be in the *order* in which these things are considered and in the *starting points* of the respective search procedures. Moreover, it should be noted that the alternative procedure was developed from the varied responses of only six real-world brand managers. Thus, it is felt that the answers to Question 5, while they do not support the model, fail to provide evidence that should lead one to reject completely the validity of the model.

Question 6: *What do you think most brand managers in the cereal industry would assume about the reactions of their competitors in contemplating the following changes in their marketing strategy?*

Respondents were then shown a card listing the changes and possible reactions:

1. *Raising their yearly advertising budget by 10 percent. In other words, what, in your opinion, do most brand managers assume about the reactions of their rivals when they think about raising their ad budget by 10 percent?*
   a. *Most brand managers would assume that competitors would react strongly to this type of change in strategy.*

b. *Most brand managers would assume that competitors would gradually adjust to this type of change in strategy.*

c. *Most brand managers would assume that competitors would not react at all to this type of change in strategy.*

d. *Most brand managers wouldn't even bother considering how competitors might react to this type of change in strategy.*

e. *Other (specify).*

2. *Raising their yearly advertising budget by 25 percent.*
   a., b., c., d., e.

3. *Raising their yearly budget for consumer-directed promotion (coupons, premiums, etc.) by 25 percent.*
   a., b., c., d., e.

4. *Raising their yearly budget for dealer-directed promotion (allowances, discounts, etc.) by 25 percent.*
   a., b., c., d., e.

5. *Raising their wholesale price by 15 percent.*
   a., b., c., d., e.

6. *Cutting their wholesale price by 5 percent.*
   a., b., c., d., e.

7. *Cutting their suggested retail price by 5 percent.*
   a., b., c., d., e.

The brand manager in the model does not expect his rivals to react strongly to his strategy changes. Instead, he conjectures that they will (1) react to his strategy changes that lower their sales by lowering their marketing expenditures and (2) react to his changes in retail price by changing their wholesale and retail prices in the same direction but by a smaller amount. Question 6 was designed to test whether real-world managers expect this kind of mild reaction from their rivals. The answers that were received tend to support the model.

The answers to each of the seven parts of this question are tabulated below:

1. Advertising, +10%: 2 b's, 2 c's, 2 d's;
2. Advertising, +25%: 2 b's, 1c, 2 d's, 1 e ("depends on brand");
3. Consumer Promotion, +25%: 1 b, 1 c, 4 d's;
4. Dealer Promotion, +25%: 2 a's, 1 b, 2 d's, 1 e ("There is none");
5. Wholesale Price, +5%: 2 a's, 2 b's, 2 d's;
6. Wholesale Price, −5%: 1 a, 1 b, 2 d's, 2 e's ("never happens");
7. Retail Price, −5%: 1 a, 3 d's, 2 e's ("never happens").

These results show that the respondents felt that most brand managers in the cereal industry do not expect strong reactions to changes in advertising or consumer-directed promotion expenditures. In addition, only two respondents felt that managers expect strong reactions to either increased spending on dealer-directed promotion or higher wholesale prices. Furthermore, only one respondent felt that managers expect strong reactions to cuts in wholesale or retail prices.

Since the managers in the model foresee stronger reactions to price changes than to other types of changes, the occurrence of "a" answers on items 5, 6, and 7 is not particularly disturbing. Morever, one of the respondents stated that he gave an "a" answer on item 4 because the use of dealer-directed promotion is so rare in the cereal industry that brand managers would naturally expect rivals to react strongly to increased spending in this area.

Question 7: *Whose competitive reaction would most brand managers be concerned about in contemplating each of the changes in the last question?*

a. *Only other brands in the same RTE category (presweetened, etc.);*
b. *Primarily other brands in the same RTE category, but to some extent all brands of cereal;*
c. *All brands of cereal;*
d. *All breakfast foods;*
e. *Would not expect any reactions (c or d answer on Question 6).*

This question served as another check (along with Question 2) on how reasonable it is to view a model that is patterned after only a segment of the cereal industry as a model of a distinct industry. If real-world brand managers in the cereal industry tend to be concerned primarily with the reactions of brands within their same category, then it becomes easier to accept the categories as being like distinct industries.

The answers to each of the seven parts of this question are tabulated below:

1. Advertising, +10%: 3 a's, 3 e's;
2. Advertising, +25%: 2 a's, 2 b's, 2 e's;
3. Consumer Promotion, +25%: 2 a's, 2 b's, 2 e's;
4. Dealer Promotion, +25%: 1 a, 3 b's, 1 c, 1 e;
5. Wholesale Price, +5%: 2 a's, 1 b, 2 c's, 1 e;
6. Wholesale Price, −5%: 2 a's, 1 b, 1 c, 1 d, 1 e;
7. Retail Price, −5%: 2 a's, 1 b, 1 d, 2 e's.

Respondents exhibited some inconsistency in the way they answered this question since all items that received "c" or "d" answers in Question 6 (i.e., no reactions expected or considered) did not receive "e" answers in this question.

Nevertheless, these results provide some mild support for the model. There were only a few respondents who stated that managers are concerned about the reactions of all cereals or all breakfast foods.

> Question 8: *Brand managers obviously face an uncertain environment. On the next card is a list of things about which a typical brand manager might be uncertain. Could you please rank order these items by giving a 1 to the item that brand managers tend to be most uncertain about at this point in time, a 2 to the item that they view as having the next most uncertainty, and so on?*

a. *Economic conditions (includes prices of raw materials);*
b. *Government intervention;*
c. *The behavior of existing competitive brands;*
d. *The behavior of potential competitive brands;*
e. *The behavior of consumers;*
f. *The behavior of dealers;*
g. *Other (specify).*

The mean ranking awarded to each item is found below:

Economic conditions: *1.2*;
Government intervention: *3.2*;
The behavior of consumers: *3.2*;
The behavior of existing competitive brands: *3.8*;
The behavior of potential competitive brands: *3.8*;
The behavior of dealers: *5.7*.

Thus, respondents felt that brand managers are most uncertain about economic conditions. This response is understandable considering the shortage (of raw materials) situation that the cereal industry was going through at the time of the interviews. Respondents also felt that managers are least uncertain about the behavior of dealers. As one person stated: "Their behavior is pretty straightforward."

For simplicity purposes, it is assumed in the model that brand managers are only uncertain about the behavior of existing and potential rivals. The answers to this question indicate that real-world managers tend to be more uncertain about economic conditions and consumer behavior than they are about the behavior of rivals. This finding suggests that future revisions of the model should place a high priority on adding uncertainty about economic conditions and consumer behavior to the decision-making situation of brand managers.

Question 9: *Brand managers presumably make some assumptions about when new, directly competitive brands might enter the market. Would you say that:*

a. Most brand managers assume that rival brands will enter when prices in their submarket reach significantly high levels.
b. Most brand managers assume that rival brands will enter when profits in their submarket reach significantly high levels.
c. Most brand managers assume that rival brands will enter when sales in their submarket reach significantly high levels.
d. Most brand managers make more complex assumptions than the above (specify).
e. Most brand managers are not very concerned about when a new rival might enter their submarket.
f. Other (specify).

How far into the future do most brand managers look when they speculate about when new rivals might enter their submarket?

In the model, it is assumed that in a given year brand managers conjecture that new rivals will enter the industry during the next four years if industry profits become high. The answers to Question 9 do not support this assumption. None of the respondents reported that real-world managers look to profits as an indicator of the likelihood of new entry. Moreover, all of the respondents reported that managers look only one to two years into the future—and not four years—when speculating about when entry might occur.

One of the respondents gave a "c" answer to this question; three others gave "d" answers; and two others gave "e" answers. The three respondents who gave "d" answers offered the following comments:

> Our managers rely on our firm's intelligence people who tell them what's going on at other firms. We've got some really good Procter & Gamble watchers.
> When the market share of a brand becomes large enough, managers expect other brands to come in and try to capture some of its share.
> The manager's assumptions will depend on the attributes of the products already in the market. Is there a brand that can be moved in on?

The two respondents who gave "e" answers added the following insights:

> The cereal market is so fragmented that managers don't worry about new entrants. Maybe in the case of a new category, like

natural cereals, they'll pay attention to it. But they won't look at prices and profits to tell them when someone is going to enter. Another reason for not worrying about entry is that there really isn't anything you can do to stop a Procter & Gamble from entering.

In many cases, managers welcome entry. The promotional effort behind a new brand can help a category to grow in size.

Thus, the model seems to have a flaw. The answers to Question 9 suggest that it should not be assumed that brand managers conjecture that new rivals will enter when profits become high. Whether this flaw should cause one to doubt the predictions of the computer runs is unclear. The decisions of the brand managers in several of the computer runs were definitely influenced by the threat of entry. However, alternative assumptions about the conjectures made by brand managers with respect to new rivals could have produced similar, entry-thwarting behavior.

> Question 10: *Which of the following criteria would you say are most closely watched by most brand managers? Put them in rank order.*

a. *Contribution to profits;*
b. *Market share;*
c. *Cash flow;*
d. *Sales;*
e. *Other (specify).*

The mean rankings awarded to the items are found below:

Contribution to profits: *1.7*;
Market share: *2.0*;
Sales: *2.2*;
Cash flow: *3.8*.

The first-place ranking of contribution to profits provides support for the model. The primary goal of the brand managers in the model is to have their brands contribute growing amounts of profits to their firms. The second-place ranking of market share also provides support for the model. Brand managers in the model use market share figures to help them make their annual decisions about whether to continue marketing their brands.

The fact that cash flow was not considered to be an important criterion to brand managers can be used to help interpret the results of the computer runs discussed in the last chapter. Giving brand managers in the model cash-flow objectives (Assumption Change 2) seemed to have a moderating effect on the impact of the advertising depreciation requirements (Runs #19 and #21).

If real-world brand managers are unlikely to have cash-flow objectives—and five of the six respondents make special mention of the fact that brand managers are *not* concerned about cash flows—then this moderating effect would be unlikely to occur when depreciation requirements were tried in the real world.

> Question 11: *There has been a running battle for years among economists over whether the decision makers within business firms are in reality "maximizers" or "satisficers."* Respondents were then shown a card describing these two terms as follows:

> 1. *Maximizers might be described as managers who continually search for ways to improve their profits, sales, market share, or some other criterion variable.* 2. *Satisficers might be described as managers who are satisfied with certain levels of profits, sales, and so on, and who generally search for ways to improve these things only when they feel satisfactory levels are not being achieved. Given this description of the two terms, would you say that most brand managers in the cereal industry are maximizers or satisficers or something else?*

Two respondents stated that most brand managers in the cereal industry are satisficers, one respondent stated that they are maximizers, and three respondents gave conditional answers. The following points came out in the conditional answers:

> Product managers are, by definition, maximizers. They are always told to do better than the guy before them. However, the managers above the product managers are definitely satisficers.
> A guy can be both the way our company is structured. It depends on the stage his brand is at in the life cycle and on the kind of leadership he is being provided with.
> The people at General Mills are maximizers while the people at Kellogg's are probably satisficers. It depends on how closely held the company is.

Since the brand managers in the model are assumed to be satisficers, these answers provide only weak support for the model.

> Question 12: *The market share of a mature, established brand in your industry is most sensitive to changes in which of the following variables? Please put them in rank order.*

a. *Retail price;*
b. *Availability;*
c. *Packaging;*

    d. *Consumer-directed promotion;*
    e. *Media advertising;*
    f. *Nutritional properties of the brand;*
    g. *Reseller support (retailer advertising, good shelf locations, etc.);*
    h. *Corporate image;*
    i. *Other (specify).*

The following scores were produced by computing the mean ranking awarded to each item:

Availability: *2.3*;
Reseller support: *2.7*;
Media advertising: *2.8*;
Consumer-directed promotion: *3.7*;
Retail price: *4.8*;
Packaging: *6.0*;
Nutritional properties of the brand: *6.2*;
Corporate image: *6.7.*

The market share response function used in the model assigns the largest sensitivity parameter to retail price (−2.0), the next largest to distribution effectiveness (1.6), the next to advertising goodwill (.5), the next to brand quality (.06) and corporate image (.06), and the next to consumer-directed promotion (.05). The answers to Question 12 indicate that it is probably correct to give distribution effectiveness such a high sensitivity parameter, but that it may be incorrect to assign such a large parameter to retail price and such a small parameter to consumer-directed promotion. If the model is revised, different retail price parameters and consumer-directed promotion parameters should therefore be tested—keeping in mind the following two additional pieces of information. First, the one respondent who worked in marketing research thought that market share in the cereal industry is highly sensitive to price changes. He ranked retail price number two behind availability on Question 12. Second, when consumer-directed promotion was given a large sensitivity parameter during the trial-and-error procedure that was used to put the model into its finalized form, brand managers started to spend unreasonable amounts on consumer-directed promotion. However, this unreasonable spending could have developed because *industry* sales were made too sensitive to changes in industry consumer-directed promotion expenditures (see the next section).

Question 13: *The total sales in pounds in your industry is most sensitive to changes in which of the following variables? Please put them in rank order.*

a. *Population;*
b. *Industry advertising expenditures;*
c. *Average industry retail price relative to prices of other breakfast foods;*
d. *Per capita income in the United States;*
e. *Industry consumer-directed promotion expenditures;*
f. *Other (specify).*

The mean ranking awarded to each item is displayed below:

Average industry retail price relative to prices of other breakfast foods: *1.3*;
Population: *2.0*;
Industry advertising expenditures: *3.3*;
Per capita income in the United States: *3.7*;
Industry consumer-directed promotion expenditures: *3.8.*

These results tend to support the model since the industry sales response function that is used makes industry sales most sensitive to changes in average industry retail price, population, industry advertising goodwill, and industry consumer-directed promotion expenditures, in that order. The only disturbing aspect of the answers to this question is that industry consumer-directed promotion expenditures were ranked lower than per capita income. This indicates that either per capita income should be included in the industry sales response function or industry consumer-directed promotion expenditures should be removed from the function. Based on the discussion under Question 12, the latter approach would seem more appropriate since it might permit the consumer-directed promotion sensitivity parameter to be increased in the market share response function.

> Question 14: *A cereal brand would probably be considered to have effective distribution if it were available in almost all retail outlets and if it were getting good reseller support in the form of retailer advertising, good shelf locations, etc. In your opinion, what are the most important determinants of whether a brand achieves effective distribution or not? (Ask about corporate image and advertising if not mentioned.)*

This open-ended question was used to provide a test of the face validity of the distribution effectiveness response function utilized in the model. The answers that were received were far ranging and difficult to categorize. Four of the responses are summarized below:

> Who the company is. If you're Kellogg's, you get what you want; if you're someone else, you have troubles. Even giants like Colgate

and Pet ran into obstacles trying to get distribution for their cereal products, and Ralston and Nabisco have always had problems in this area. . . . Heavy advertising is important for getting a new brand on the shelf, but once they're up there, advertising doesn't make that much difference.

The market share of the company selling the product is the most important thing. Next comes the advertising and promotion expenditures behind the brand. The third most important determinant is sales force activity.

Good stock turnover and strong advertising and promotion support are the most important determinants. A good sales force—like Kellogg's—can also help to prolong the life of a product. [after prompting] . . . The corporate name *is* important. Kellogg's, for example, can keep a "sick" brand on the shelves while others can't.

Advertising dollars are spent to reach retailers as much as they are to reach consumers. A good ad program can be a tremendous tool for getting distribution. [after prompting] . . . A good corporate image gets you in the door, but there has to be more than that. Procter & Gamble is hated by the trade, yet still gets pretty much what it wants.

The other two respondents felt that corporate image was no longer the important factor that it used to be in determining whether a brand got on the shelves. Both pointed to the successful entry of Pet (Heartland) and Colgate-Palmolive (Alpen) into the natural cereal market as evidence of this.

It is difficult to say whether the responses to Question 14 provide support for the model. The response function that is used in the model is a "catch-all" equation that includes most of the variables that the respondents cited as determinants of distribution effectiveness. However, it is not clear that the response function gives each variable its correct amount of influence. Based on some of the responses, it seems proper to have made corporate image (or the company's market share) the most important determinant of distribution effectiveness. But other responses indicate that corporate image should not have been made so influential. Clearly, further testing of the validity of the distribution effectiveness response function is needed.

Question 15: *The current antitrust suit against the four major cereal manufacturers could have a number of different outcomes. Some people have suggested that your industry should have its advertising expenditures limited or restricted in some way as part of a settlement in this case.*

1. *How do you think most brand managers would alter the various variables in their "marketing mix" if they were required to . . .*

a. *Pay, say, a 5 percent to 10 percent tax on their advertising?*
b. *Pay some sort of progressive tax on their advertising?*
c. *Limit their advertising to some fixed percentage of sales? (New brands would be exempted for their first three years.)*
d. *Capitalize and depreciate their advertising expenditures?*
2. *Do you think the number and type of entrants to the industry would change if cereal manufacturers were required to do any of the above?*
3. *Is there anything else that you can see would occur within the industry if the manufacturers were required to do any of the above?*

This question was used to test the face validity of the model's predictions. The responses tended to fall within two categories. One group of responses consisted of general comments about the potential effects of advertising controls. The second group of responses consisted of comments about the specific controls listed in the question. In general, the responses would support a claim that the model has predictive validity.

Four general comments that were made about the potential effects of placing controls on the advertising expenditures of firms in the cereal industry are found below:

> They would slow down the growth rate of the industry.
> An escalation would occur temporarily in the use of other marketing tools as everyone would respond to everyone else. But the basic structure of the market wouldn't change.
> None of these measures would alter the strength of the franchise the big firms have with consumers and dealers.
> Some firms would spend so much time and money trying to get around the controls that prices would have to go up.

The first three forecasts are reasonably accurate descriptions of what occurred when controls were tested using the model. In most cases, the controls (1) caused industry sales to grow more slowly, (2) encouraged flurries of competitive activity that did not change the structure of the industry, and (3) allowed large brands to maintain their entrenched position with retailers and consumers.

As for comments about specific controls, the respondents were unable to give a confident prediction about what would occur if a 5 to 10 percent straight tax were introduced. One individual thought that the cost might be passed on to consumers, while another suggested that brand managers might use some of the funds allocated for promotion to pay the tax. A third person thought that managers might start spending more on dealer-directed promotion instead of advertising and that this would lead to lower retail prices. But none of these three predictions were offered with great confidence. The respondents simply had no clear idea of what a straight tax might do to the industry.

With respect to a progressive tax, the respondents were a little less cautious about making predictions. Three of them definitely felt that a progressive tax would cause managers to spend less on advertising and a little more on promotion. One of these three respondents also stated that some managers "would really get mashed" with a large tax bill as a result of a progressive tax and that firms would be less likely to bring out new brands because of the tax. As for the other three respondents, one of them refused to make a prediction; another thought that nothing would change; and a third insisted that the tax experts in the industry would find a way to get around it. These findings do not contradict the results of the computer runs that tested a progressive tax (Runs #7, #8, and #9). In these runs, managers spent less on advertising and a little more on promotion. Entry by new brands was also delayed in two of these runs.

The predictions that were made about the effects of limiting advertising expenditures to a fixed percentage of sales were not very useful for testing the predictive validity of the model. For example, one respondent simply claimed that this type of control would never be used (it would be too difficult to administer). Similarly, another stated that such a control would lead companies to demand more creativity from their advertising agencies. The two responses that *were* of some use pointed out that (1) limits on the advertising-sales ratio would give an unfair advantage to large firms and (2) firms would tend to reduce their advertising expenditures and take higher profits if limits of this type were imposed. The results of the computer runs that tested limits on the advertising-sales ratio (Runs #10 to #14) were reasonably consistent with these latter two responses. The limits were found to give the larger brands a strong advantage because they could spend more. Also, with a 20 percent limit, the larger brands were able to earn higher returns on sales.

Three of the respondents were unsure about what would happen if a depreciation requirement was introduced. Another two respondents stated that the requirement would have no impact because brand managers are not concerned about cash flows. The last respondent predicted that a depreciation requirement would encourage managers to spend more on advertising. He felt that since product managers do not have cash-flow responsibilities, they would take advantage of not having to expense all of their advertising outlays and would spend more than they would otherwise. This prediction by the last respondent is quite consistent with the results of the computer runs which tested depreciation requirements (Runs #17 to #21).

Summary of Interview Findings

Six personal interviews were used to help test the validity of the model. The model stood up reasonably well to this test of its validity. However, four flaws in the model were discovered while examining the findings of the interviews:

1. The decision procedure employed by the brand managers in the model for determining marketing expenditures and prices differs somewhat from the procedures reported in the interviews.
2. The brand managers in the model are not uncertain about economic conditions and the behavior of consumers, while their real-world counterparts tend to be more uncertain about these things than anything else.
3. Unlike the managers in the model, real-world managers do not conjecture that new rivals will enter the industry if profits become too high.
4. In the market-share response function used in the model, the sensitivity parameter assigned to prices is probably too high and the one assigned to consumer-directed promotion is probably too low.

While these flaws are disturbing, the model would have to be revised and the experiments rerun to find out exactly how much they influence the model's output. Since this study was only designed to be an *exploratory* investigation, such a revision was not undertaken.

THE BENCHMARK RUN VS. REAL-WORLD DATA

In this section, the output of the benchmark run of the model is compared to the limited amount of data that was available on the nutritional cereal submarket and on the entire ready-to-eat cereal industry. Since this same data was used to help develop the model, this comparison represents a weak test of the model's predictive validity. Ideally, different bodies of data should be used to create and to validate a model.

In Figure 5-2, a graphical comparison of the industry sales figures generated by the model and actual sales figures for the nutritional submarket is presented. As shown in the exhibit, the model produced industry sales figures that can be considered reasonable. The real-world data used here for the years 1965 through 1967 was taken from the "Life Cereal Case."[9] The data for the remaining years was computed from information on brand shares and total ready-to-eat cereal sales found in trade journal articles by John C. Maxwell.[10] A slight downward bias exists in the real-world data because sales of three brands ("Kaboom," "100% Bran-Flakes," and "Charged Bran") were not included. The market shares of these brands were not large enough to be reported in the Maxwell data.

A comparison of the entrants to the simulated industry and the real-world submarket is found in Table 5-1. As shown in the table, entry by nonestablished firms did not occur either in the benchmark run or in historical experience (only the six largest cereal companies brought out brands). Furthermore, new brands tended to enter on a one-per-year basis in both situations. However, three more new brands entered the real-world submarket than the

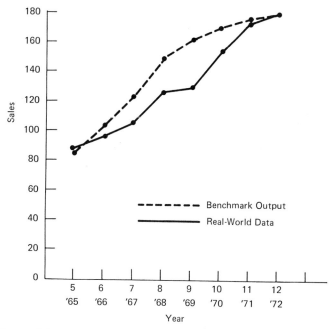

Figure 5-2. Industry Sales in Pounds: Benchmark Run vs. Real-World Data.

simulated industry. Also, some of the real-world firms were able to bring out a second (Kellogg and Quaker) and even a third (General Mills) nutritional brand before all of the six major cereal companies had marketed a nutritional brand. In the benchmark run, all six established firms brought out brands before Firm 1 brought out a second brand. On balance, it must be said that the model did only a fair job of simulating how entry occurred in the real-world submarket.

Graphical comparisons of market-share figures are displayed in the next two figures (5-3 and 5-4). The dotted lines represent the paths of the market shares of the brands in the simulated market and the smooth lines represent the paths of the shares of real-world brands. As shown in Figure 5-3, the market shares of Brand 1 and "Special K" matched up reasonably well, while the shares of Brands 2 and 3 remained somewhat lower than those of "Life" and "Total." The reason why Brands 2 and 3 did poorer than their real-world counterparts was because new brands tended to attain higher initial market shares in the simulation, thereby hurting Brands 2 and 3 in the process (see Figure 5-4). In short, the model did not do a good job of duplicating real-world market-share figures. As a result, the concentration ratios produced by the benchmark run were not close to the concentration ratios of the real-world submarket (see Table 5-2).

Because the market-share figures generated by the benchmark run

**Table 5-1. Entrants to Markets: Benchmark Run vs.
Real-World Data**

The Simulated Industry	Year of Entry	The Nutritional Submarket
Original Brands:		Original Brands:
Brand 1 of Established Firm 1		"Special K" of Kellogg
Brand 2 of Established Firm 2		"Life" of Quaker
Brand 3 of Established Firm 3		"Total" of General Mills[a]
Entrants:		Entrants:
Brand 4 of Established Firm 4	5 — '65	"Fortified Oat Flakes" of Post (General Foods)
Brand 5 of Established Firm 5	6 — '66	"Product 19" of Kellogg
Brand 6 of Established Firm 6	7 — '67	
Brand 7 of Established Firm 1	8 — '68	"Kaboom" of General Mills
	9 — '69	"King Vitamin" of Quaker
	10 — '70	"Buck-Wheats" of General Mills
	11 — '71	"100% Bran Flakes" of Nabisco "Charged Bran" of Ralston
	12 — '72	

[a]Corn Total was brought out by General Mills in 1971.

differed from those of the real-world submarket, it would not be appropriate to make direct comparisons between the marketing expenditures of simulated and real-world brands. It would be more meaningful to compare the *ratios* of marketing expenditures to sales that were generated by the model to the ratios that occurred in the real world. Unfortunately, this could not be done in a precise way. Only a limited amount of data was available on how much each real-world brand spent on advertising, consumer-directed promotion, and sales calls during the years 1965 to 1972. The "Life Cereal Case" only contains data on how much "Life" spent in these areas from 1965 to 1967 and on how much "Special K," "Total," and "Fortified Oats" spent during 1965.[11] In addition, the data on advertising expenditures provided by *National Advertising Investments* is extremely incomplete.[12] To make matters worse, there are no data sources available that provide information on the amount of *dollar* sales achieved by individual brands.

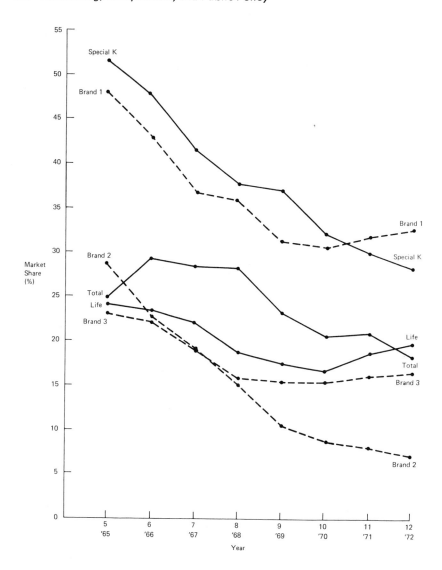

*Source: Milton P. Brown *et al*, "Life Cereal Case," *Problems in Marketing* (New York: McGraw-Hill, 1968), pp. 161-65; John C. Maxwell, "Cereals," *Marketing/Communications* (March 1970), p. 37ff.; and John C. Maxwell, "Cold Cereals Industry Goes Through Growth Year," *Advertising Age* (March 26, 1973), p. 3.

Figure 5-3.   Market Shares of Original Brands

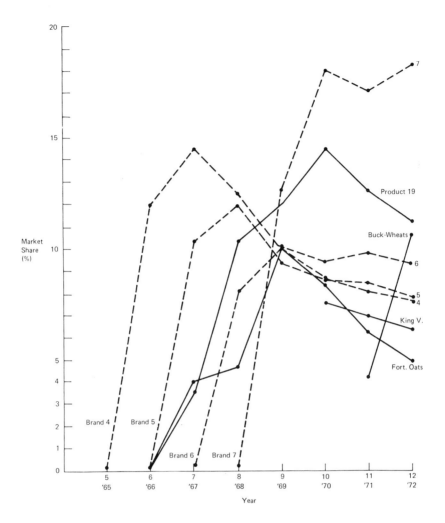

Figure 5-4. Market Shares of New Brands.

Thus, it was necessary to compare the spending ratios produced by the computer run to the average spending ratios for the entire ready-to-eat cereal industry reported in the National Commission on Food Marketing study.[13] As shown in Table 5-3, the spending ratios tended to be slightly higher in the benchmark run. This disparity can be explained, however, by the fact that the simulated industry experienced a growth stage during the simulated time period. To spur on their growth, the brands in the simulation could be expected to spend slightly more on marketing than the average, real-world cereal brand.

Table 5-2. Concentration Ratios: Benchmark Run vs. Real-World Data

		\			*Year*				
		5	6	7	8	9	10	11	12
Ratios:		'65	'66	'67	'68	'69	'70	'71	'72
2-Firm C.R.	(B)	.77	.66	.56	.52	.60	.64	.65	.68
	(RW)	.77	.77	.72	.76	.72	.72	.69	.68
2-Brand C.R.	(B)	.77	.66	.56	.52	.47	.49	.49	.51
	(RW)	.77	.77	.69	.66	.60	.53	.51	.48
3-Firm C.R.	(B)	1.00	.88	.75	.67	.70	.74	.75	.77
	(RW)	1.00	1.00	.94	.95	.90	.92	.94	.95
3-Brand C.R.	(B)	1.00	.88	.75	.67	.60	.64	.65	.68
	(RW)	1.00	1.00	.91	.85	.78	.70	.70	.66

B = Data from Benchmark Run
RW = Data from Real-World

Table 5-3. Ratios of Marketing Expenditures to Sales: Benchmark Run vs. Real-World Data

Simulated Data:	*Range of Advertising/ Sales Ratio*	*Range of Consumer-Dir. Promotion/ Sales Ratio*	*Range of Dealer-Dir. Promotion/ Sales Ratio*	*Range of Sales Calls/ Sales Ratio*
Brand:				
Brand 1	.170 - .235	.018 - .031	.009 - .025	.028 - .038
Brand 2	.180 - .225	.028 - .034	.009 - .013	.028 - .045
Brand 3	.187 - .258	.028 - .038	.010 - .047	.037 - .050
Brand 4[a]	.206 - .242	.028 - .034	.010 - .038	.041 - .047
Brand 5[a]	.208 - .239	.030 - .035	.010 - .035	.040 - .046
Brand 6[a]	.190 - .211	.028 - .030	.095 - .101	.038 - .040
Brand 7[a]	.192 - .199	.025 - .027	.027 - .028	.027 - .050
All Brands	.170 - .258	.018 - .038	.009 - .101	.027 - .050
Real-World Data:				
Average Ratios in Industry – 1964[b]	.178	.015	.007	.035

[a]Ranges of ratios do not include figures from the brand's test market, first, or second year.

[b]Source: National Commission on Food Marketing, *Studies of Organization and Competition in Grocery Manufacturing, Technical Study No. 6* (Washington, D.C.: U.S. Government Printing Office, 1966), pp. 206-07.

During the years 1965 to 1972, none of the real-world cereal firms altered the quality of their nutritional brands.[f] The small changes in brand quality that occurred during the benchmark run were therefore somewhat unrealistic (see Appendix B).[g]

A comparison of the wholesale prices, retail prices, and after-tax returns on sales generated by the benchmark run to figures available on real-world prices and returns on sales is presented in Table 5-4. It appears that the prices in the benchmark run tended to start out at somewhat high levels. However, the after-tax returns on sales earned by the brands in the benchmark run seemed reasonable.

In the final exhibit of this section, Table 5-5, a comparison is made between the ratios of marketing expenditures to sales (for new brands) produced by the benchmark run and data supplied by Buzzell and Nourse in their study on new-product innovation in food processing.[14] Although the ratios generated by the simulation are a little on the high side, they are still quite reasonable.

In summary, it appears that the benchmark run of the model produced data that was reasonable, but not necessarily the same, as the available data on the nutritional cereal submarket and the entire cereal industry. This finding is disturbing, but it should not lead one to heavily discount the conclusions of this study. There are many people who feel that too much emphasis can be placed on the need to duplicate real-world data with the output of a simulation model. Preston and Collins, for example, have warned of the following two dangers:

(1) Simulation studies may become so heavily directed toward a goal of replication that the possibilities of exploring the properties of complex, general models may be neglected.
(2) The comparison of simulation output with some record of observed experience may come to be accepted as the only basis for evaluating simulation studies.[15]

Clearly, models of hypothetical systems can be just as useful for

[f]In 1974, Kellogg's increased the amount of nutrients of "Product 19." Thus, the firms in the cereal industry *do* consider changing the quality of their brands.

[g]The brand quality indices that were assigned to the three brands at the start of each computer run were computed by using data on the quantities of vitamins, minerals, and protein in six nutritional cereal brands ("Special K," "Life," "Total," "Fortified Oats," "Product 19," and "King Vitamin"). A brand was assigned an index of 101 if it had either (1) a total vitamin and mineral content that was one standard deviation greater than the average total vitamin and mineral content of the six brands or (2) a protein content that was one standard deviation greater than the average protein content of the six brands. Additional points were added or subtracted, if appropriate, where nutrient quantities were more (or less) standard deviations away from the averages.

Table 5-4.   **Wholesale and Retail Prices, Returns on Sales:
Benchmark Run vs. Real-World Data**

Simulated Data:	Range of Wholesale Prices per Pound	Range of Retail Prices per Pound	Range of After-Tax Returns on Sales (%)
Brand:			
Brand 1	.639 - .702	.760 - .862	9.4 - 12.4
Brand 2	.490 - .564	.625 - .725	−1.7 - 3.1
Brand 3	.630 - .671	.750 - .816	5.2 - 7.2
Brand 4	.582 - .603	.701 - .770	−0.4 - 1.9[a]
Brand 5	.583 - .602	.697 - .770	−0.1 - 0.6[a]
Brand 6	.588 - .625	.701 - .732	0.2 - 1.7[a]
Brand 7	.591 - .605	.705 - .721	8.1 - 8.2[a]
Real-World Data:			
Approximate 1966 Prices per Pound:[b]			
"Special K"	.63	.77	
"Life"	.45	.57	
"Total"	.58	.70	
"Fortified Oats"	.47	.59	
Average After-Tax Return on Sales for RTE Cereals–1964[c]			7.2

[a]Range does not include figures from the brand's test market, first, and second year.

[b]Source: Milton P. Brown *et al.*, "Life Cereal Case," *Problems in Marketing* (New York: McGraw-Hill, 1963), pp. 161-95.

[c]Source: National Commission on Food Marketing, *Studies of Organization and Competition in Grocery Manufacturing, Technical Study No. 6* (Washington, D.C.: U.S. Government Printing Office, 1966), pp. 206-07.

certain purposes as models of real systems. Since the purpose of this study was merely to *explore* the potential consequences of putting controls on advertising expenditures, a model of a hypothetical industry that was like a real-world market was felt to be adequate.

A FINAL CRITIQUE OF THE MODEL

Throughout Chapters Three, Four, and Five, the flaws of this model have received considerable attention. In this section, these flaws are given a final evaluation. Some discussion is also presented on the strong points of the model.

Ten flaws in the model stand out as being more disturbing than the

Table 5-5. New Brand Marketing Expenditures: Benchmark Run vs. Real-World Data

Simulated Data:	Ratio of First-Year Marketing Expenditures to Sales	Ratio of Second-Year Marketing Expenditures to Sales
Brand:		
Brand 4	.534	.391
Brand 5	.547	.418
Brand 6	.587	.493
Brand 7	.412	.333
Real-World Data:		
Average Ratios for New Cereal Brands–1954-1964[a]	.51	.30

[a]Source: Robert D. Buzzell and Robert E.M. Nourse, *Product Innovation in Food Processing: 1954-1964* (Cambridge, Mass.: Harvard Business School, 1967), p. 117.

others. Each of these ten flaws is listed below. Most of them have been discussed earlier, although a few are mentioned for the first time. The order in which they are presented is of no significance.

1. The brand managers in the model are only uncertain about the behavior of their rivals. The interviews suggested that real-world managers tend to be more uncertain about economic conditions and the behavior of consumers than they are about the behavior of rivals.

2. The computer running time of the model is too long. This makes it expensive to perform any experiments with the model. The lengthy search procedures that the brand managers go through seem to be responsible for the long running times. If these search procedures were shortened—which may be an appropriate step to take in making the model more realistic (see item #3 below)—then the running time could be made more acceptable.

3. The decision procedure employed by the brand managers in the model for determining marketing expenditures and prices differs somewhat from the procedures reported in the interviews. The procedure described earlier in this chapter may be a more correct approximation of real-world behavior.

4. Unlike the brand managers in the model, real-world managers do not seem to conjecture that new rivals will enter their industry when profits become high.

5. The potential rival manufacturers' submodel is too simple. Potential rivals should be allowed to consider the consequences of using several postentry marketing strategies instead of just a single strategy.

6. The retailers' submodel is too simple and it is not based on

real-world data. For one thing, retailers, and not manufacturers, should make the final decisions on retail prices somewhere in this submodel. In addition, two endogenous variables—availability and reseller support—should replace the single endogenous variable (distribution effectiveness) that is used in this submodel.

7. Industry sales in the model are sensitive to changes in only one exogenous variable—population. All other exogenous variables are assumed to always remain constant. The industry sales response function should be revised to make industry sales sensitive to changes in other exogenous variables such as price levels, advertising expenditures of close-substitute products, or GNP. In addition, consideration should be given to making other variables in the model sensitive to exogenous factors.

8. In the market-share response function used in the model, the sensitivity parameter assigned to price is probably too high and the parameter assigned to consumer-directed promotion is probably too low. It might also be necessary to allow all of the parameters to take on different values at different stages of the product life cycle.

9. The brand managers in the model abandon their brands if specific market share levels are not reached. They do this no matter how large industry sales might grow. The abandonment rule should be revised to allow managers to lower their minimum acceptable share level if industry sales grow substantially.

10. The benchmark run does only a fair job of replicating available real-world data on the nutritional cereal submarket and the entire ready-to-eat cereal industry.

These flaws have been pointed out so that public policy makers or other individuals will know where to turn in revising the model. Although it is felt that the model, in spite of its flaws, is a reasonably valid approximation of a grocery manufacturing industry and that its predictions are therefore fairly accurate and useful, it is recognized that the model needs further development and refinement before policy decisions can be made based on its predictions.

It should be noted that the model used in this study, even with its flaws, represents an improvement over many models of oligopolistic behavior that have appeared in the economics literature. The model is more realistic than many of the models from economics since it has oligopolists making decisions in seven major marketing areas rather than in just one or two. Although it is important to keep models simple, sometimes they can be made too simple to be useful to public policy makers, business decision makers, or anyone else.

Before concluding this critique, mention should be made of one other potential flaw in the model. It is possible that the *act* of introducing controls on advertising expenditures might disturb an entire industry so much that major changes would occur in people's basic behavior patterns. Manufacturers might develop totally new objectives, potential rivals might begin to look at entry in a completely different way, and retailers and consumers might start to respond differently to manufacturers and to each other. The possibility that controls on advertising expenditures could inspire major changes in basic behavior patterns should, of course, be kept in mind while reading the final conclusions of this study. These conclusions are presented in the next chapter.

SUMMARY

The validity of the model that was used in this study must be tested before one can judge the accuracy of the predictions of the last chapter. The validation procedure used was tailored to the specific needs and characteristics of this study. The three steps of the validation procedure discussed in this chapter are (1) the viability run, (2) the personal interviews, and (3) the comparison of the output of the benchmark run to real-world data.

The viability run contained an eight-year extension of the benchmark run. During these eight years, the model was found to produce results that were reasonable and nonexplosive. By the end of this run, the industry had reached the late-maturity stage of its life cycle and only two firms, marketing two brands apiece, had survived. All four surviving brands were earning good profits.

The personal interviews tested the face validity and predictive validity of the model. Respondents were asked about the process used by brand managers in making decisions and about several other subjects. The findings of the interviews provided a reasonable amount of support for the model. However, four flaws in the model were discovered as a result of the interviews. These flaws had to do with (1) the decision procedures used by the brand managers; (2) the assumption about the uncertainty faced by the brand manager; (3) the conjectures about potential rivals made by brand managers; and (4) the size of the parameters in the market-share response function.

The output of the benchmark run of the model did only a fair job of matching available real-world data on the nutritional cereal submarket and the entire ready-to-eat cereal industry. However, the output of the benchmark run was still quite reasonable.

Ten flaws in the model that appeared to be more disturbing than the others were cited at the end of this chapter. In the future, these flaws should be corrected. The revised model could then be used to make more accurate predictions about the competitive consequences of controlling advertising expenditures than the predictions made in this study.

NOTES TO CHAPTER FIVE

1. Richard L. Van Horn, "Validation of Simulation Results," *Management Science* (January 1971), p. 248.

2. Thomas H. Naylor and J.M. Finger, "Validation," in Thomas H.

Naylor, *Computer Simulation Experiments with Models of Economic Systems* (New York: Wiley, 1971), Ch. 5.

3. Ibid., p. 157.

4. Charles P. Bonini, *Simulation of Information and Decision Systems in the Firm* (Englewood Cliffs, N.J.: Prentice-Hall, 1963), p. 22.

5. Naylor and Finger, "Validation," p. 157.

6. Van Horn, "Validation," p. 251.

7. Naylor and Finger, "Validation," p. 158.

8. A.M. Turing, "Computing Machinery and Intelligence," *MIND* (October 1950), pp. 433-60.

9. Milton P. Brown et al., "Life Cereal Case," *Problems in Marketing* (New York: McGraw-Hill, 1968), pp. 161-95.

10. John C. Maxwell, "Cereals," *Marketing Communications* (March 1970), p. 37 ff.; and John C. Maxwell, "Cold Cereals Industry Goes Through Growth Year," *Advertising Age* (March 26, 1973), p. 3.

11. Brown et al., "Life."

12. *National Advertising Investments* (New York: Leading National Advertisers, 1965-1972).

13. National Commission on Food Marketing, *Studies of Organization and Competition in Grocery Manufacturing, Technical Study No. 6* (Washington, D.C.: U.S. Government Printing Office, 1966).

14. Robert D. Buzzell and Robert E.M. Nourse, *Product Innovation in Food Processing: 1954-1964* (Cambridge, Mass.: Harvard Business School, 1967).

15. Lee E. Preston and Norman R. Collins, *Studies in a Simulated Market* (Berkeley: Institute of Business Economic Research, 1966), p. 1.

Chapter Six

Conclusions, Implications, and Future Directions

The major conclusions that can be drawn from this study are presented in this chapter. The implications of these conclusions are also discussed. At the end of the chapter, some suggestions are made of areas where future research could be conducted that would build upon what has been done in this study.

CONCLUSIONS

Because of a shortage of past systematic research that has examined the competitive consequences of controlling advertising expenditures, this study was designed to be exploratory. As such, its conclusions could only be expected to be tentative. Nevertheless, it is felt that the simulation model that was used has enough validity to make the following conclusions worthy of the attention of public policy makers and others concerned about the competitive effects of advertising.

The results of the computer runs and the validation steps that were carried out during this study indicate that if certain types of controls on advertising expenditures were introduced in a growing, oligopolistic industry with unequal-sized firms and nonincreasing returns to advertising, it is unlikely that vigorous competition would develop. More specifically, it appears that:

1. A straight tax on advertising could discourage new rivals from entering the industry and could also be more of a burden to small firms than large firms.
2. A progressive tax of 2 percent per million dollars spent on advertising *might* lead to a small increase in competition. However, the more sensitive industry sales are to advertising, the less likely it is that this tax would stimulate increased competition.
3. A limit on the advertising-sales ratio could penalize the small firms in the industry more than the large firms. It could also encourage competitive

activity that would help large firms at the expense of small firms. Furthermore, if the limit were set too low, it could discourage new rivals from entering the industry even if they were given a three-year exemption from the limit.

4. A dollar limit on advertising expenditures could lead to competitive activity that would help large firms at the expense of small firms.

5. A depreciation requirement for advertising could encourage firms to spend much more on advertising, and it could also discourage new rivals from entering the industry.[a]

None of these controls appear to have the ability to eliminate the advantage that large firms with strong corporate images have in getting effective distribution for their brands. In fact, some of the controls could amplify this advantage.[b] Without controls, the simulated industry became a duopoly with rather stable sales in the long run. With controls, the industry's progression toward becoming a duopoly was not sidetracked and, in some cases, was accelerated.

The above conclusions are not stated in more certain terms because the model that was used in this study has a number of flaws. These flaws are listed at the end of Chapter Five. Without actually repairing these flaws and repeating the computer runs, it is impossible to tell how much they influence the predictions of the model. However, it is felt that none of these flaws should lead one to reject the above statements as highly plausible hypotheses in need of further systematic testing.

Of course, it must be noted that the controls on advertising expenditures that were tested in this study might work differently in other types of industries. For example, these controls might help prevent a mature industry made up of numerous, equal-sized firms from drifting toward oligopoly. It is also possible that other types of controls, such as a very steep progressive tax or a limit on the advertising-sales ratio that exempts firms below a certain size might do an excellent job of encouraging competition in an industry. However, in this study, it was only possible to explore how a few controls on advertising expenditures would affect competition in growing industries that have unequal-sized firms and nonincreasing returns to advertising.

---

[a]The effects of a depreciation requirement would probably be different if brand managers were to become concerned about the cash flows generated by their brands. However, the findings of the interviews that were conducted in this study indicate that brand managers are not very concerned about cash flows.

[b]Bauer and Greyser came to a similar conclusion in their short examination of the effects of limiting advertising expenditures. They stated: "On the whole it would seem that any patterns of restriction on the level of advertising expenditure would *benefit* the dominant firm in any market." They felt that firms in entrenched positions with dealers would not be hurt by any limits. See Raymond A. Bauer and Stephen A. Greyser, *Advertising in America: The Consumer View* (Boston: Harvard Business School, 1968), p. 375.

There is one other important conclusion to be drawn from this study: computer simulation experiments *can* be useful in exploring the potential effects of public policy changes and in studying oligopolistic behavior. Even if one is unwilling to accept the validity of the model that was used, one should agree that this study has shown that it is definitely possible to build a computer simulation model of an industry that can yield interesting, valuable, and sometimes counterintuitive insights. Thus, at the very least, this study has demonstrated an approach that someone with access to a rich data base could use to make accurate predictions of the consequences of controlling expenditures on advertising.

IMPLICATIONS

The conclusions of this study imply that there is a need for public policy makers to be extremely cautious about using controls on advertising expenditures as a means of encouraging competition in oligopolistic industries. Aside from the administrative problems and enforcement costs that controls on advertising expenditures could be expected to generate, there is a strong possibility that controls of this type would simply not work. Competition could be suppressed rather than stimulated. Policy makers should, therefore, systematically study all the consequences of putting controls on advertising expenditures—preferably by using a computer simulation approach similar to the one used in this study— before any industries are required to pay taxes on, limit, or depreciate their advertising expenditures.

The conclusions of this study also imply that public policy makers should look to actions other than putting controls on advertising expenditures as ways to encourage competition in manufacturing industries. Advertising controls of any type may not be able to break down the strong franchise that certain manufacturers—particularly certain grocery products manufacturers—have with their dealers. In order to find a way to break down this franchise and possibly encourage more competition in some industries as a result, policy makers should develop a better understanding of vertical marketing relationships. For example, the relationship between the giant chain stores and the giant grocery manufacturers needs to be analyzed. What causes the firm-loyal buying patterns of the chain stores? Why are some manufacturers continually given better shelf locations, more shelf space, and better retail advertising by chain stores? How sensitive are chain stores to the various marketing strategies that can be used by manufacturers? What can public policy makers do to make chain stores less firm loyal? These are questions to which policy makers should seek answers. Unfortunately, there has been very little reported research that has explored these issues.[c]

---

[c]Four of the few empirical studies that have examined the relationship between manufacturers and chain stores are David B. Montogomery, "New Product

FUTURE DIRECTIONS

The most obvious follow-up to this study would involve correcting the flaws in the model—especially those listed at the end of Chapter Five. Access to a large amount of real-world data on a grocery manufacturing industry should be obtained, and this data should then be used to revise the model's response functions. Furthermore, additional interviews should be conducted with real-world brand managers to help refine the decision process that brand managers go through in the model. Interviews should also be conducted with chain store executives and potential entrants to the industry to help refine the retailers' submodel and the potential rivals' submodel. When a valid model has finally been constructed, the hypotheses generated by this study should be tested.

Another direction for further research would be to build models of other types of industries. Industries that have equal-sized firms, that are not in a growth stage, or that are not made up of grocery manufacturers should be modeled. These models could then be used to test not only controls on advertising expenditures, but also proposed measures such as a graduated corporate income tax.[d] The models could also be used to gain insights into the *unregulated* behavior of firms in different kinds of industries.

In the long run, revisions and extensions of the model used in this study, and of others like it, could lead to the development of a simulation model that could easily be adapted to almost any industry by making a few changes in its structure, parameters, or input data. Such a model could be tremendously useful to public policy makers, marketing managers, and consumers. Policy makers could use it to pretest changes in policy; marketing managers could use it to predict how their rivals are going to behave in various situations; and consumers could use it to help them understand the behavior of sellers—which could, in turn, help them to become more efficient buyers. Clearly, the development of this type of general model of *marketer* behavior (or marketing theory of the firm) is a goal that researchers in the field of marketing should seek to attain.[e] This study should help these researchers in their efforts to attain this goal.

Distribution: An Analysis of Supermarket Buyer Decisions," a paper presented at the 1973 American Marketing Association Doctoral Consortium, Michigan State University, August 1973; Leonard J. Parsons, "An Econometric Analysis of Advertising, Retail Availability, and Sales of a New Brand," *Management Science* (February 1974), pp. 938-47; George H. Haines and Alvin J. Silk, "Does Consumer Advertising Increase Retail Availability of a New Product?" *Journal of Advertising Research* (September 1967), pp. 9-15; and Michael E. Porter, "Consumer Behavior, Retailer Power and Market Performance in Consumer Goods Industries," *Review of Economics and Statistics* (November 1974), pp. 419-36.

[d]Such a tax is proposed in Julian L. Simon, "Antitrust and the 'Size' Problem: The Graduated Corporate Income Tax as an Anti-Bigness Device," *Antitrust Law and Economics Review* (Winter 1972-73), pp. 53-66.

[e]For a more elaborate discussion of this point, see Paul N. Bloom, "Toward a Model of Marketer Behavior in Oligopolistic Industries," in Edward Mazze, ed., *1975 Combined Proceedings* (Chicago: American Marketing Association, 1976).

Appendixes

Appendix A:

The Computer Program

The computer program used in the study is found on the following pages. The program contains one main program and ten subroutines. The program is written in FORTRAN IV. Numerous comment cards are found throughout the program to help make it easier to understand. In addition, the key variables used in the program are defined in Table 3-1.

```
                  PROGRAM ADREG (INPUT,OUTPUT)
000003            DIMENSION  NDROP(30),LOOK(20),PVO(20),NO(20,30),NEW(20,30),
                 1X1(7),YA(20),YCP(20),YDP(20),YSC(20),YR(20),YPW(20),YPR(20),H(20,3
                 20),PV1(20)
000003            COMMON  NF(30),FZ(20,30),N(30),LIVE(20,30),NBRND(30),ID(20),
                 1 NAGE(20,30),CI(20,30),NFRM(30),A(20,30),CP(20,30),DP(20,30),
                 2 SC(20,30),B(20,30),PW(20,30),PR(20,30),P(7,20),SB(20,30),
                 3 VC(20,30),FC(20,30),Q(20,30),TA(30),TCP(30),APR(30),FSR(20,30),
                 4 FA(20,30),CC(20,30),D(20,30),R(20,30),EFFORT(20,30),SHARE(20,30),
                 5 SI(30),Z(20,30),M,SIGN,VL,NUMB,NOLD,NX,LIM,SID(30),SAT,IDF(20),
                 6 MOLD,AG(20,30),TAG(30),POP(30),FSH(20,30),KX,EPR,EA,ECP,ER,ED,
                 7 EREV,ESC,DIV,ADREV,ECI
               C  **** READ IN DATA, INITIALIZE VARIABLES **********************
000003            READ 999,JEND,SAT,LIM,G,MOLD,JCON
000023        999 FORMAT(I2,F10.2,I2,F3.2,2I2)
000023            READ 300,(N(J),J=1,7)
000035        300 FORMAT(/I2)
000036            DO 310  J=1,4
000037            NDROP(J)=0
000040            NBRND(J)=0
000041            NFRM(J)=0
000042            NF(J)=N(J)
000044            NA=N(J+3)
000045            DO 310  I=1,NA
000047            LIVE(I,J)=0
000052            NO(I,J)=0
000055            NEW(I,J)=0
000057            H(I,J)=0
000062            READ  2,ID(I),NAGE(I,J),IDF(I),A(I,J),CP(I,J),DP(I,J),SC(I,J),
                 1B(I,J),PW(I,J),PR(I,J),CI(I,J),SHARE(I,J),FSH(I,J),D(I,J),Z(I,J),
                 2SB(I,J)
000135          2 FORMAT(I2,2X,2I2,2X,5F10.2,2F10.3,/,F5.1,3F5.3,3F10.2,F12.2)
000145            IF(I,LE,N(J)) LIVE(I,J)=1
000153        310 CONTINUE
000160            SI(2)=50000000.00
000161            TAG(2)=4900000.
000163            TCP(2)=750000.
000164            APR(2)=.66
000166            READ 400,(POP(J),J=2,30),EPR,EA,ECP,ER,ED,EREV,ESC,DIV,ADREV,ECI
000223        400 FORMAT(8F10.0,/,8F10.0,/,8F10.0,/,5F10.0,5F5.2,/,2F5.2,F5.1,F10.2,
                 1F5.2)
000223            PRINT 401,EPR,EA,ECP,ER,ED,EREV,ESC,DIV,ADREV,SAT,G,ECI
000237        401 FORMAT(1H1,30X,*PARAMETERS*,//,4X,*EPR*,10X,*EA*,9X,*ECP*,10X,*ER*
                 1,10X,*ED*,9X,*EREV*,8X,*ESC*,9X,*DIV*,8X,*ADREV*,//,9F12.2,//,4X,*
                 2SAT*,10X,*G*,12X,*ECI*,//,3F12.2)
000257            PRINT 1
000263          1 FORMAT(1H1,35X,*DATA ON POTENTIAL ENTRANTS*,//,25X,*ACTUAL BEHAVIO
                 1R*,40X,*CONJECTURED BEHAVIOR*,//,20X,*TYPE OF*,12X,*NET PRESENT*,/
                 2,20X,*ENTRANT*,12X,*VALUE OF ENTRY*,/)
000263            NX=0
000264            LREG=0
000265            J=3
000266            CALL PROFITS (I,J)
000270            J=4
000271            CALL PROFITS(I,J)
000273            NUMB=NF(J)
000275            NOLD=NF(J)
               C  **** START OF YEAR *****************************************
000277         10 J=J+1
000301            IF(J.EQ.JCON) LREG=1
000304            N(J)=N(J-1)
000306            NF(J)=NF(J-1)
000310            NDROP(J)=0
000311            NBRND(J)=0
000312            NFRM(J)=0
000313            I=0
000314            KX=0
000315            L=J
000316            GO TO 26
               C  **** CONJECTURES MADE ABOUT POTENTIAL RIVALS ****************
000316         25 CALL ENTRY1(L)
000320         26 NA=N(L)
               C  **** START LOOP WHERE CONJECTURES MADE ABOUT EXISTING RIVALS *****
000322            DO 20  K=1,NA
               C  **** IS BRAND K ALIVE *************************************
000324            H(K,J)=0
```

```
000327              IF(LIVE(K,L-1).EQ.1) GO TO 14
000333              LIVE(K,L)=0
000336              GO TO 20
000336          14  LIVE(K,L)=1
000342              NAGE(K,L)=NAGE(K,L-1)+1
000347              IF(K.EQ.I) GO TO 12
000351              IF(L.GT.J) GO TO 35
         C          **** SHOULD BRAND BE KILLED ***********************************
000354              NC=NAGE(K,L)
000356              IF(NC.GT.4) NC=4
000361              GO TO (31,32,33,34),NC
000371          31  IF(SHARE(K,L-1).GE.0.001) GO TO 35
000376              LIVE(K,L)=0
000401              GO TO 20
000401          32  IF(SHARE(K,L-1).GE.0.03) GO TO 35
000406              GO TO 36
000407          33  IF(SHARE(K,L-1).GE.0.05) GO TO 35
000414              GO TO 36
000415          34  IF(SHARE(K,L-1).GE.0.07) GO TO 35
000422              GO TO 36
000423          35  IF(NAGE(K,L).LT.5) GO TO 11
000430              IF(L.EQ.J) GO TO 13
000432              IF(NAGE(K,L).EQ.5) CALL PARAM (K,L)
000437              GO TO 12
000440          13  IF(Z(K,L-1).GT.0.0) GO TO 18
000445              IF(Z(K,L-2).GT.0.0) GO TO 18
000451              IF(Z(K,L-3).GT.0.0) GO TO 18
000455              IF(Z(K,L-4).GT.0.0) GO TO 18
000461          36  LIVE(K,L)=0
000465              NDROP(L)=NDROP(L)+1
000467              GO TO 20
000467          18  IF(IDF(K).GT.1) MOLD=MOLD+1
000473              IF(IDF(K).GT.1) H(K,J)=IDF(K)
000502              IF(IDF(K).GT.1) IDF(K)=1
000506              GO TO 21
         C          **** DETERMINE CONJECTURED MIX OF K FOR YEAR L ****************
000507          11  CALL FIRST(K,L)
000511              GO TO 19
000512          21  CALL PARAM (K,L)
000514          12  CALL MIX (K,L)
         C          **** CHECK FOR AD LIMITATION *********************************
000516          19  IF(LIM.LT.5) GO TO 20
000521              LIMP=LIM-4
000523              GO TO (301,302,303),LIMP
000531         301  IF(A(K,L).GT.3000000.) A(K,L)=3000000.
000541              GO TO 305
000542         302  CRIT=.10*SB(K,L-1)
000547              GO TO 304
000547         303  CRIT=.20*SB(K,L-1)
000554         304  IF(NAGE(K,L).LT.4) GO TO 20
000561              IF(A(K,L).GT.CRIT) A(K,L)=CRIT
000570         305  IF(L.EQ.J) P(1,K)=A(K,L)/SB(K,L-1)
000602          20  CONTINUE
         C          **** COMPUTE EXPECTED PROFITS FOR YEAR L *********************
000605          30  CALL PROFITS (I,L)
000607              IF(L.EQ.J+3) GO TO 40
000612              L=L+1
         C          **** MAKE CONJECTURES FOUR YEARS INTO FUTURE *****************
000613              GO TO 25
000614          40  L=J
000616              IF(I.GT.0) GO TO 55
         C          **** FIND BRANDS THAT WILL UNDERGO SEARCH ********************
000620              NA=N(J)
000621              DO 5    K=1,NA
000622              IF(LIVE(K,J).EQ.0) GO TO 50
000625              CC(K,J)=0.10
000630              AVZ=Z(K,J-1)
000633              IF(NAGE(K,J).GT.4) GO TO 45
000640              NC=NAGE(K,J)
000642              GO TO (42,42,43,44), NC
000652          42  LOOK(K)=3
000654              GO TO 50
000655          45  IF(Z(K,J-4).GT.AVZ) AVZ=Z(K,J-4)
000665          44  IF(Z(K,J-3).GT.AVZ) AVZ=Z(K,J-3)
000675          43  IF(Z(K,J-2).GT.AVZ) AVZ=Z(K,J-2)
000705              ZMIN=.05*SB(K,J-1)
```

```
000712          IF(AVZ.LT.ZMIN) AVZ=ZMIN
000715          PVY(K)=(AVZ*(1.+G))/(1.+CC(K,J))+(AVZ*(1.+G)**2.)/((1.+CC(K,J))**2
               1.)+(AVZ*(1.+G)**3.)/((1.+CC(K,J))**3.)+(AVZ*(1.+G)**4.)/((1.+CC(K,
               2J))**4.)
000752          PV=(Z(K,J)/(1.+CC(K,J))+(Z(K,J+1)/((1.+CC(K,J))**2.))+(Z(K,J+2)/(
               1(1.+CC(K,J))**3.))+(Z(K,J+3)/((1.+CC(K,J))**4.))
001017          PVL(K)=PV
001021          IF(PV.GE.PV0(K)) GO TO 49
001023          LOOK(K)=1
001024          GO TO 50
001025       49 LOOK(K)=2
001027       50 CONTINUE
001032       52 I=I+1
001034          IF(I.GT.N(J)) GO TO 80
001037          IF(LIVE(I,J).EQ.0) GO TO 52
001041          NO(I,J)=0
001044          NEW(I,J)=0
001046          NSRCH=0
001047          NC=LOOK(I)
001051          GO TO (53,63,99), NC
            C    **** BEGIN SEARCH PROCEDURE FOR ESTABLISHED BRAND I *************
001057       53 IF(NAGE(I,J).GT.4) GO TO 57
001065          LZ=J+1
001066          CALL PARAM (I,LZ)
001070       57 DO 54  M=1,7
001072       54 X1(M)=P(M,I)
001101          M=7
001102          LAST=2
001103          PL=P(M,I)
001106          PVL=PVL(I)
001110          PV=PVL
001111          GO TO 56
            C    **** COMPUTE PRESENT VALUE OF EXPECTED PROFITS ****************
001111       55 PV=(Z(I,J)/(1.+CC(I,J)))+(Z(I,J+1)/((1.+CC(I,J)**2.))+(Z(I,J+2)/(
               1(1.+CC(I,J))**3.))+(Z(I,J+3)/((1.+CC(I,J))**4.))
            C    **** IS IT A SATISFACTORY MIX ***********************
001146          IF(PV.GE.PV0(I)) GO TO 69
001151       56 NO(I,J)=NO(I,J)+1
            C    **** IF LAST STEP AN IMPROVEMENT, REPEAT *****************
001156          IF(PV.GT.PVL) GO TO 65
001161          IF(NO(I,J).GE.75) GO TO 64
001166          NSRCH=NSRCH+1
001167          IF(NSRCH.EQ.15) GO TO 50
            C    **** IF LAST STEP NO IMPROVEMENT, SWITCH DIRECTION OR TRY ANOTHER*
001171          GO TO (62,63,63), LAST
001200       62 P(M,I)=PL-0.01
001205          IF(P(M,I).LE.0.0) P(M,I)=0.01
001212          PLIM=X1(M)-.20
001215          IF(P(M,I).LT.PLIM) P(M,I)=PLIM
001223          CALL REVISE (I,J)
001225          LAST=2
001226          GO TO 30
            C    **** SWITCH DIRECTION ****************************************
001227       63 P(M,I)=PL
001233          CALL REVISE (I,J)
001235          IF(M.EQ.7) M=0
001240          M=M+1
001242          PL=P(M,I)
001245          P(M,I)=PL+0.01
001250          PLIM=X1(M)+.20
001252          IF(P(M,I).GT.PLIM) P(M,I)=PLIM
001260          CALL REVISE (I,J)
001262          LAST=1
001263          GO TO 30
001264       64 P(M,I)=PL
001270          CALL REVISE (I,J)
001272          GO TO 69
001273       65 NSRCH=0
001274          PL=P(M,I)
001300          PVL=PV
001301          GO TO (66,67,66), LAST
            C    **** SEARCH IN POSITIVE DIRECTION ***************************
001310       66 P(M,I)=PL+0.01
001315          PLIM=X1(M)+.20
001317          IF(P(M,I).GT.PLIM) P(M,I)=PLIM
001325          CALL REVISE (I,J)
```

```
001327          LAST=3
001330          GO TO 30
        C       **** SEARCH IN NEGATIVE DIRECTION ****************************
001331   67     P(M,I)=PL-0.01
001336          IF(P(M,I).LE.0.0) P(M,I)=0.01
001343          PLIM=X1(M)-.20
001346          IF(P(M,I).LT.PLIM) P(M,I)=PLIM
001354          CALL REVISE (I,J)
001356          LAST = 2
001357          GO TO 30
        C       **** BEGIN SEARCH PROCEDURE FOR NEW BRAND I ****************
001360   99     CALL PROFITS (I,J)
001362          IF(Z(I,J).GT.0.0) GO TO 69
001367          NEW(I,J)=NEW(I,J)+1
001372          IF(NEW(I,J).GT.1) GO TO 110
001376          M=7
001377          VL=B(I,J)
001402          ZL=Z(I,J)
001405          LAST=2
001406          NX=1
001407   110    IF(Z(I,J).GT.ZL) GO TO 150
001415          NSRCH=NSRCH+1
001416          IF(NSRCH.EQ.14) GO TO 140
001420          IF(NEW(I,J).GE.75) GO TO 140
001424          GO TO (120,130,130), LAST
001433   120    NINC=0
001434          SIGN=-1.
001436          CALL FIX(I,J)
001440          LAST=2
001441          GO TO 99
001442   130    NINC=0
001443          SIGN=0.0
001444          CALL FIX (I,J)
001446          IF(M.EQ.7) M=0
001451          M=M+1
001453          CALL UPDATE (I,J)
001455          SIGN=1.
001457          CALL FIX (I,J)
001461          LAST=1
001462          GO TO 99
001463   140    SIGN=0.
001464          CALL FIX (I,J)
001466          GO TO 69
001467   150    NSRCH=0
001470          NINC=NINC+1
001472          CALL UPDATE (I,J)
001474          ZL=Z(I,J)
001500          IF(NINC.EQ.5) GO TO 130
001502          GO TO (160,170,160), LAST
001511   160    SIGN=1.
001513          CALL FIX (I,J)
001515          LAST=3
001516          GO TO 99
001517   170    SIGN=-1.
001521          CALL FIX(I,J)
001523          LAST=2
001524          GO TO 99
        C       **** STORE MIX SELECTED IN SEARCH ****************************
001525   69     YA(I)=A(I,J)
001531          YCP(I)=CP(I,J)
001534          YDP(I)=DP(I,J)
001537          YSC(I)=SC(I,J)
001542          YB(I)=B(I,J)
001545          YPW(I)=PW(I,J)
001550          YPR(I)=PR(I,J)
001553          IF(LOOK(I).EQ.3) GO TO 75
001555          IF(LREG.EQ.1) GO TO 71
001557          L1=J+1
001561          L2=J+2
001563          L3=J+3
        C       **** PRINT CONJECTURES MADE ABOUT POTENTIAL RIVALS ***********
001565          PRINT 800,J,I,L1,NBRND(L1),L2,NBRND(L2),L3,NBRND(L3)
001610   800    FORMAT(60X,*IN YEAR*,I3,4X,*BY BRAND*,I3,*ABOUT YEAR*,I3,*NEW BRAN
               1DS EXPECTED*/95X,I3,19X,I3//95X,I3,19X,I3)
001610   71     IF(NO(I,J).EQ.0) GO TO 75
        C       **** BRING BACK CONJECTURED PARAMETERS AND MIX **************
```

```
001614          DO 70  M=1,7
001615       70 P(M,I)=X1(M)
001624          CALL MIX (I,J)
001626          GO TO 52
001627       75 IF(NEW(I,J).EQ.0) GO TO 52
001633          CALL FIRST (I,J)
001635          IF(LIM.EQ.5) CALL ADLIM(I,J)
001641          NX=0
001642          GO TO 52
         C    **** GO ON TO ANOTHER BRAND *********************************
         C    **** IF CONTROL INTRODUCED THIS YEAR, OTHER CONJECTURES MADE *****
001643       80 IF(LREG.EQ.0) GO TO 81
001644          LREG=0
001645          NA=N(J)
001647          DO 82  I=1,NA
001650          IF(LIVE(I,J).EQ.0) GO TO 82
001653          A(I,J)=YA(I)
001656          CP(I,J)=YCP(I)
001662          DP(I,J)=YDP(I)
001665          SC(I,J)=YSC(I)
001671          B(I,J)=YB(I)
001674          PW(I,J)=YPW(I)
001700          PR(I,J)=YPR(I)
001703          IF(NAGE(I,J).LT.3) GO TO 82
001710          LZ=J+1
001712          CALL PARAM (I,LZ)
001714       82 CONTINUE
001717          L=J
001720          I=0
001721          GO TO 30
         C    **** WILL A NEW BRAND ACTUALLY ENTER ************************
001721       81 CALL ENTRY2 (J)
         C    **** BRING BACK ACTUAL DECISIONS ***************************
001723          NA=N(J)-NBRND(J)
001726          DO 90  I=1,NA
001727          IF(LIVE(I,J).EQ.0) GO TO 90
001732          A(I,J)=YA(I)
001735          CP(I,J)=YCP(I)
001741          DP(I,J)=YDP(I)
001744          SC(I,J)=YSC(I)
001750          B(I,J)=YB(I)
001753          PW(I,J)=YPW(I)
001757          PR(I,J)=YPR(I)
001752       90 CONTINUE
         C    **** COMPUTE ACTUAL PROFITS, ETC. FOR YEAR J ******************
001765          CALL PROFITS (I,J)
001767          IF(NBRND(J).EQ.0) GO TO 700
001771          NA=N(J)-NBRND(J)+1
001773          NB=N(J)
001775          DO 600  I=NA,NB
001777          B(I,J)=0
002002          NO(I,J)=0
002005          NEW(I,J)=0
002007          IF(SHARE(I,J).GE.0.001) GO TO 600
002013          NDROP(J)=NDROP(J)+1
002015      600 CONTINUE
         C    **** GO TO ANOTHER YEAR ***********************************
002020      700 IF(J.LT.JEND) GO TO 10
         C    **** PRINT INDUSTRY DATA **********************************
002023          PRINT 410
002026      410 FORMAT(1H1,52X,*INDUSTRY DATA*,//,20X,*SALES*,4X,*ADVERTISING*,6X,
                1*CONSUMER*,2X,*AVERAGE PRICE    AD GOODWILL  NUMBER OF  NUMBER OF
                2 NUMBER OF*,/,20X,*LBS*,22X,*DIRECTED*,32X,*NEW BRANDS NEW FIRMS
                3 EXITS*,/,46X,*PROMOTION*,/)
002026          DO 405  J=3,JEND
002030          PRINT 420,J,SI(J),TA(J),TCP(J),APR(J),TAG(J),NBRND(J),NFRM(J),
                1NDROP(J)
002055      420 FORMAT(3X,*YEAR*,I3,3F15.2,F15.4,F15.2,I8,2I11)
002055      405 CONTINUE
         C    **** PRINT BRAND DATA *************************************
002060          NA=N(JEND)
002061          DO 430  I=1,NA
002063          PRINT 440,I,ID(I)
002073      440 FORMAT(1H1,45X,*DATA ON BRAND*,I3,* OF FIRMS*,I3,//,22X,*SALES*,8X,*P
                1ROFITS    DOLLAR SALES    POUND SALES    MARKET SHARE  VARIABLE COST
```

```
                   2    FIXED COST*,/)
002072                  DO 450  J=3,JEND
002074                  IF(I.GT.N(J)) GO TO 450
002100                  IF(LIVE(I,J).EQ.0) GO TO 455
002102                  PRINT 460,J,NAGE(I,J),Z(I,J),SB(I,J),Q(I,J),SHARE(I,J),VC(I,J),
                   1FC(I,J)
002137          460 FORMAT(3X,*YEAR*,I3,I15,3F15.2,2F15.5,F15.2)
002137          450 CONTINUE
002142          455 PRINT 470
002146          470 FORMAT(//,47X,*MARKETING MIX DECISIONS*,//,12X,*ADVERTISING*,7X,
                   1*C-D PROMOTION*,7X,*D-D PROMOTION*,9X,*SALES CALLS*,7X,*BRAND QUAL
                   2ITY    W-S PRICE    R-T PRICE*,/)
002146                  DO 480  J=3,JEND
002150                  IF(I.GT.N(J)) GO TO 480
002154                  IF(LIVE(I,J).EQ.0) GO TO 485
002156                  ASR=A(I,J)/SB(I,J)
002163                  CPSR=CP(I,J)/SB(I,J)
002166                  DPSR=DP(I,J)/SB(I,J)
002170                  SCSR=SC(I,J)/SB(I,J)
002173                  PRINT 490,J,A(I,J),ASR,CP(I,J),CPSR,DP(I,J),DPSR,SC(I,J),SCSR,
                   1B(I,J),PW(I,J),PR(I,J)
002235          490 FORMAT(2X,*YEAR*,I3,4(F13.2,F7.3),F13.2,2F13.4)
002235                  IF(NAGE(I,J).LT.2) GO TO 430
002242                  P1=A(I,J)/SB(I,J-1)
002247                  P2=CP(I,J)/SB(I,J-1)
002252                  P3=DP(I,J)/SB(I,J-1)
002254                  P4=SC(I,J)/SB(I,J-1)
002257                  P5=B(I,J)/B(I,J-1)
002261                  P6=PW(I,J)/APR(J-1)
002264                  P7=PR(I,J)/APR(J-1)
002266                  PRINT 900,P1,P2,P3,P4,P5,P6,P7
002307          900 FORMAT(4F20.3,14X,3F13.3)
002307          480 CONTINUE
002312          485 PRINT 500
002316          500 FORMAT(//,14X,*ADVERTISING  CORPORATE*,     4X,      *DISTRIBUTI
                   1ON  MKTG EFFORT  LENGTH OF  TYPE OF*,/,14X,*GOODWILL
                   2  IMAGE*,             36X,*SEARCH  SEARCH-NEW FIRM*,/)
002316                  DO 510  J=3,JEND
002320                  IF(I.GT.N(J)) GO TO 510
002324                  IF(LIVE(I,J).EQ.0) GO TO 430
002326                  PRINT 520,J,AG(I,J),CI(I,J),        D(I,J),EFFORT(I,J),NO(I,J),NEW(
                   1I,J),IDF(I),H(I,J)
002365          520 FORMAT(2X,*YEAR*,I3,F15.2,F10.2,    F15.3,E15.4,3I10,I2)
002365          510 CONTINUE
002370          430 CONTINUE
            C       **** PRINT FIRM DATA ******************************************
002373                  PRINT 3
002376            3 FORMAT(1H1)
002376                  NA=NF(JEND)
002400                  DO 550  MF=1,NA
002402                  PRINT 540,MF
002407          540 FORMAT(//, 52X,*DATA ON FIRM*,I3,//,10X,*INDUSTRY SALES  IN DOLLARS
                   1   DOLLAR SALES      SHARE*,9X,*PROFITS      ADVERTISING*)
002407                  DO 530  J=3,JEND
002411                  IF(MF.GT.NF(J)) GO TO 530
002415                  PRINT 560,J,SID(J),FSB(MF,J),FSH(MF,J),FZ(MF,J),FA(MF,J)
002442          560 FORMAT(3X,*YEAR*,I3,10X,3F15.2,F15.4,3F15.2)
002442          530 CONTINUE
002445          550 CONTINUE
002447                  STOP
002451                  END


                   SUBROUTINE  PROFITS (I,J)
000005                 DIMENSION DREV(20,30),DE(30)
000005                 COMMON  NF(30),FZ(20,30),N(30),LIVE(20,30),NBRND(30),ID(20),
                   1 NAGE(20,30),CI(20,30),NFRM(30),A(20,30),CP(20,30),DP(20,30),
                   2 SC(20,30),B(20,30),PW(20,30),PR(20,30),P(7,20),SB(20,30),
                   3 VC(20,30),FC(20,30),Q(20,30),TA(30),TCP(30),APR(30),FSB(20,30),
                   4 FA(20,30),CC(20,30),D(20,30),R(20,30),EFFORT(20,30),SHARE(20,30),
                   5 SI(30),Z(20,30),M,SIGN,VL,NUMB,NOLD,NX,LIM,SID(30),SAT,IDF(20),
                   6 MOLD,AG(20,30),TAG(30),POP(30),FSH(20,30),KX,EPR,EA,ECP,ER,ED,
                   7 EREV,ESC,DIV,ADREV,ECI
            C       **** COMPUTES EXPECTED AND ACTUAL BRAND PROFITS ****************
```

```
         C     **** INITIALIZE VARIABLES ***********************************
000005         TA(J)=0.0
000006         TCP(J)=0.0
000007         TPR=0.0
000010         SID(J)=0.0
000011         TEFF=0.0
000012         BRANDS=0.0
000013         OLD=0.0
000014         TDREV=0.0
000015         TSC=0.0
000016         TAG(J)=0.0
000017         FIRMS=0.0
000020         NA=NF(J)
000021         DO 9  MF=1,NA
000023         FSH(MF,J)=0.0
000026         FSB(MF,J)=0.0
000031         FZ(MF,J)=0.0
000033       9 FA(MF,J)=0.0
000040         NA=N(J)
000041         DO 5  K=1,NA
000043         IF(LIVE(K,J).EQ.0) GO TO 5
000046         BRANDS=BRANDS+1
000050         TA(J)=TA(J)+A(K,J)
000054         TCP(J)=TCP(J)+CP(K,J)
000057         TPR=TPR+PR(K,J)
         C     **** RESPONSE FUNCTIONS ************************************
000063         MF=ID(K)
000064         CI(K,J)=CI(K,J-1)+((FSH(MF,J-1)-FSH(MF,J-2))*10.)
000076         JX=J-3
000100         IF(J.EQ.3)JX=1
000102         AG(K,J)=.4*A(K,J)+.3*A(K,J-1)+.2*A(K,J-2)+.1*A(K,JX)
000120         TAG(J)=TAG(J)+AG(K,J)
000123         DE(K)=D(K,J-1)
000125         IF(NAGE(K,J).LE.1) DE(K)=CI(K,J)/DIV
000133         IF(NAGE(K,J).EQ.0) AG(K,J)=100.*AG(K,J)
000140         IF(NAGE(K,J).EQ.0) CP(K,J)=100.*CP(K,J)
000145         EFFORT(K,J)=(PR(K,J)*EPR)*(AG(K,J)**EA)*(CP(K,J)**ECP)*(B(K,J)**E
              1R)*(DE(K)**ED)*(CI(K,J)**ECI)
000210         IF(NAGE(K,J).EQ.0) EFFORT(K,J)=.01*EFFORT(K,J)
000215         TEFF=TEFF+EFFORT(K,J)
000221       5 CONTINUE
000224         APR(J)=TPR/BRANDS
000226         ETA=.85-.000000010*TAG(J)
000231         SI(J)=SI(J-1)*((TAG(J)/TAG(J-1))**ETA)*((TCP(J)/TCP(J-1))**.05)*((
              1APR(J)/APR(J-1))**-1.5)*(POP(J)/POP(J-1))**1.0)
000261         DO 200 K=1,NA
000262         IF(LIVE(K,J).EQ.0) GO TO 200
000265         DREV(K,J)=(SI(J)*(EFFORT(K,J)/TEFF)*(PR(K,J)-PW(K,J)-.10))+DP(K,J)
000303         IF(DREV(K,J).LE.0.0) DREV(K,J)=1.0
000307         IF(NAGE(K,J).LT.2) GO TO 200
000312         OLD=OLD+1.
000314         TSC=TSC+SC(K,J)
000317     200 CONTINUE
000322         ASC=TSC/OLD
000324         TEFF=0.*
000325         DO 10  K=1,NA
000326         IF(LIVE(K,J).EQ.0) GO TO 10
000331         IF(NAGE(K,J).EQ.0) DREV(K,J)=100.*DPEV(K,J)
000340         D(K,J)=(CI(K,J)/DIV)*((DREV(K,J)/ADREV)**EREV)*((SC(K,J)/ASC)**ESC
              1)
000362         IF(D(K,J).LT.0.01) D(K,J)=0.01
000367         EFFORT(K,J)=(PR(K,J)*EPR)*(AG(K,J)**EA)*(CP(K,J)**ECP)*(B(K,J)**E
              1R)*(D(K,J)**ED)*(CI(K,J)**ECI)
000433         IF(NAGE(K,J).GT.0) GO TO 16
000437         EFFORT(K,J)=.01*EFFORT(K,J)
000441         AG(K,J)=.01*AG(K,J)
000443         CP(K,J)=.01*CP(K,J)
000445         SC(K,J)=.01*SC(K,J)
000447         D(K,J)=.01*D(K,J)
000451      16 TEFF=TEFF+EFFORT(K,J)
000456      10 CONTINUE
         C     **** COMPUTATION OF MARKET SHARES ************************
000461         DO 70 K=1,NA
000462         IF(LIVE(K,J).EQ.0) GO TO 70
000465         SHARE(K,J)=EFFORT(K,J)/TEFF
000472      70 CONTINUE
```

```
              C       **** COMPUTATION OF BRAND SALES AND PROFITS ***********************
000475                IF(NX.EQ.0) GO TO 75
000476                K=I
000477                GO TO 85
000477         75 K=0
000500         80 K=K+1
000502         85 IF(LIVE(K,J).EQ.0) GO TO 100
000506                Q(K,J)=SHARE(K,J)*SI(J)
000513                SB(K,J)=PW(K,J)*Q(K,J)
000516                SID(J)=SID(J)+SB(K,J)
000520                VC(K,J)=.18+.0002*B(K,J)+.10*D(K,J)
000527                FC(K,J)=2000000.
000532                IF(NAGE(K,J).EQ.0) FC(K,J)=1000000.
000535                Z(K,J)=(SB(K,J)-(VC(K,J)*Q(K,J))-FC(K,J)-A(K,J)-CP(K,J)-DP(K,J)-SC
                     1(K,J))*.52
000557                IF(J.LT.5) GO TO 300
000561                IF(LIM.GT.0) CALL ADLIM(K,J)
000566        300 MF=ID(K)
000570                FSH(MF,J)=FSH(MF,J)+SHARE(K,J)
000575                FSB(MF,J)=FSB(MF,J)+SB(K,J)
000600                FZ(MF,J)=FZ(MF,J)+Z(K,J)
000603                FA(MF,J)=FA(MF,J)+A(K,J)
000606                IF(NX.EQ.1) GO TO 110
000610        100 IF(K.LT.N(J)) GO TO 80
000613        110 RETURN
000614                END


                      SUBROUTINE ENTRY1(J)
000003                COMMON  NF(30),FZ(20,30),N(30),LIVE(20,30),NBRND(30),ID(20),
                     1 NAGE(20,30),CI(20,30),NFRM(30),A(20,30),CP(20,30),DP(20,30),
                     2 SC(20,30),B(20,30),PW(20,30),PR(20,30),P(7,20),SB(20,30),
                     3 VC(20,30),FC(20,30),Q(20,30),TA(30),TCP(30),APR(30),FSB(20,30),
                     4 FA(20,30),CC(20,30),D(20,30),R(20,30),EFFORT(20,30),SHARE(20,30),
                     5 SI(30),Z(20,30),M,SIGN,VL,NUMB,NX,LIM,SID(30),SAT,IDF(20),
                     6 MOLD,AG(20,30),TAG(30),POP(30),FSH(20,30),KX,EPR,EA,ECP,ER,ED,
                     7 EREV,ESC,DIV,ADREV,ECI
              C       **** CONJECTURES MADE ABOUT POTENTIAL RIVALS ***********************
000003                NF(J)=NF(J-1)
000005                IF(KX.GT.0) GO TO 100
000007                TZ=0.0
000007                BRANDS=0.0
000010                NFRM(J)=0
000011                NA=NF(J-1)
000013                DO 10  I=1,NA
000014         10 TZ=TZ+FZ(I,J-1)
000023                NA=N(J-1)
000024                DO 20  I=1,NA
000026                IF(LIVE(I,J-1).EQ.0) GO TO 20
000031                BRANDS=BRANDS+1.
000033         20 CONTINUE
              C       **** HOW MANY NEW BRANDS ***********************************************
000036                CRIT=SAT*BRANDS
000040                NBRND(J)=(TZ-CRIT)/SAT
000044                IF(NBRND(J).LT.1) GO TO 40
000046                IF(NBRND(J).GT.3) NBRND(J)=3
000052        100 N(J)=N(J-1)+NBRND(J)
000055                NA=N(J-1)+1
000057                NB=N(J)
000060                DO 3   I=NA,NB
              C       **** WHICH FIRMS GET NEW BRANDS *************************************
000062                IF(KX.GT.0) GO TO 200
000064                LIVE(I,J-1)=1
000067                NAGE(I,J-1)=0
000072                NC=I-N(J-1)
000073                GO TO (11,12,13),NC
000102        200 KY=IDF(I)
000104                GO TO (11,12,13),KY
000112         11 IDF(I)=1
000114                IF(KX.LT.2) GO TO 75
000117                NUMB=NUMB+1
000120                IF(NUMB.GT.MOLD) NUMB=1
000123                IF(NUMB.GT.NOLD) GO TO 16
000126                NZ=0
000126                ND=N(J-1)
```

```
000130          DO 14  K=1,ND
000131          IF(IDF(K).EQ.1) NZ=NZ+1
000134          IF(NUMB.EQ.NZ) ID(I)=ID(K)
000141          IF(NUMB.EQ.NZ) CI(I,J-1)=CI(K,J-1)
000150       14 CONTINUE
000153          GO TO 29
000153       75 IF(NOLD.LT.MOLD) GO TO 15
000156          NQ=NUMB+1
000160          IF(NQ.GT.MOLD) NQ=1
000162          NZ=0
000163          ND=N(J-1)
000165          DO 80  K=1,ND
000166          IF(IDF(K).EQ.1) NZ=NZ+1
000171          IF(NQ.EQ.NZ) ID(I)=ID(K)
000176          IF(NQ.EQ.NZ) CI(I,J-1)=CI(K,J-1)
000205       80 CONTINUE
000210          GO TO 29
000210       16 NOLD=NOLD+1
000212          IF(NOLD.GT.MOLD) NOLD=MOLD
          C     **** INITIALIZE VARIABLES FOR CONJECTURED NEW BRANDS ***************
000215       15 CI(I,J-1)=105.
000221          GO TO 17
000222       12 IDF(I)=2
000224          CI(I,J-1)=100.
000230          GO TO 17
000230       13 IDF(I)=3
000232          CI(I,J-1)=90.
000236       17 NF(J)=NF(J)+1
000240          NFRM(J)=NFRM(J)+1
000242          ID(I)=NF(J)
000244          MF=ID(I)
000245          FSH(MF,J-1)=0.0
000250          FSH(MF,J-2)=0.0
000252       29 A(I,J-1)=0.0
000256          A(I,J-2)=0.0
000260          A(I,J-3)=0.0
000263          SHARE(I,J-1)=.001
000266       30 CONTINUE
000270          GO TO 50
000271       40 N(J)=N(J-1)
000273          NBRND(J)=0
000274       50 RETURN
000275          END


                SUBROUTINE ENTRY2 (J)
000003          DIMENSION MTEST(3)
000003          COMMON  NF(30),FZ(20,30),N(30),LIVE(20,30),NBRND(30),ID(20),
               1 NAGE(20,30),CI(20,30),NFRM(30),A(20,30),CP(20,30),DP(20,30),
               2 SC(20,30),B(20,30),PW(20,30),PR(20,30),P(7,20),SB(20,30),
               3 VC(20,30),FC(20,30),Q(20,30),TA(30),TCP(30),APR(30),FSB(20,30),
               4 FA(20,30),CC(20,30),D(20,30),R(20,30),EFFORT(20,30),SHARE(20,30),
               5 SI(30),Z(20,30),M,SIGN,VL,NUMB,NOLD,NX,LIM,SID(30),SAT,IDF(20),
               6 MOLD,AG(20,30),TAG(30),POP(30),FSH(20,30),KX,EPR,EA,ECP,ER,ED,
               7 EREV,ESC,DIV,ADREV,ECI
          C     **** ACTUAL BEHAVIOR OF POTENTIAL RIVALS ***********************
000003          NA=N(J)
000005          I=NA+1
000007          CALL PROFITS (I,J)
          C     **** THREE POTENTIAL ENTRANTS ***********************
000011          DO 120  KY=1,3
000014          MTEST(KY)=0
000015          L=J+1
000017          IDF(I)=KY
000020          PVNET=0.0
000021          NBRND(L)=1
000023          KX=1
          C     **** ASSIGN A NUMBER AND FIRM TO POTENTIAL ENTRANT **************
000024          CALL ENTRY1 (L)
000026          L1=J+1
000031          L2=J+10
          C     **** MAKE CONJECTURES TEN YEARS INTO FUTURE **********************
000033          DO 70  L=L1,L2
000035          N(L)=N-1
000037          NF(L)=NF(J+1)
000041          IF(L.GT.L1) NBRND(L)=0
```

```
000044              LIVE(I,L)=1
000050              NAGE(I,L)=L-J
000053              CALL FIRST (I,L)
000055              DO 60 KA=1,NA
000060              IF(LIVE(KA,L-1).EQ.1) GO TO 10
000064       36     LIVE(KA,L)=0
000070              GO TO 60
000070       10     LIVE(KA,L)=1
000074              NAGE(KA,L)=NAGE(KA,L-1)+1
000101              NC=NAGE(KA,L)
000103              IF(NC.GT.4) NC=4
000106              GO TO (31,32,33,34),NC
000116       31     IF(SHARE(KA,L-1).GE.0.001) GO TO 35
000123              GO TO 36
000124       32     IF(SHARE(KA,L-1).GE.0.03) GO TO 35
000131              GO TO 36
000132       33     IF(SHARE(KA,L-1).GE.0.05) GO TO 35
000137              GO TO 36
000140       34     IF(SHARE(KA,L-1).GE.0.07) GO TO 35
000145              GO TO 36
000146       35     NC=NAGE(KA,L)
000152              IF(NC.EQ.5) CALL PARAM(KA,L)
000157              IF(NC.GT.4) GO TO 40
000163              CALL FIRST (KA,L)
000165              GO TO 50
000167       40     CALL MIX (KA,L)
000171       50     IF(LIM.LT.5) GO TO 60
000175              LIMP=LIM-4
000177              GO TO (301,302,303),LIMP
000205      301     IF(A(KA,L).GT.3000000.) A(KA,L)=3000000.
000215              GO TO 60
000216      302     CRIT=.10*SB(KA,L-1)
000223              GO TO 304
000223      303     CRIT=.20*SB(KA,L-1)
000230      304     IF(NAGE(KA,L).LT.4) GO TO 60
000235              IF(A(KA,L).GT.CRIT) A(KA,L)=CRIT
000244       60     CONTINUE
000247              CALL PROFITS (I,L)
000251              YR=L-J
000254              RATE=1.20
000256              IF(KY.EQ.1) RATE=1.10
000261              IF(LIM.EQ.1) Z(I, L)=Z(I, L)-(.4*A(I, L))+(.15*A(I, L-1))+(.15*A(I
                   1, L-2))+(.10*A(I, L-3))
000307              IF(LIM.EQ.2) Z(I, L)=Z(I, L)-(.7*A(I, L))+(.30*A(I, L-1))+(.20*A(I
                   1, L-2))+(.20*A(I, L-3))
000335              PVNET=PVNET+((Z(I,L)+(.25*FC(I,J+1)))/(RATE**YR))
000352       70     CONTINUE
            C       **** COMPUTE NET PRESENT VALUE OF ENTRY ****************************
000354              PVNET=PVNET-(2.5*FC(I,J+1))
000362              IF(KY.EQ.1) PVNET=PVNET+1000000.
000366              IF(PVNET.GE.0) MTEST(KY)=1
            C       **** PRINT ACTUAL BEHAVIOR OF POTENTIAL RIVALS *****************
000372              PRINT 200,J,KY,PVNET
000404      200     FORMAT (3X,*YEAR*,I3,10X,I5,10X,F15.2)
000404      120     CONTINUE
            C       **** INITIALIZE VARIABLES AND DETERMINE MIX OF NEW RIVALS *********
000407              DO 300 KY=1,3
000411              IF(MTEST(KY).EQ.0) GO TO 300
000412              NBRND(J)=NBRND(J)+1
000414              N(J)=N(J)+1
000416              I=N(J)
000417              IDF(I)=KY
000420              LIVE(I,J)=1
000423              NAGE(I,J)=0
000426              CALL FIRST (I,J)
000430              A(I,J)=.01*A(I,J)
000436              CP(I,J)=.01*CP(I,J)
000441              DP(I,J)=.01*DP(I,J)
000444      300     CONTINUE
000446              IF(NBRND(J).EQ.0) GO TO 400
000450              KX=2
000451              CALL ENTRY1 (J)
000452      400     RETURN
000453              END
```

```
              SUBROUTINE FIRST (I,J)
000005        COMMON  NK(30),FZ(20,30),N(30),LIVE(20,30),NBRND(30),ID(20),
            1 NAGE(20,30),CI(20,30),NFRM(30),A(20,30),CP(20,30),DP(20,30),
            2 SC(20,30),B(20,30),PW(20,30),PR(20,30),P(7,20),SB(20,30),
            3 VC(20,30),FC(20,30),Q(20,30),TA(30),TCP(30),APR(30),FSB(20,30),
            4 FA(20,30),CC(20,30),D(20,30),R(20,30),EFFORT(20,30),SHARE(20,30),
            5 SI(30),Z(20,30),M,SIGN,VL,NUMB,NOLD,NX,LIM,SID(30),SAT,IDF(20),
            6 MOLD,AG(20,30),TAG(30),POP(30),FSH(20,30),KX,EPR,EA,ECP,ER,ED,
            7 EREV,ESC,DIV,ADREV,ECI
       C      **** COMPUTE CONJECTURED MIX OF A NEW BRAND IN FIRST YEAR ********
000005        TAA=0.0
000006        TCPA=0.0
000007        TDPA=0.0
000010        TSCA=0.0
000011        BRANDS=0.0
000012        NA=N(J-1)-NBRND(J-1)
000014        DO 5 L=1,NA
000016        IF(LIVE(L,J-1).EQ.0) GO TO 5
000021        TAA=TAA+A(L,J-1)
000025        TCPA=TCPA+CP(L,J-1)
000030        TDPA=TDPA+DP(L,J-1)
000033        TSCA=TSCA+SC(L,J-1)
000037        BRANDS=BRANDS+1.
000041      5 CONTINUE
000044        KA=IDF(I)
000046        IF(NAGE(I,J).GT.2) GO TO 50
000053        GO TO (10,20,30),KA
       C      **** IF CEREAL COMPANY BRAND **********************************
000061     10 A(I,J)=(TAA/BRANDS)*1.25
000066        CP(I,J)=TCPA/BRANDS
000071        DP(I,J)=(TDPA/BRANDS)*2.
000075        SC(I,J)=TSCA/BRANDS
000100        IF(NAGE(I,J).EQ.2) GO TO 65
000104        PW(I,J)=APR(J-1)*.82
000107        PR(I,J)=APR(J-1)
000112        B(I,J)=100.
000115        GO TO 40
       C      **** IF CONSUMER PRODUCTS MARKETER BRAND *********************
000116     20 A(I,J)=(TAA/BRANDS)*1.5
000123        CP(I,J)=(TCPA/BRANDS)*1.2
000130        DP(I,J)=(TDPA/BRANDS)*3.
000136        SC(I,J)=(TSCA/BRANDS)*1.2
000143        IF(NAGE(I,J).EQ.2) GO TO 65
000146        PW(I,J)=APR(J-1)*.82
000151        PR(I,J)=APR(J-1)
000154        B(I,J)=104.
000157        GO TO 40
       C      **** IF PRIVATE BRAND ****************************************
000160     30 A(I,J)=(TAA/BRANDS)*.25
000165        CP(I,J)=(TCPA/BRANDS)*.25
000172        DP(I,J)=TDPA/BRANDS
000175        SC(I,J)=TSCA/BRANDS
000200        IF(NAGE(I,J).GE.2) GO TO 65
000204        PW(I,J)=APR(J-1)*.50
000207        PR(I,J)=APR(J-1)*.70
000213        B(I,J)=95.
000216        GO TO 40
000216     50 GO TO (60,60,30),KA
000225     60 A(I,J)=TAA/BRANDS
000231        CP(I,J)=TCPA/BRANDS
000234        DP(I,J)=TDPA/BRANDS
000237        SC(I,J)=TSCA/BRANDS
000242     65 PW(I,J)=PW(I,J-1)
000247        PR(I,J)=PR(I,J-1)
000252        B(I,J)=B(I,J-1)
000254     40 RETURN
000255        END


              SUBROUTINE PARAM (I,J)
000005        COMMON  NF(30),FZ(20,30),N(30),LIVE(20,30),NBRND(30),ID(20),
            1 NAGE(20,30),CI(20,30),NFRM(30),A(20,30),CP(20,30),DP(20,30),
            2 SC(20,30),B(20,30),PW(20,30),PR(20,30),P(7,20),SB(20,30),
            3 VC(20,30),FC(20,30),Q(20,30),TA(30),TCP(30),APR(30),FSB(20,30),
            4 FA(20,30),CC(20,30),D(20,30),R(20,30),EFFORT(20,30),SHARE(20,30),
            5 SI(30),Z(20,30),M,SIGN,VL,NUMB,NOLD,NX,LIM,SID(30),SAT,IDF(20),
```

```
           6 MOLD,AG(20,30),TAG(30),POP(30),FSH(20,30),XX,EPR,EA,ECP,ER,ED,
           7 EREV,ESC,DIV,ADREV,ECI
         C    **** COMPUTE CONJECTURED DECISION PARAMETERS *****************
000005        P(1,I)=A(I,J-1)/SB(I,J-2)
000013        P(2,I)=CP(I,J-1)/SB(I,J-2)
000017        P(3,I)=DP(I,J-1)/SB(I,J-2)
000023        P(4,I)=SC(I,J-1)/SB(I,J-2)
000027        P(5,I)=PR(I,J-1)/APR(J-2)
000032        P(6,I)=PW(I,J-1)/APR(J-2)
000036        P(7,I)=1.00
         C    **** ROUND OFF DECISION PARAMETERS ********************
000040        DO 15  K=1,7
000042        MA=P(K,I)*100.
000047        P1=MA
000050        P2=P(K,I)*100.-P1
000053        IF(P2.GE.0.50) GO TO 20
000056        P(K,I)=P1*0.01
000061        GO TO 10
000062     20 P(K,I)=P1*0.01+0.01
000067     10 IF(P(K,I).LE.0.,1) P(K,I)=0.01
000077        IF(P(K,I).GT.1.5) P(K,I)=1.5
000106     15 CONTINUE
000110        RETURN
000111        END


              SUBROUTINE MIX (I,J)
000005        COMMON  NF(30),FZ(20,30),N(30),LIVE(20,30),NBRND(30),ID(20),
           1 NAGE(20,30),CI(20,30),NFRM(30),A(20,30),CP(20,30),DP(20,30),
           2 SC(20,30),B(20,30),PW(20,30),PR(20,30),P(7,20),SB(20,30),
           3 VC(20,30),FC(20,30),Q(20,30),TA(30),TCP(30),APR(30),FSB(20,30),
           4 FA(20,30),CC(20,30),D(20,30),R(20,30),EFFORT(20,30),SHARE(20,30),
           5 SI(30),Z(20,30),M,SIGN,VL,NIUMB,NOLD,NX,LIM,SID(30),SAT,IDF(20),
           6 MOLD,AG(20,30),TAG(30),POP(30),FSH(20,30),KX,EPR,EA,ECP,ER,ED,
           7 EREV,ESC,DIV,ADREV,ECI
         C    **** MARKETING MIX DECISION RULES *****************
000005        A(I,J)=P(1,I)*SB(I,J-1)
000014        CP(I,J)=P(2,I)*SB(I,J-1)
000017        DP(I,J)=P(3,I)*SB(I,J-1)
000023        SC(I,J)=P(4,I)*SB(I,J-1)
000027        PR(I,J)=P(5,I)*APR(J-1)
000033        PW(I,J)=P(6,I)*APR(J-1)
000037        B(I,J)=P(7,I)*B(I,J-1)
000044        IF(B(I,J).LE.95.) B(I,J)=95.
000050        RETURN
000051        END


              SUBROUTINE  ADLIM (I,J)
000005        COMMON  NF(30),FZ(20,30),N(30),LIVE(20,30),NBRND(30),ID(20),
           1 NAGE(20,30),CI(20,30),NFRM(30),A(20,30),CP(20,30),DP(20,30),
           2 SC(20,30),B(20,30),PW(20,30),PR(20,30),P(7,20),SB(20,30),
           3 VC(20,30),FC(20,30),Q(20,30),TA(30),TCP(30),APR(30),FSB(20,30),
           4 FA(20,30),CC(20,30),D(20,30),R(20,30),EFFORT(20,30),SHARE(20,30),
           5 SI(30),Z(20,30),M,SIGN,VL,NIUMB,NOLD,NX,LIM,SID(30),SAT,IDF(20),
           6 MOLD,AG(20,30),TAG(30),POP(30),FSH(20,30),KX,EPR,EA,ECP,ER,ED,
           7 EREV,ESC,DIV,ADREV,ECI
         C    **** CONTROLS ON ADVERTISING EXPENDITURES *****************
000005        GO TO (1,2,3,4,5,6,7),LIM
000020      1 Z(I,J)=Z(I,J)+.52*(A(I,J)-(.6*A(I,J))-(.15*A(I,J-1))-(.15*A(I,J-2)
           1)-(.1*A(I,J-3)))
000043        GO TO 20
000044      2 Z(I,J)=Z(I,J)+.52*(A(I,J)-(.3*A(I,J))-(.30*A(I,J-1))-(.20*A(I,J-2)
           1)-(.2*A(I,J-3)))
000067        GO TO 20
000070      3 Z(I,J)=Z(I,J)-.05*A(I,J)
000077        GO TO 20
000077      4 Z(I,J)=Z(I,J)-(.02*(A(I,J)/1000000.))*A(I,J)
000110        GO TO 20
000110      5 IF(A(I,J).GT.3000000.) A(I,J)=3000000.
000120        GO TO 20
000121      6 CRIT=.10*SB(I,J)
000125        GO TO 8
000126      7 CRIT=.20*SB(I,J)
000132      8 IF(NAGE(I,J).LT.4) GO TO 20
```

```
000137        IF(A(I,J).GT.CRIT) Z(I,J)=Z(I,J)-(A(I,J)-CRIT)
000152     20 RETURN
000153        END


              SUBROUTINE  REVISE (I,J)
000005        COMMON  NF(30),FZ(20,30),N(30),LIVE(20,35),NBRND(30),ID(20),
             1 NAGE(20,30),CI(20,30),NFRM(30),A(20,30),CP(20,30),DP(20,30),
             2 SC(20,30),B(20,30),PW(20,30),PR(20,30),P(7,20),SB(20,30),
             3 VC(20,30),FC(20,30),Q(20,30),TA(30),TCP(30),APR(30),FSB(20,30),
             4 FA(20,30),CC(20,30),D(20,30),R(20,30),EFFORT(20,30),SHARE(20,30),
             5 SI(30),Z(20,30),M,SIGN,VL,NUMB,NOLD,NX,LIM,SID(30),SAT,IDF(20),
             6 MOLD,AG(20,30),TAG(30),POP(30),FSH(20,30),KX,EPR,EA,ECP,ER,ED,
             7 EREV,ESC,DIV,ADREV,ECI
       C      ****  CHANGE APPROPRIATE DECISION VARIABLE **********************
000005        GO TO (1,2,3,4,5,6,7), M
000020      1 A(I,J)=P(1,I)*SB(I,J-1)
000027        IF(LIM.EQ.5) CALL ADLIM (I,J)
000034        GO TO 10
000035      2 CP(I,J)=P(2,I)*SB(I,J-1)
000044        GO TO 10
000045      3 DP(I,J)=P(3,I)*SB(I,J-1)
000054        GO TO 10
000055      4 SC(I,J)=P(4,I)*SB(I,J-1)
000064        GO TO 10
000065      5 PR(I,J)=P(5,I)*APR(J-1)
000072        GO TO 10
000073      6 PW(I,J)=P(6,I)*APR(J-1)
000100        GO TO 10
000101      7 B(I,J)=P(7,I)*B(I,J-1)
000110        IF(B(I,J).LE.95.) B(I,J)=95.
000115     10 RETURN
000116        END


              SUBROUTINE  UPDATE (I,J)
000005        COMMON  NF(30),FZ(20,30),N(30),LIVE(20,35),NBRND(30),ID(20),
             1 NAGE(20,30),CI(20,30),NFRM(30),A(20,30),CP(20,30),DP(20,30),
             2 SC(20,30),B(20,30),PW(20,30),PR(20,30),P(7,20),SB(20,30),
             3 VC(20,30),FC(20,30),Q(20,30),TA(30),TCP(30),APR(30),FSB(20,30),
             4 FA(20,30),CC(20,30),D(20,30),R(20,30),EFFORT(20,30),SHARE(20,30),
             5 SI(30),Z(20,30),M,SIGN,VL,NUMB,NOLD,NX,LIM,SID(30),SAT,IDF(20),
             6 MOLD,AG(20,30),TAG(30),POP(30),FSH(20,30),KX,EPR,EA,ECP,ER,ED,
             7 EREV,ESC,DIV,ADREV,ECI
       C      ****  ASSIGN PROPER VALUE TO LAST DECISION VARIABLE CHANGED *******
000005        GO TO (1,2,3,4,5,6,7), M
000020      1 VL=A(I,J)
000024        GO TO 10
000024      2 VL=CP(I,J)
000030        GO TO 10
000030      3 VL=DP(I,J)
000034        GO TO 10
000034      4 VL=SC(I,J)
000040        GO TO 10
000040      5 VL=PR(I,J)
000044        GO TO 10
000044      6 VL=PW(I,J)
000050        GO TO 10
000050      7 VL=B(I,J)
000054     10 RETURN
000055        END


              SUBROUTINE  FIX (I,J)
000005        COMMON  NF(30),FZ(20,30),N(30),LIVE(20,35),NBRND(30),ID(20),
             1 NAGE(20,30),CI(20,30),NFRM(30),A(20,30),CP(20,30),DP(20,30),
             2 SC(20,30),B(20,30),PW(20,30),PR(20,30),P(7,20),SB(20,30),
             3 VC(20,30),FC(20,30),Q(20,30),TA(30),TCP(30),APR(30),FSB(20,30),
             4 FA(20,30),CC(20,30),D(20,30),R(20,30),EFFORT(20,30),SHARE(20,30),
             5 SI(30),Z(20,30),M,SIGN,VL,NUMB,NOLD,NX,LIM,SID(30),SAT,IDF(20),
             6 MOLD,AG(20,30),TAG(30),POP(30),FSH(20,30),KX,EPR,EA,ECP,ER,ED,
             7 EREV,ESC,DIV,ADREV,ECI
       C      ****  CHANGE VALUE OF APPROPRIATE DECISION VARIABLE ***************
000005        GO TO (1,2,3,4,5,6,7), M
000020      1 A(I,J)=VL+1.00000.*SIGN
```

```
000026          IF(A(I,J).LE.0.0) A(I,J)=1000.
000035          IF(LIM.EQ.5) CALL ADLIM (I,J)
000042          GO TO 10
000043       2  CP(I,J)=VL+10000.*SIGN
000051          IF(CP(I,J).LE.0.0) CP(I,J)=1000.
000060          GO TO 10
000061       3  DP(I,J)=VL+10000.*SIGN
000067          IF(DP(I,J).LE.0.0) DP(I,J)=1000.
000076          GO TO 10
000077       4  SC(I,J)=VL+10000.*SIGN
000105          IF(SC(I,J).LE.0.0) SC(I,J)=1000.
000114          GO TO 10
000115       5  PR(I,J)=VL+.01*SIGN
000123          IF(PR(I,J).LE.0.0) PR(I,J)=.02
000132          GO TO 10
000133       6  PW(I,J)=VL+.01*SIGN
000141          IF(PW(I,J).LE.0.0) PW(I,J)=.01
000150          GO TO 10
000151       7  B(I,J)= VL+.01*SIGN
000157          IF(B(I,J).LE.95.) B(I,J)=95.
000166      10  RETURN
000167          END
```

The Benchmark Run

A copy of the computer output from the benchmark run (Run #1) of the model is found in the following pages. The output should be self-explanatory except for the items listed below.

1. Any output listed for years 3 and 4 represents data that was read into the computer program. The run started in year 5.
2. The numbers found immediately to the right of the values of the marketing mix decision variables in the data on individual brands represent the ratios of the variables to sales.
3. The numbers found immediately below the values of the marketing mix decision variables in the data on individual brands represent the values of the decision parameters used in the appropriate decision rules.
4. The left-hand side of the data on potential entrants shows the net present value of entry computed by an established company brand, consumer products marketer brand, and private brand, in that order. The right-hand side of the data on potential entrants shows how many new entrants existing brands expect to enter the industry in future years when they make their decisions for a given year.

INDUSTRY DATA

YEAR	SALES -LBS	ADVERTISING	CONSUMER-DIRECTED PROMOTION	AVERAGE PRICE	AD GOODWILL	NUMBER OF NEW BRANDS	NUMBER OF NEW FIRMS	NUMBER OF EXITS
YEAR 3	67704904.93	7722041.26	1445168.29	.7133	6426378.67	0	0	0
YEAR 4	74704225.90	7705406.54	1423783.78	.7101	7102519.79	0	0	1
YEAR 5	84722549.68	9678329.18	1426941.92	.7116	8310073.89	1	1	1
YEAR 6	102641086.22	13451483.10	1429927.76	.7169	10596404.23	1	1	1
YEAR 7	123967625.97	17085059.49	1978593.32	.7210	13575188.62	1	1	1
YEAR 8	149299094.44	21740125.19	2636623.47	.7255	17479697.46	1	1	0
YEAR 9	163244737.92	22858437.75	3036656.68	.7391	20427572.87	0	0	0
YEAR 10	170927938.25	24176014.07	3091591.30	.7531	22584467.94	0	0	0
YEAR 11	174154133.74	23962916.10	3110448.21	.7626	23536670.73	0	0	0
YEAR 12	179997908.97	26365840.13	3337287.07	.7886	24855257.47	0	0	0

DATA ON BRAND 1 OF FIRM 1

YEAR	AGE	DOLLAR SALES	POUND SALES	PROFITS	MARKET SHARE	VARIABLE COST	FIXED COST
YEAR 3	8	21561946.79	33659291.85	2432738.79	.49715	.29385	2000000.00
YEAR 4	9	23326199.31	36384672.35	2652828.00	.48705	.28794	2000000.00
YEAR 5	10	25956658.10	46626638.65	3212162.64	.47945	.28864	2000000.00
YEAR 6	11	28093950.89	43895784.67	3483325.64	.42766	.29007	2000000.00
YEAR 7	12	29405520.60	45577116.00	3591643.89	.36764	.29119	2000000.00
YEAR 8	13	34762754.27	53374198.20	3393347.36	.35884	.29745	2000000.00
YEAR 9	14	34025084.97	50986049.43	3187536.92	.31233	.30335	2000000.00
YEAR 10	15	35569080.57	52369985.23	3866745.39	.30638	.30481	2000000.00
YEAR 11	16	38476379.26	55519998.11	4560787.10	.31879	.30661	2000000.00
YEAR 12	17	41221165.62	58754511.64	4557746.02	.32642	.30881	2000000.00

MARKETING MIX DECISIONS

YEAR	ADVERTISING	C-D PROMOTION	D-D PROMOTION	SALES CALLS	BRAND QUALITY	W-S PRICE	R-T PRICE
YEAR 3	3604777.42 (.167)	360477.74 (.017)	168295.33 (.008)	839305.10 (.039)	100.10	.6400	.7300
YEAR 4	4137297.30 (.178)	414054.05 (.018)	192432.43 (.008)	964324.32 (.041)	100.10	.6400	.7600
YEAR 5	4424376.16 (.170)	465723.81 (.018)	232461.90 (.009)	931447.61 (.036)	100.10	.6390	.7597
YEAR 6	4931751.74 (.176)	519131.76 (.018)	259565.88 (.009)	1038263.52 (.037)	100.10	.6400	.7609
YEAR 7	5337831.67 (.182)	561817.02 (.019)	280938.51 (.010)	1123756.04 (.038)	100.10	.6452	.7671
YEAR 8	7351580.15 (.211)	882165.62 (.025)	882165.62 (.025)	1176220.82 (.034)	100.10	.6499	.7714
YEAR 9	7995533.48 (.235)	1042882.63 (.031)	347427.54 (.031)	1042288.63 (.031)	99.10	.6673	.8197
YEAR 10	7825769.54 (.220)	1020752.55 (.029)	340750.85 (.029)	1020752.55 (.029)	99.10	.6800	.8352

YEAR 11	8190265.63	.213	1068295.52	.028	35609?.51	.009	1068295.52	.028	99.10	.6930	.8512		
	.230		.030		.010		.030		1.000	.920	1.130		
YEAR 12	9619094.82	.233	1154291.38	.028	384763.79	.009	1154291.38	.028	99.10	.7016	.8617		
	.250	.230	.030		.010		.030		1.000	.920	1.130		
									1.000	.920	1.130		

	ADVERTISING GOODWILL	CORPORATE IMAGE	DISTRIBUTION	MKTG EFFORT	LENGTH OF SEARCH	LENGTH OF SEARCH-NEW	TYPE OF FIRM	
YEAR 3	3281108.11	141.37	.938	9.0459E+03	0	0	1	0
YEAR 4	3664395.83	139.42	.879	9.1291E+03	0	0	1	0
YEAR 5	4046873.11	139.32	.886	9.7822E+03	0	0	1	0
YEAR 6	4487950.75	139.24	.901	1.0592E+04	0	0	1	0
YEAR 7	4913263.15	138.73	.912	1.1164E+04	0	0	1	0
YEAR 8	5597068.52	138.13	.974	1.3337E+04	11	0	1	0
YEAR 9	6964328.95	138.06	1.035	1.4700E+04	51	0	1	0
YEAR 10	7532997.06	138.84	1.050	1.5044E+04	0	0	1	0
YEAR 11	7958061.83	139.32	1.068	1.5339F+04	0	0	1	0
YEAR 12	8669414.87	139.35	1.090	1.6203E+04	2	0	1	0

DATA ON BRAND 2 OF FIRM 2

	AGE	PROFITS	DOLLAR SALES	POUND SALES	MARKET SHARE	VARIABLE COST	FIXED COST
YEAR 3	3	144247.79	11767917.31	24516494.39	.36211	26415	2000000.00
YEAR 4	4	420646.41	11662545.78	23047053.71	.38851	26293	2000000.00
YEAR 5	5	51925.63	11934156.44	24360392.81	.28753	26292	2000000.00
YEAR 6	6	28815.69	12030368.51	25507222.03	.29902	26307	2000000.00
YEAR 7	7	38571A.58	12496220.32	23877960.71	.19261	26542	2000000.00
YEAR 8	8	315104.65	12081565.25	22954411.03	.15375	26580	2000000.00
YEAR 9	9	-10026.49	9043h4.27	17760334.64	.16679	26350	2000000.00
YEAR 10	10	-12538.77	8418080.59	15912225.23	.09005	26157	2000000.00
YEAR 11	11	-10135.20	7980595.99	14316565.89	.08221	26084	2000000.00
YEAR 12	12	-131126.40	7551997.61	13382550.91	.07435	26077	2000000.00

MARKETING MIX DECISIONS

	ADVERTISING	C-D PROMOTION	D-D PROMOTION	SALES CALLS	BRAND QUALITY	W-S PRICE	R-T PRICE
YEAR 3	2043431.05 (.314 / .174)	600454.31 (.092 / .051)	58631.92 (.009 / .005)	273615.64 (.042 / .023)	100.30	.4860 (1.000 / .727)	.6200 / .939
YEAR 4	1292272.97 (.110 / .117)	562162.16 (.048 / .051)	1081.08 (.000 / .000)	326486.49 (.028 / .030)	100.30	.4800 (1.000 / .673)	.6200 / .869
YEAR 5	2655020.59 (.240 / .222)	331877.57 (.030 / .028)	110625.86 (.010 / .009)	331187.57 (.028 / .028)	100.30	.4899 (1.000 / .690)	.6248 / .880
YEAR 6	2744855.98 (.230 / .225)	358024.69 (.030 / .029)	119341.56 (.010 / .010)	358002.69 (.029 / .029)	95.00 (.947)	.5191 (.730)	.6613 / .930
YEAR 7	2566250.69 (.210 / .205)	366092.96 (.030 / .029)	122030.99 (.010 / .010)	366092.96 (.030 / .029)	95.00 (1.000)	.5233 (.730)	.6811 / .930
YEAR 8	2499244.06 (.230 / .207)	374886.61 (.030 / .031)	124962.20 (.010 / .010)	374886.61 (.030 / .031)	95.00	.5263 (.730)	.5849 / .950

	ADVERTISING GOODWILL		CORPORATE IMAGE	DISTRIBUTION		MKTG EFFORT					LENGTH OF SEARCH		LENGTH OF SEARCH-NEW	TYPE OF FIRM
	.200	.030					.030							
YEAR 9	1691421.24	24163171		.026	120115.85	362447.56	.039	95.00	1.000	.5295	.730	.6818	.950	
	.140	.020			.010	.010	.030							
YEAR 10	1880A60.85	28212913		.034	94443.04	37672.17	.045	95.00	1.000	.5469	.730	.7022	.940	
	.200	.030			.010	.010	.040							
YEAR 11	1767799.92	25254242		.032	84180.81	36723.22	.042	96.90	1.000	.5574	.740	.7156	.950	
	.210					.010	.040							
YEAR 12	1675925.16	23941.88		.032	79905.96	319223.84	.042	98.84	1.020	.5643	.740	.7245	.950	
	.210	.030			.011		.040							

	ADVERTISING GOODWILL	CORPORATE IMAGE	DISTRIBUTION	MKTG EFFORT	LENGTH OF SEARCH	LENGTH OF SEARCH-NEW	TYPE OF FIRM
YEAR 3	2315733.45	105.59	.641	6.588E+03	0	0	1
YEAR 4	1907866.01	106.15	.629	5.782E+03	0	0	1
YEAR 5	2136780.17	105.62	.629	5.865E+03	15	0	1
YEAR 6	2357386.27	105.41	.641	5.472E+03	75	0	1
YEAR 7	2508081B.48	104.82	.664	5.849E+03	28	0	1
YEAR 8	2562966.09	104.46	.668	5.292E+03	18	0	1
YEAR 9	2213357.73	104.07	.645	5.125E+03	33	0	1
YEAR 10	2015884.80	103.62	.626	4.422E+03	48	0	1
YEAR 11	1859585.82	103.43	.615	3.955E+03	30	0	1
YEAR 12	1746023.50	103.35	.610	3.695E+03	30	0	1

DATA ON BRAND 3 OF FIRM 3

	AGE	PROFITS	DOLLAR SALES	POUND SALES	MARKET SHARE	VARIABLE COST	FIXED COST
YEAR 3	1	-833294.13	6003344.77	9529118.69	.14074	.26172	2000000.00
YEAR 4	2	115465.02	9621674.90	15272499.84	.20444	.26677	2000000.00
YEAR 5	3	70078.61	12350417.12	19603933.70	.23139	.26852	2000000.00
YEAR 6	4	96211.13	14463885.34	22958849.12	.22368	.27032	2000000.00
YEAR 7	5	865881.53	15085803.42	23643040.47	.19073	.26892	2000000.00
YEAR 8	6	808040.07	15222223.26	23723344.32	.15890	.26929	2000000.00
YEAR 9	7	117950.07	16313032.79	25555948.79	.15655	.28119	2000000.00
YEAR 10	8	890950.14	17233271.02	26498779.48	.15501	.28246	2000000.00
YEAR 11	9	1227975.49	18773530.64	28320344.66	.16262	.28374	2000000.00
YEAR 12	10	1374742.70	20169343.30	30055578.44	.16697	.28546	2000000.00

MARKETING MIX DECISIONS

	ADVERTISING	C-D PROMOTION	D-D PROMOTION	SALES CALLS	BRAND QUALITY	W-S PRICE	R-T PRICE
	.345	.081	.046				
YEAR 3	2073803.79	48256.24	27472.96	276872.96	103.10	.6300	.7400
	.236	.047	.028				
YEAR 4	2270270.27	44567.57	26106.11	339459.46	103.10	.6300	.7500
	.378 .075	.045	.012	.057		1.000	.883 1.051
YEAR 5	2566846.85	47494.59	153873.87	543423.42	103.10	.6300	.7500
	.208	.038 .049 .016	.056				
YEAR 6	321541.53	424065.32	165787.21	60249.54	103.10	.6300	.887 1.056
	.222 .260 .034	.029	.013 .049		1.000		.836 1.055

YEAR 7–12 (main/second-line values)

YEAR											
7	3760610.35 / .260	.249	433916.58 / .030	.029	144639.86 / .010	.010	723194.30 / .050	.048	103.10 / 1.000	.6380 / .890	.7527 / 1.050
8	3922308.89 / .260	.258	452557.10 / .030	.030	158858.03 / .010	.010	754290.17 / .050	.050	103.10 / 1.000	.6417 / .890	.7570 / 1.050
9	3044484.65 / .260	.187	456672.70 / .030	.028	76112.16 / .040	.047	608896.93 / .040	.037	104.13 / 1.010	.6393 / .880	.7761 / 1.070
10	4241588.53 / .200	.246	469390.98 / .030	.028	65252.31 / .040	.038	652521.31 / .040	.038	104.13 / 1.000	.6504 / .880	.7908 / 1.070
11	4480650.46 / .260	.239	516698.13 / .030	.028	68933.84 / .040	.037	689330.84 / .040	.037	104.13 / 1.000	.6629 / .880	.8060 / 1.070
12	4881117.97 / .260	.242	563205.92 / .030	.028	750941.23 / .040	.037	750941.23 / .040	.037	104.13 / 1.000	.6711 / .880	.8160 / 1.070

DATA ON BRAND 4 OF FIRM 4

YEAR	ADVERTISING GOODWILL	CORPORATE IMAGE	DISTRIBUTION	MKTG EFFORT	LENGTH OF SEARCH	LENGTH OF SEARCH-NEW	TYPE OF FIRM
3	829533.12	119.70	.611	2.569E+03	0	0	1
4	1539255.94	121.11	.661	3.339E+03	0	0	1
5	2122586.38	121.74	.679	4.721E+03	0	0	1
6	2717657.20	122.01	.697	5.539E+03	0	0	1
7	3209264.89	121.64	.683	5.916E+03	0	0	1
8	3596874.25	121.61	.687	6.120E+03	0	0	1
9	3468150.05	121.29	.804	7.362E+03	73	0	1
10	3770423.62	121.27	.816	7.613E+03	11	0	1
11	4065804.56	121.25	.829	7.826E+03	0	0	1
12	4449368.50	121.33	.846	8.288E+03	0	0	0

YEAR	AGE	PROFITS	DOLLAR SALES	POUND SALES	MARKET SHARE	VARIABLE COST	FIXED COST
5	0	-516357.99	8015818.18	1376181.51	.00163	.20060	1000000.00
6	1	-962882.33	7069195.59	1212002.61	.11811	.25931	200000.00
7	2	-200701.69	10447867.86	1791716.37	.14453	.24473	200000.00
8	3	209694.13	11036211.08	1866767.80	.12504	.26657	200000.00
9	4	153850.57	9656088.48	1641074.24	.10065	.26647	200000.00
10	5	-34306.49	8790689.73	1484880.77	.08698	.26639	200000.00
11	6	34926.05	8565634.82	1421039.19	.08160	.26552	200000.00
12	7	129116.68	8374986.91	1391663.21	.07723	.26583	200000.00

MARKETING MIX DECISIONS

YEAR	ADVERTISING	C-D PROMOTION	D-D PROMOTION	SALES CALLS	BRAND QUALITY	W-S PRICE	R-T PRICE
5	32085.59 / .400	4745.95	3577.48 / .059	5434.23 / .068	100.00	.5822	.7100
6	251926.16 / .356	326065.32	43574.42 / .046	50229.54 / .071	99.90	.5831	.7011
7	2691028.25 / .258	306327.78 / .043	56834.54 / .029	525196.82 / .050	99.80	.5831	.7011
8	2403009.61 / .391 / .230	313436.04 / .030	417914.71 / .080 / .040	522393.39 / .074 / .050	97.80 / .999 / .980	.5912 / .813 / .820	.7354 / .992 / 1.020

FIRM SUMMARY (YEAR 9–12)

YEAR	(ADV GOODWILL)							(W-S)	(R-T)
9	1986517.99 (.180)	331086.33 (.030)	.206	.034	220724.22	.023	441448.44	.046	100.74 (.030)
10	2123898.14 (.220)	289622.47 (.030)	.242	.033	96540.82 (.020)	.011	386163.30 (.040)	.044	103.76 (.030)
11	2021835.64 (.230)	263717.69 (.030)	.236	.031	87905.90 (.010)	.010	351423.59 (.040)	.041	106.87 (.030)
12	1969613.01 (.230)	256906.04 (.030)	.235	.031	85635.35 (.010)	.010	342541.39 (.040)	.041	109.01 (1.020)

YEAR	W-S PRICE		R-T PRICE	
9	.5876	.810	.7399	1.020
10	.5913	.800	.7613	1.030
11	.6026	.800	.7684	1.020
12	.6024	.790	.7702	1.010

YEAR	ADVERTISING GOODWILL	CORPORATE IMAGE	DISTRIBUTION	LENGTH OF SEARCH	LENGTH OF SEARCH-NEW	TYPE OF FIRM
5	12834.23	105.00	.006	0	0	1 0
6	1017332.94	105.02	.593	0	75	1 0
7	1838608.87	106.18	.648	0	75	1 0
8	2275574.51	106.45	.670	62	0	1 0
9	2305642.55	106.25	.663	67	0	1 0
10	2195219.40	106.01	.656	48	0	1 0
11	2039508.26	105.87	.641	32	0	1 0
12	2017827.32	135.82	.640	42	0	1 0

DATA ON BRAND 5 OF FIRM 5

AGE	PROFITS	DOLLAR SALES	POUND SALES	MKTG EFFORT	MARKET SHARE	VARIABLE COST	FIXED COST
0	-516826.74	91274.85	156527.75	3.3156E+01	.00153	.20061	1000000.00
1	-998702.91	751048.04	1290585.55	2.9253E+03	.10318	.26027	2000000.00
2	-32388.04	1055763.71	1795464.95	4.388AE+03	.12027	.26555	2000000.00
3	54776.04	9145084.57	1537495.74	4.8213E-03	.09418	.26564	2000000.00
4	-8662.54	881313.18	1421102.80	4.7373E-03	.08612	.26516	2000000.00
5	14270.32	8785741.05	1474340.54	4.2270E+03	.08477	.26675	2000000.00
6	10687.32	8497207.42	1414506.92	3.9261E+03 / 3.8336E+03	.07836	.26609	2000000.00

MARKETING MIX DECISIONS

YEAR	ADVERTISING	C-D PROMOTION	D-D PROMOTION	SALES CALLS	BRAND QUALITY	W-S PRICE	R-T PRICE
6	40192.68 (.440)	4240.65 (.046)	3315.74 (.036)	6622.50 (.066)	100.00	.5831	.7111
7	2691028.25 (.358)	306321.78 (.030)	58013.54 (.078)	529196.82 (.070)	99.90	.5879	.6969
8	2760787.30 (.262)	314906.02 (.030)	781150.97 (.074)	552086.99 (.052)	99.80	.5879	.7069
9	189994.47 (.367 / .180)	316657.91 (.042 / .030)	3165.91 (.035)	422210.55 (.074 / .040)	101.80 (.999 / 1.020)	.5948 (.815)	.7399 (.980)
10	2103360.45 (.239 / .230)	274352.54 (.030)	182201.69 (.021)	365803.38 (.040)	104.85 (1.020)	.5987 (.820)	.7539 (1.020)
11	2027021.78 (.231 / .230)	264594.15 (.030)	176262.76 (.026 / .020)	355525.53 (.040)	105.90 (1.010)	.5951 (.810)	.7684 (1.020)
12	2020720.44 (.238 / .230)	263572.23 (.030)	87857.41 (.010)	351429.64 (.040)	108.02 (1.020)	.6024 (.790)	.7702 (1.010)

	ADVERTISING GOODWILL	CORPORATE IMAGE	DISTRIBUTION	MKTG EFFORT	LENGTH OF SEARCH	LENGTH OF SEARCH-NEW	TYPE OF FIRM
YEAR 6	16077.07	105.00	.006	3.7770E-01	0	0	1
YEAR 7	1088469.11	105.02	.603	3.1130E-03	0	76	1
YEAR 8	1919661.93	106.03	.656	4.6373E-03	0	75	1
YEAR 9	2130440.10	106.20	.653	4.432RE-03	75	0	1
YEAR 10	2232592.31	105.94	.642	4.2301E-03	69	0	1
YEAR 11	2097887.77	105.86	.656	4.0790E-03	31	0	1
YEAR 12	2027063.35	105.85	.645	3.8996E-03	32	0	0

DATA ON BRAND 6 OF FIRM 6

	AGE	PROFITS	DOLLAR SALES	POUND SALES	MARKET SHARE	VARIABLE COST	FIXED COST
YEAR 7	0	-51689.77	95771.98	162916.86	.00131	.20063	1000000.00
YEAR 8	1	-111645.45	730793.70	1215667.24	.08142	.26037	2000000.00
YEAR 9	2	-662512.02	1099282.45	1652863.81	.10122	.26602	2000000.00
YEAR 10	3	82757.02	1010816.62	1628111300	.09525	.26492	2000000.00
YEAR 11	4	175875.47	1665179.29	1724220.05	.08902	.26522	2000000.00
YEAR 12	5	16204.21	1577901.50	1691574.18	.09398	.26597	2000000.00

MARKETING MIX DECISIONS

	ADVERTISING	C-D PROMOTION	D-D PROMOTION	SALES CALLS	BRAND QUALITY	W-S PRICE	R-T PRICE
YEAR 7	41910.28 / .438	4063.22 / .042	4481.35 / .051	6251.97 / .065	100.00	.5879	.7169
YEAR 8	276787.30 / .378	294906.02 / .040	68150.97 / .093	55286.99 / .076	99.90	.6012	.7010
YEAR 9	302031.11 / .299	288812.40 / .029	113300.84 / .110	55552.50 / .055	99.80 / .999	.6112 / .843	.7110 / .980
YEAR 10	191885.67 / .413	302978.47 / .040	1009928.25 / .152	403971.30 / .040	99.80 / 1.000	.6209 / .840	.7243 / .980
YEAR 11	202162.36 / .190	303244.40 / .030	1010814.68 / .100	404325.87 / .038	99.80 / 1.000	.6177 / .820	.7232 / .960
YEAR 12	223673.65 / .200 / .210	319553.38 / .030 / .030	1065177.93 / .100 / .100	426071.17 / .040 / .040	99.80 / 1.000	.6253 / .820	.7321 / .960

	ADVERTISING GOODWILL	CORPORATE IMAGE	DISTRIBUTION	MKTG EFFORT	LENGTH OF SEARCH	LENGTH OF SEARCH-NEW	TYPE OF FIRM
YEAR 7	16764.11	105.00	.006	3.9906E-01	0	0	1
YEAR 8	1116688.01	105.01	.604	3.1394E-03	0	77	1
YEAR 9	2044744.69	105.81	.661	4.7641E-03	0	80	1
YEAR 10	2229988.79	106.01	.650	4.6784E-03	74	0	1
YEAR 11	2264452.80	105.95	.653	4.7644E-03	67	0	1
YEAR 12	2187042.61	105.99	.660	4.6649E-03	17	0	1

DATA ON BRAND 7 OF FIRM 1

	AGE	PROFITS	DOLLAR SALES	POUND SALES	MARKET SHARE	VARIABLE COST	FIXED COST
YEAR 8	0	-499909.75	157984.65	267229.91	.00179	.20088	1000000.00
YEAR 9	1	-284989.38	1246671.88	2061213.21	.12627	.28512	2000000.00
YEAR 10	2	824247.78	18629741.70	30827940.63	.18021	.28726	2000000.00
YEAR 11	3	1459991.74	18001341.30	29780459.96	.17100	.27772	2000000.00
YEAR 12	4	1640039.67	19888225.74	32883753.66	.18269	.27845	2000000.00

MARKETING MIX DECISIONS

	ADVERTISING	C-D PROMOTION	D-D PROMOTION	SALES CALLS	BRAND QUALITY	W-S PRICE	R-T PRICE
YEAR 8	42667.87 / .270	3949.06 / .025	6815.51 / .043	6526.87 / .041	100.00	.5912	.7210
YEAR 9	322016.11 / .258	348812.40 / .028	101300.84 / .081	55527.50 / .045	99.90	.6048	.7054
YEAR 10	4081863.88 / .219	432365.15 / .023	111220.96 / .060	56948.73 / .031	99.90	.6048	.7054
	.327	.035	.089	.046	1.000	.818	.954
YEAR 11	3453716.30 / .192	441655.90 / .025	498350.99 / .028	539318.96 / .030	99.90	.6048	.7054
	.185	.024	.027	.029	1.000	.803	.936
YEAR 12	3962495.09 / .199	540340.24 / .027	540340.24 / .027	534591.93 / .027	99.90	.6048	.7054
	.220	.030	.030	.030	1.000	.793	.925

	ADVERTISING GOODWILL	CORPORATE IMAGE	DISTRIBUTION	MKTG EFFORT	LENGTH OF SEARCH	LENGTH OF SEARCH-NEW	TYPE OF FIRM
YEAR 8	17043.15	138.13	.009	6.9017E+01	0	0	1
YEAR 9	1300908.81	138.06	.851	5.9430E+03	0	75	1
YEAR 10	2607361.96	138.84	.873	8.8513E+03	0	0	1
YEAR 11	3254369.69	139.32	.777	8.2280E+03	0	0	1
YEAR 12	3759517.31	139.35	.785	9.0683E+03	7	0	1

DATA ON FIRM 1

	INDUSTRY SALES IN DOLLARS	DOLLAR SALES	SHARE	PROFITS	ADVERTISING
YEAR 3	39313208.87	21541946.79	.4971	2432738.79	3604777.42
YEAR 4	43970450.98	23286190.31	.4876	2652628.00	4137297.30
YEAR 5	50321319.84	25956588.10	.4795	3212162.64	4424376.16
YEAR 6	61921305.78	28093850.89	.4277	3438325.64	4931751.74
YEAR 7	75050232.23	29405520.60	.3676	3551643.89	5337831.67
YEAR 8	91124135.93	34920738.93	.3606	2901437.61	7393988.02
YEAR 9	101107583.41	46491796.84	.4386	2902547.53	11215749.59
YEAR 10	107602818.60	54239592.27	.4866	4692993.17	11907633.43
YEAR 11	111242902.35	56487720.56	.4898	6020778.84	11643981.93
YEAR 12	116280828.10	61109391.36	.5091	6197785.69	13581589.90

DATA ON FIRM 2

	INDUSTRY SALES IN DOLLARS	DOLLAR SALES	SHARE	PROFITS	ADVERTISING
YEAR 3	39313208.87	11767917.31	.3621	164247.79	2043431.05
YEAR 4	43970450.98	11062585.78	.3085	426464.41	1292972.97
YEAR 5	50321319.84	11934156.44	.2875	51923.63	2655020.59
YEAR 6	61921305.78	12203099.51	.2290	228157.69	2744855.98
YEAR 7	75050232.23	12496220.32	.1926	385718.58	2562650.69
YEAR 8	91124135.93	12081585.25	.1538	315104.65	2499244.06
YEAR 9	101107583.41	9404304.27	.1088	160269.49	1691421.94
YEAR 10	107602818.60	8418080.59	.0900	-125338.77	1880860.85
YEAR 11	111242902.35	7980595.99	.0822	-101356.20	1767796.92
YEAR 12	116280828.10	7551997.61	.0743	-131126.40	1675925.16

DATA ON FIRM 3

	INDUSTRY SALES IN DOLLARS	DOLLAR SALES	SHARE	PROFITS	ADVERTISING
YEAR 3	39313208.87	6003344.77	.1407	-833294.13	2073832.79
YEAR 4	43970450.98	9621674.90	.2044	115465.02	2270270.27
YEAR 5	50321319.84	12350417.12	.2314	700738.61	2566846.85
YEAR 6	61921305.78	14463885.94	.2237	962112.13	3215414.53
YEAR 7	75050232.23	15085803.42	.1907	865881.53	3780610.35
YEAR 8	91124135.93	15222423.26	.1589	808040.07	3922308.89
YEAR 9	101107583.41	16313032.79	.1565	1172933.07	3044484.65
YEAR 10	107602818.60	17233271.02	.1550	890950.14	4241388.53
YEAR 11	111242902.35	18773530.64	.1626	1227975.49	4480650.46
YEAR 12	116280828.10	20169343.30	.1670	1374742.70	4881117.97

DATA ON FIRM 4

	INDUSTRY SALES IN DOLLARS	DOLLAR SALES	SHARE	PROFITS	ADVERTISING
YEAR 5	50321319.84	80159.18	.0016	-516257.99	320R5.59
YEAR 6	61921305.78	7069195.59	.1181	-962822.33	2519268.16
YEAR 7	75050232.23	10447867.86	.1445	-200701.69	2691028.21
YEAR 8	91124135.93	11036211.08	.1250	209694.13	2403009.61
YEAR 9	101107583.41	9654082.48	.1007	153850.57	1986517.99
YEAR 10	107602818.60	8790589.73	.0870	-34306.49	2123898.14
YEAR 11	111242902.35	8563534.82	.0816	34026.05	2021835.64
YEAR 12	116280828.10	8374986.91	.0772	12911.68	1969613.01

DATA ON FIRM 5

	INDUSTRY SALES IN DOLLARS	DOLLAR SALES	SHARE	PROFITS	ADVERTISING
YEAR 6	61921305.78	91274.85	.0015	-516826.74	40192.68
YEAR 7	75050232.23	7519048.04	.1032	-998702.91	2691028.25
YEAR 8	91124135.93	10555263.71	.1203	-323368.04	2760787.30
YEAR 9	101107583.41	9145084.57	.0942	54776.04	1899947.47
YEAR 10	107602818.60	8813138.18	.0861	-8662.54	2103369.45
YEAR 11	111242902.35	8785741.05	.0848	14270.32	2027021.78
YEAR 12	116280828.10	8497207.42	.0784	10387.32	2020720.44

DATA ON FIRM 6

	INDUSTRY SALES IN DOLLARS	DOLLAR SALES	SHARE	PROFITS	ADVERTISING
YEAR 7	75050232.23	95771.98	.0013	-516390.77	41910.28
YEAR 8	91124135.93	7307913.70	.0814	-1116415.45	2760787.30
YEAR 9	101107583.41	10099282.45	.1012	-662512.09	3020316.11
YEAR 10	107602818.60	10108146.82	.0953	82757.02	1918863.67
YEAR 11	111242902.35	10651779.29	.0990	175375.47	2021629.36
YEAR 12	116280828.10	10577901.50	.0940	16204.21	2236873.65

DATA ON POTENTIAL ENTRANTS

ACTUAL BEHAVIOR			CONJECTURED BEHAVIOR			
	TYPE OF ENTRANT	NET PRESENT VALUE OF ENTRY		ABOUT YEAR	NEW BRANDS	EXPECTED
YEAR 5	1	3017424.90	IN YEAR 5 BY BRAND 1	6		0
YEAR 5	2	-2147685.25		7		1
YEAR 5	3	-3359077.95		8		0
			IN YEAR 5 BY BRAND 2	6		0
				7		1
				8		0
			IN YEAR 5 BY BRAND 3	6		0
				7		1
				8		0
YEAR 6	1	2446950.06	IN YEAR 6 BY BRAND 1	7		0
YEAR 6	2	-2626668.66		8		1
YEAR 6	3	-7560725.05		9		0
			IN YEAR 6 BY BRAND 2	7		0
				8		1
				9		0
			IN YEAR 6 BY BRAND 3	7		0
				8		1
				9		0
YEAR 7	1	2183401.13	IN YEAR 7 BY BRAND 1	8		0
YEAR 7	2	-2881570.66		9		1
YEAR 7	3	-7686484.96		10		0
			IN YEAR 7 BY BRAND 2	8		0
				9		1
				10		0
			IN YEAR 7 BY BRAND 3	8		0
				9		1
				10		0
YEAR 8	1		IN YEAR 8 BY BRAND 1	9		0
YEAR 8	2			10		0
YEAR 8	3			11		2
			IN YEAR 8 BY BRAND 2	9		0
				10		0
				11		2
			IN YEAR 8 BY BRAND 3	9		0
				10		0
				11		2

IN YEAR 8 BY BRAND 4ABOUT YEAR 9NEW BRANDS EXPECTED   10   0
                                                        11   0
                                                             1

IN YEAR 9 BY BRAND 1ABOUT YEAR 10NEW BRANDS EXPECTED   11   0 0 0 0 0

IN YEAR 9 BY BRAND 2ABOUT YEAR 10NEW BRANDS EXPECTED   11   0 0 0 0 0
                                                        12
                                                        11
                                                        12

IN YEAR 9 BY BRAND 3ABOUT YEAR 10NEW BRANDS EXPECTED   10   0 0 0 0 0 0
                                                        12

IN YEAR 9 BY BRAND 4ABOUT YEAR 10NEW BRANDS EXPECTED   10   0 0 0 0 0
                                                        12

IN YEAR 9 BY BRAND 5ABOUT YEAR 10NEW BRANDS EXPECTED   11   0 0 0 0 0
                                                        12
                                                        11
                                                        12

IN YEAR 10 BY BRAND 1ABOUT YEAR 11NEW BRANDS EXPECTED   11   0 0 0 0 0 0 0 0 0 0 0 0 0 0 0 1 0 0 0
                                                        12
                                                        13

IN YEAR 10 BY BRAND 2ABOUT YEAR 11NEW BRANDS EXPECTED   11
                                                        12
                                                        13

IN YEAR 10 BY BRAND 3ABOUT YEAR 11NEW BRANDS EXPECTED   11
                                                        12
                                                        13

IN YEAR 10 BY BRAND 4ABOUT YEAR 11NEW BRANDS EXPECTED   11
                                                        12
                                                        13

IN YEAR 10 BY BRAND 5ABOUT YEAR 11NEW BRANDS EXPECTED   11
                                                        12
                                                        13

IN YEAR 10 BY BRAND 6ABOUT YEAR 11NEW BRANDS EXPECTED   11
                                                        12
                                                        13

IN YEAR 11 BY BRAND 1ABOUT YEAR 12NEW BRANDS EXPECTED   12   0 1 0 0 1 0
                                                        13
                                                        14

IN YEAR 11 BY BRAND 2ABOUT YEAR 12NEW BRANDS EXPECTED   13
                                                        14

YEAR 8   1   14510367.30
YEAR 8   2   -3703108.85
YEAR 8   3   -805543.70

YEAR 9   1   -5747302.64
YEAR 9   2   -7831168.13
YEAR 9   3   -10128295.39

YEAR 10   1   -2849483.88
YEAR 10   2   -5556680.36
YEAR 10   3   -9375269.49

```
IN YEAR 11   BY BRAND 3ABOUT YEAR 12NEW BRANDS EXPECTED    0
                                    13                     1
                                    14                     0
IN YEAR 11   BY BRAND 4ABOUT YEAR 12NEW BRANDS EXPECTED    0
                                    13                     1
                                    14                     0
IN YEAR 11   BY BRAND 5ABOUT YEAR 12NEW BRANDS EXPECTED    0
                                    13                     0
                                    14                     1
IN YEAR 11   BY BRAND 6ABOUT YEAR 12NEW BRANDS EXPECTED    0
                                    13                     0
                                    14                     1
IN YEAR 11   BY BRAND 7ABOUT YEAR 12NEW BRANDS EXPECTED    0
                                    13                     0
                                    14                     1

IN YEAR 12   BY BRAND 1ABOUT YEAR 13NEW BRANDS EXPECTED    0
                                    14                     1
                                    15                     0
IN YEAR 12   BY BRAND 2ABOUT YEAR 13NEW BRANDS EXPECTED    0
                                    14                     1
                                    15                     0
IN YEAR 12   BY BRAND 3ABOUT YEAR 13NEW BRANDS EXPECTED    0
                                    14                     0
                                    15                     1
IN YEAR 12   BY BRAND 4ABOUT YEAR 13NEW BRANDS EXPECTED    0
                                    14                     0
                                    15                     0
IN YEAR 12   BY BRAND 5ABOUT YEAR 13NEW BRANDS EXPECTED    0
                                    14                     1
                                    15                     0
IN YEAR 12   BY BRAND 6ABOUT YEAR 13NEW BRANDS EXPECTED    0
                                    14                     1
                                    15                     0
IN YEAR 12   BY BRAND 7ABOUT YEAR 13NEW BRANDS EXPECTED    1
                                    14                     0
                                    15                     0
```

```
                -1042538.86        1
                -4366557.62        2      YEAR 11
                -8722434.22        3      YEAR 11
                                          YEAR 11
```

```
                -541129.08         1
                -4107325.48        2      YEAR 12
                -8281218.32        3      YEAR 12
                                          YEAR 12
```

Index

About the Author

Paul N. Bloom is Assistant Professor of Marketing in the College of Business and Management of the University of Maryland. He received his Ph.D. in marketing from Northwestern University and his M.B.A. in finance from The Wharton School of the University of Pennsylvania. His major research interests are in public policy toward marketing and marketing for nonprofit organizations. His articles have appeared in the *Harvard Business Review*, *Journal of Marketing*, *Journal of Consumer Affairs*, and several other publications.